14 February 2019

Steve,

I hope you enjoy reading about my military journey of 30 years, nine months, and twenty-one days.

Steve Stephens

When in Charge, Take Charge!

Brigadier General (Ret)
Robert L. "Steve" Stephens, Jr.

Tapestry Press, Ltd.
Littleton, MA 01460

Printed in the United States of America.

ISBN 978-1-59830-477-0

For book orders, author appearance inquiries, and interviews, please contact the author by mail at:

Steve Stephens
2819 Players Drive
Jonesboro, GA 30236

Contents

Invictus

Out of the night that covers me,
Black as the Pit from pole to pole,
I thank whatever gods may be
For my unconquerable soul.

In the fell clutch of circumstance
I have not winced nor cried aloud.
Under the bludgeonings of chance
My head is bloody, but unbowed.

Beyond this place of wrath and tears
Looms but the Horror of the shade,
And yet the menace of the years
Finds, and shall find, me unafraid.

It matters not how strait the gate,
How charged with punishments the scroll.
I am the master of my fate:
I am the captain of my soul.

—William Ernest Henley

INTRODUCTION

Friday, the 10th of August 1962 began as a bright sunny morning for me and Olivia in our little rented house just off the campus of West Virginia State College (WVSC) a small historically black college set in the middle of the Kanawha Valley, eight miles west of Charleston, West Virginia. The reason that particular Friday morning was going to be so special was because I was going to be commissioned a second lieutenant of Infantry in the Regular United States Army and graduate from WVSC with a Bachelor of Science degree in Education. I was going to be the first one in my family to graduate from college, and the first to be commissioned in the United States Army, ever. My wife of exactly sixty days, Delores Olivia Bennett-Stephens had already established the standard in her family. She was the first one in her family to earn a college degree. She had marched in the graduation ceremonies, along with everyone else in my class, down the center of campus on the 6th of June. Three days later, on the 9th of June we were married in her hometown of Bishop, West Virginia.

We arrived for the commissioning ceremony about fifteen minutes early and Staff Sergeants Bailey and Henson and the man who was my personal role model and mentor, Major Samuel Kelly, greeted us. Staff Sergeant Bailey had official papers for me to sign designating me as a Regular Army Officer and financial forms to start my pay. Sergeant Henson was there to collect a dollar as the first noncommissioned officer to salute a newly commissioned officer, a military tradition that dates back many years. Major Samuel Kelly was there because he cared about cadets. Until that day he had been for me the toughest, straightest, and neatest military officer that I had known. He was completely no-nonsense in the purest sense of the word. I wanted to be an Army officer in his image. In my eyes Major Sam Kelly was a man of integrity, a man of honor, and above all, a professional soldier. I wanted to be just like him.

Since I was attending summer school at West Virginia State, there would not be a graduation ceremony, only the commissioning ceremony for those cadets receiving commissions and Bachelor degrees as a result of completing their academic requirements in summer school. Actually, I had been quite successful in college in many ways. As a junior I was selected by my classmates to be the class president. From all accounts I did a good job. Also during my junior year I was selected to represent my fraternity, Alpha Phi Alpha, Inc in the campus-wide pan Hellenic council. So coming up to my senior year I was well known and liked by my peers. And I had the respect and support of the college faculty and staff. After all I had been awarded the prize position for a male student on that campus. The Professor of Military Science and Tactics (PMS&T), Lieutenant Colonel (LTC) Edward Hinkson, appointed me to the position of Cadet Colonel and Commanding Officer of the 540 man Reserve Officer Training Corps (ROTC) Cadet Battle Group. That meant that I had, far and away, the most influential student leadership position on campus.

I had come to West Virginia State from Warrior Mines, West Virginia. Warrior Mines is a hollow that moves southeast toward Virginia out of War, West Virginia. While I was on active duty in the military and led numerous parades, I smiled broadly when I was introduced at the reviewing stand area as Colonel or General Stephens from War, West Virginia. Somehow that always got an extra measure of applause from the crowds and I strutted just a little taller. The local high school in War for Negroes was Excelsior High School. Excelsior was a consolidated school in Big Creek District in McDowell County, the southern most county in West Virginia. Excelsior had a rather distinguished faculty and staff with many of its teachers boasting master's degrees in their chosen fields. At the time I attended Excelsior there were approximately 20 Negro high schools in the state of West Virginia, and four of them were located in McDowell County. McDowell County was the cradle of the black population in West Virginia that had been brought in by the infamous coal barons to mine coal by hand in the billion dollar coal fields. Later in life I would go to work as the Director of Personnel for the state of West Virginia and discover that the total minority population for the entire state was only 3.69 percent. That's when I found out that most of the minorities were located in McDowell County. In fact, the population of McDowell County in the mid-1950s was approximately 139,000 residents. Black citizens owned convenience stores, service stations, restaurants, barber shops, hair salons, auto repair garages and grocery stores. We had black preachers, policemen, firemen, lawyers, federal judges, undertakers and members of the state legislature and of course our prize crop of professional educators. We did not suffer from a lack of black role models in McDowell County. We saw leadership first hand and we knew that it was every student's obligation to graduate and become a God fearing, useful member of society seeking leading roles in the different schemes of leadership in the county. The real leaders in high school were identified early and put in tracts that would offer the best chance for the development of their full potential. The criteria for selection were usually simple—could your parents afford to assist you through college? In addition to being selected for early leadership positions I managed to excel in the trades at the U. H. Prunty Trade School. Aside from being the regional president of the National Honor Society, class president as a junior and captain of the football team as a senior, I was appointed as the shop foreman for the auto body and fender class at trade school. So the appointment to a leadership position at West Virginia State was a logical progression that folks back home in McDowell County expected from me. In fact over a span of about eight years I was the fourth of six students from McDowell County at West Virginia State selected to command the ROTC Cadet Command at West Virginia State College. Four of us were graduates of Excelsior High School. The other three were Ray Owens and James Revels, both from Bishop, West Virginia and Herman Jones from Coalwood, West Virginia.

I was so excited that August morning in 1962 I do not remember much about my commissioning ceremony except it was held on a bright sun shiny morning. My parents drove the three hours from McDowell County to Institute, and my wife Olivia, was absolutely beautiful in her little silk suit—hat and gloves—the universal signature for an officer's wife, at that time. The ceremony began at ten o'clock sharp and was presided over by the professor of military science and tactics (PMS&T), Lieutenant Colonel Edward Hinkson. LTC Hinkson was a quiet, unassuming man who did not display his awards and badges on his uniforms. On the other hand, he insisted that I wear every cadet award that I had earned on my uniform every day, a habitual trait that followed me throughout my career. As cadets we knew very little about Colonel Hinkson; however, later in my life, when I became a lieutenant colonel and he was retired he and I became very close friends. As a cadet, the only thing I knew was that his integrity was beyond reproach; he was always immaculately dressed even in civilian clothes, and when he told you something you could take it to the bank. He was a bachelor who never married and an avid reader of novels. He invited me and my fiancee over to his house for brunch one Sunday before we were married and that day still sticks in our minds as one of our most unforgettable experiences in college. Olivia was coached on what to say and how to act by Carol Bowie, the spouse of Captain Walter Bowie, a member of the ROTC staff. Our wedding gift from Colonel Hinkson was a sterling silver butter dish that we still use occasionally after more than forty-eight years of marriage.

The commissioning ceremony was being held to commission the only two Regular Army officers commissioned at West Virginia State for that school year. In actuality, WVSC only commissioned ten to thirteen lieutenants a year. However, only one or two were awarded the coveted Regular Army (RA) commission. So I started my career off as a "Regular." What this meant was that I was in line for a thirty-year career with the U.S. Army, if I wanted it. I would have to make certain gates/milestones, e.g., complete an initial three-year probationary period and undergo a periodic review and evaluation of my performance management reports every seven years to determine if I passed muster. After each evaluation period I would be extended for another seven years up to a maximum of thirty years. I did not know at the time but there were other cadets who understood this system far better than I did who were willing to sell their souls for the opportunity to become a Regular Army Officer.

I was in a unique position that morning but I did not know it. I had the world by the tail and of course I had Olivia and my mother and father standing at my side that morning. I think that my mother stepped back and let Olivia pin the lieutenant's bar on me. I honestly do not remember who pinned on my rank insignia that day. What I do remember is how happy I was to be commissioned and how proud I was to be called a Lieutenant of Infantry. Hell, I was so happy that I gave Sergeant Henson the dollar for saluting me without comment. I guess he never really knew that I disliked him immensely. He was an officer retread who had been reduced back to sergeant after the Korean War and was serving out his time for retirement. He was bitter with the system for reducing him and never missed an opportunity to be sarcastic with cadets. He was the only ROTC staff member who constantly talked down to us and I determined very early that he would not be one of leaders after whom I would pattern my career. The commissioning ceremony lasted less than 30 minutes. I did not know in those days that when you are honored you are supposed to provide refreshments for your guests and a bouquet of flowers for your spouse. It was kind of a moot point that day, for I only had the dollar that my mother had given me to give the first noncommissioned officer (NCO) who saluted me. Little did I know that we were being launched on a journey that would take Olivia and me thirty years, nine months and 21 days to complete. It would also provide us with experiences, observations and educations that would last us for a lifetime. I was given twenty-four hours to get to my first duty station and report on active duty. Actually, I had a little longer because it was Friday and I didn't have to report to Fort Benning, Georgia, until Monday, the 13th of August 1962.

As I look back at my college days it is clear that almost every day and every activity in which I participated was somehow connected to the day that I would be commissioned a second lieutenant. Even as a freshman I knew that I could excel in the ROTC, pronounced "RotorC" in historically black schools and "RotC" at other campuses. ROTC was a required course at WVSC for all male students during their freshman and sophomore years. On drill day (every Monday at 0900 hours,) there would be 400 to 500 cadets on the parade field (college quad) in all stages of military dress and undress. The full cadre would be on hand to supervise the cadet staff and the cadet band would play when we marched in review. The elite campus military unit was the Pershing Rifles Military Honorary Society and Drill Team, referred to by everyone on campus as the PRs. The unique thing about the PRs was you had to volunteer to participate, and you had to survive a rigorous initiation period during college "hell week" conducted by all of the WVSC fraternities and sororities to get in. I signed up for it the first week. There were two things that I didn't know when I signed up. They were: as a freshman we would be required to drill twice a day five days a week; and second, there was a secret deal being worked on by the college administration for our unit, Company, H1, to march during half-time at a Cleveland Browns football game in Cleveland, Ohio. Before that semester would end I had an opportunity to be seen by my parents, at home, on television on a Sunday afternoon. That was exciting! The only catch was that I had to compete with every other freshman cadet in the PRs and be selected by the cadet company commander and his staff to go on the trip. As only college students can do we coined a phrase that said "You're ready even if you don't get to go."

The cadet company commander was Cadet Captain Peter Ridley from Washington, District of Columbia (DC). Pete had attended Dunbar High School in DC and knew the U.S.

Army Field Manual 22-5 inside and out. He had been a Cadet Company Commander at Dunbar High School before attending college. He was the only WVSC junior commanding a cadet company that year. The second in command (SIC) was Cadet First Lieutenant Lucius (Peanuts) Reeves from Miami, Florida. Peanuts did not have previous ROTC training; however, his older brother was a recent WVSC graduate and had taught him the ropes. The Company First Sergeant was Cadet First Sergeant Christopher Thorn from New York City whose major asset was his loud mouth. Tall, gaunt, fair skinned with a close-cropped haircut he was a man to be feared. The most important and impressive figure associated with the Pershing Rifles at WVSC at that time was an active duty Army Captain named Tapia. He was the PR faculty advisor. I think that Captain Tapia was from the Philippines. He was by far the neatest person I had met to date. Of course, I had not yet met then Major Samuel Kelly, the commandant of cadets. In any case I was thoroughly impressed with the PRs and I wanted to be one of them.

The selection process for the PRs was really quite simple. You had to finish the mid-semester with a 2.00 grade point average (GPA). You had to apply to the organization personally and you had to be initiated into the "fraternity" during hell week. The initiation process was absolutely grueling. First, we were treated as "pledges" roughly patterned along the lines of acting like "Plebes" at West Point or "Rats" at Virginia Military Institute. Of course none of the cadets in charge had ever visited either of these institutions, not even as tourists, so they kind of made up the scenario as they went along and either added, deleted, or changed processes as the whim hit them. The other part to this process was that all of the other campus fraternities and sororities required an overall 2.50 GPA to be inducted into their organizations. The guys in the PRs were generally, normally, usually, almost always, far from becoming 2.50 students. Because a majority of the members found it difficult to get the 2.50 to join other organizations, the PRs was their identity and life on campus and they made it tough, if not almost impossible for new members to "walk in." Now that I am older and reflecting on my youth I believe it was fortuitous for me to join the PRs the first semester that I was in college. If I had waited until my second semester I would not have joined. As part of the initiation we were abused, verbally and physically, insulted with statements unfavorable to our ancestry, and literally beaten with wooden paddles and slapped around by the "brothers." Even after I applied, if it had not been for the prospect of a road trip to perform at the Cleveland Brown's football game, I would have quit. I still marvel at the thought that I let the likes of cadets like Reginald Bellinger, Chris Thorn, Kenny Whitfield, and Wade Hamlin physically and mentally abuse me the way they did with wooden paddles, cigarette burns and exhausting physical drills and later address me as "brother." I didn't like it then, and I don't like it today. I went on to pledge and be initiated into Alpha Phi Alpha Fraternity, Incorporated the following year and did not receive the same degree of abuse.

The PR initiation was called "walking-the-line." Fortuitously, it only lasted one semester and we were inducted into the organization during a candlelit, very formal, ceremony that was attended by all of the active duty ROTC staff members and other campus brothers within the fraternity. In fact the induction ceremony was so well done that one sort of forgot the former abuses until you took a shower and saw all of the bruises and welts that were the results of the beatings. The drill team selection process was a little different and required skill, coordination and timing. As mentioned before, we drilled twice a day; at six o'clock in the mornings and five o'clock in the evenings. We were getting ready to go to Cleveland, Ohio and there would only be thirty-six cadets selected to go. One of the pledges that I remember very well was John Franklin Hailey from Aracoma High School in Logan, West Virginia. John was a rather mature student for his age and worked along side of me, washing dishes, in the campus dining hall. We worked for a self styled tyrant named Gwendolyn Goldston. Everyone called her "Ma Goldston." She tried so hard to act tough with students but in reality she was one of the nicest, most softhearted persons on the campus. John and I convinced her that we had to leave work early to attend drill in the evenings. She complained and threatened to fire us. She even said that she would dock our pay. She did neither. To end the story, John and I were selected to go on the Cleveland trip. He was selected to go as number thirty-five and I stood next to him as number thirty-six, the last man in the last rank. Until his untimely death in 2003, John lived only about 10 miles from me in the Atlanta, Georgia, area where we played golf together regularly and we talked a lot about our college days. We laughed a lot about how we used to sit on the dormitory steps with another friend, John Gravely, my roommate as a senior, and plan on how we would graduate from college and someday earn $10,000 dollars per year. That was our goal.

Because my study habits were so bad coupled with the fact that I was pledging the PRs and working in the dining room, my first semester grades were disastrous. Although I worked hard the following semesters to improve my grade point average I never recovered enough to satisfy my own personal goals. My grades were good enough, however, to apply and be initiated into Alpha Phi Alpha, Incorporated my sophomore year. That is when I memorized the poem *Invictus*, and took charge of my life. In the same year, 1959, I became the guidon bearer for the PRs and during the second semester I became the company first sergeant. That set me up to be selected by the ROTC cadre as the PR company commander the next year. Now if one assumes that the Pershing Rifles Company was the best marching and most disciplined unit in the student Battle Group and I was appointed the company commander, then one could only logically conclude that I was the best company commander on campus in 1961. The cadre certainly must have felt that way because I walked away with every award that was possible for a college junior to earn that year. Just before the school year ended Lieutenant Colonel Hinkson called me into his office and asked me point blank "What leadership position do you want next year?" I told him that I wanted to be the Battle

Group Executive Officer (XO) or second in command (SIC). Colonel Hinkson laughed and replied, "You're not telling me the truth, why do you want to be the XO?" I hemmed and hawed and finally said I'd really like to be the Battle Group Commander. Colonel Hinkson laughed again, as only he could and said "Well you can't have both jobs." I answered, "Sir?" He explained that I could not have the cadet corps commander's job and also be president of the student body. He went on to say, "don't answer me today, but come back and let me know in a couple of days." I never knew that I had a choice. The reason that I was hesitant to ask for the commander's position was that I knew there were at least three other cadets that had a better grade point averages than I did. I also knew, however, that neither of them could touch me for leadership ability. I didn't know until my daughter was a cadet at the United States Military Academy at West Point, New York that most military schools and ROTC programs evaluate students from both sides of the spectrum. The cadre evaluates academic strength as well as leadership ability. Evidently, in my case, my leadership ability overshadowed the other cadet's academic marks. Before leaving his office that day I told LTC Hinkson that I wanted to be the cadet corps commander. LTC Hinkson made my appointment contingent upon doing well at ROTC Summer Camp at Fort Knox, Kentucky. And, when I left WVSC for ROTC Summer Camp I knew that I could march troops and call cadence as well as any cadet in the country and I had a chance to become the Cadet Colonel, Commander of the student detachment. I was starting to get "cocky." Secretly I would say to myself "I can do this."

The reader may notice that I have spent very little time talking about other things that happened to me in college. It is really because ROTC was everything to me at college. It was because of the childhood experience that I had running through the woods playing Army with playmates in the coalfields of McDowell County. To be fair, I will mention some of the other things that I accomplished in college, but they truly paled in relationship to the real prize—a Regular Army Commission—in the United States Army. At different points I served as the president of my class, president of my fraternity and vice president of the Pan Hellenic Council of Fraternities and Sororities. My grades after the first semester were well above average. I never failed a course and I received only one D in the entire four years and that was during my freshman year. I always had a work-study job and played intramural sports. I served as a student representative on the West Virginia State College Scholarship Committee, chaired by mine and Olivia's dear friend and mentor, Dr. Grace I. Woodson. Through that committee I was able to funnel three scholarships back to my high school in McDowell County for Freddie McLauglin, Levy Morgan, and a girl whose last name was Smith. I do not remember her first name. Finally, I was selected to the prestigious Who's Who in American Universities and Colleges for the school year 1962.

Olivia and I left the beautiful campus of WVSC on the 10th of August 1962 with everything that we owned in my parent's car. We were completely broke, but we both had jobs. I could borrow money. We went back to my parent's two-bedroom house in Warrior Mines, WV, to spend the weekend. Late that afternoon, my Dad let me use his car to take Olivia to see her parents in Bishop, WV, and while we were out we went to the Tazewell, Virginia County Fair. I wore the uniform that I was commissioned in that morning and Olivia held on to my arm like I was a prize bull. I won her a stuffed animal toy by shooting a rifle. The next morning, Saturday, I went to the local Bank of War with my Dad and borrowed $300.00. I am certain that the redneck that ran the bank required my Dad to co-sign the loan. It would take another five years and a tour of duty in Vietnam before I decided to tell those folks at that bank that if they wanted to continue to do business with me, they would have to stop asking my Dad to come in and co-sign even if all I wanted to do was cash a check. I don't think they realized how insulting they were to me. I was making more money than my Dad and probably even had a larger savings account at a bank twenty miles away. That was one of the first steps of my resolution to refuse to be pushed around by prejudiced white folks after I returned from the war in Vietnam. After borrowing the money on my initial trip to the bank I returned to my parent's house and gave Olivia half of the money. I knew that she needed it because she would be going to Cleveland, Ohio to start her career as a teacher in the famed Shaker Heights District, within one week. In the meantime, I started packing my bags for my trip to my initial entry station, Fort Benning, Georgia, the next day.

SECTION I

THE COMPANY GRADE YEARS

Being presented a Certificate of Achievement from the 101st Airborne Division, 1965.

Being promoted to Captain in 8th Special Forces Group, Panama, April 1966.

Being promoted to 1st Lt. in the 1st Brigade, 101st Airborne Division on 10 February 1964.

Escorting and hosting the USARSO G-3 for Operations and the Commander, 8th Special Forces Group at graduation exercises in Panama, Canal Zone—1966.

Easter Sunday 1968 photo in the Republic of Vietnam with the other company commanders of the 1st Battalion, 7th Cavalry (Gary Owen)—1968.

1st day of duty in the 327th Battle Group,
101st Airborne Division,
Fort Campbell, KY—27 Nov 1962.

Commandant of the USARSO
NCO Academy in Coco Solo,
Panama, Canal Zone in 1966.

Official Army Photograph as a Captain
in the 8th SFG in Panama—1966.

US Airborne Jump School student at
Fort Benning, GA—August 1962.

Stephens in the 3rd grade at Excelsior Elementary School in War, WV–1949.

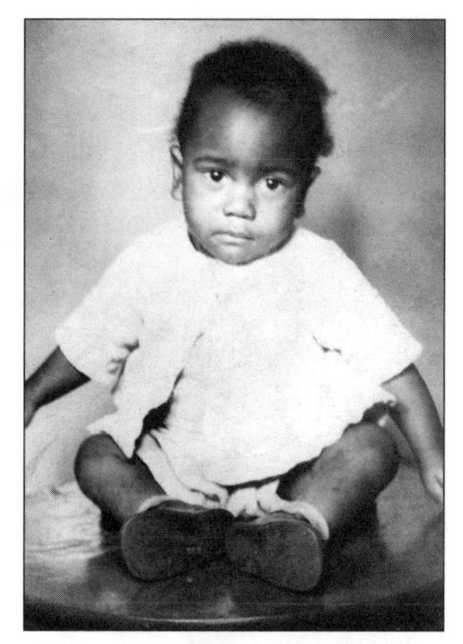

Nine months old, Robert L. Stephens, Jr.—1941.

With Mom and Dad, 1943.

Wedding day at Little Zion Baptist Church, Bishop WV—09 June 1962.

With Olivia after being promoted to Captain in Panama, CZ.

THE COMPANY GRADE YEARS

The dictionary defines company grade officers as junior commissioned officers having the rank of second lieutenant, first lieutenant, or captain in the U.S. Army, Air Force, or Marine Corps. In the Army, the company grade officer ranks begin with second lieutenant and rise to the rank of captain. Normally, usually, generally, almost always, company grade officers are in the learning mode for positions of higher responsibility. A lieutenant, for example, may be a platoon leader for his/her principal duty. However, he will also be assigned a number of ancillary duties which may include, the company transportation officer, supply officer, material readiness officer, voting officer, area beautification officer and a list of other functions. I am positive that there were times when I was loaded up with these duties by my first company commander in an effort to wash me out of the Army. However, I did all of them well.

At the time I entered the Army an airborne company like I was assigned to, consisted of four rifle platoons and one weapons platoon. Each rifle platoon had one officer (second lieutenant) and 46 enlisted men, one of whom was the platoon sergeant. The weapons platoon consisted of one seasoned officer (first lieutenant) and about thirty-five enlisted men. The company headquarters had a company commander (captain) and an executive/operations officer (first lieutenant) and several enlisted men in various administrative positions. In my first company, the fourth rifle platoon was referred to as the "ghost platoon" because it was not filled to full strength.

Work life for a company grade officer was very hectic and always uncertain in terms of how much time one would spend on a job/mission. If you had a decent company commander you could sort of plan your time at work. However, if you had a "dud" for a company commander, the boss imposed requirements or better known, short fuse orders, were never ending.

For the first five to seven years of my career, I was a company grade officer and I attempted to learn everything that I could about the Army. That learning experience included leading a Special Forces "A Team" in Panama, commanding two companies in combat during the Vietnam War and doing ordinary staff duty as a lower level action officer. Because of the number of airborne assignments at the time I performed the duties of Departure Airfield Control Officer (DACO) and Drop Zone Safety Officer (DZSO) many times during my early career. While in Panama I was also assigned to special duty (SD) with the US Army Southern Command Noncommissioned Officer Academy, first as the administration and supply officer and later as the Commandant.

For me, the company grade years were challenging. There were a lot of family separations for training, a tremendous time for learning about the Army, but most of all, deciding where my family would fit in the Army if I made it a career.

I arrived in Columbus, Georgia, late in the afternoon on the 13th of August, 1962. The overnight ride on a Trailways bus had been uneventful. It was hard to say goodbye to Olivia and realize that I would not see her for a while. After all we had only been married two months and I had really gotten used to being around her all the time. I dismounted from the Trailways and went into the segregated bus station in Columbus, Georgia, and changed into my uniform in the restroom. Major Sam Kelly had taught me that you report for duty in uniform, not in civilian clothes. I repacked my bags and went out to catch a local bus to Fort Benning—the Home of the Infantry—the Queen of Battle. Fort Benning was also the location for training people to jump, with parachutes, out of perfectly good flying airplanes. Later in life I would affectionately refer to Fort Benning as "Fort Beginning" because that is where every Infantryman got his start. That is true even today. On the way to Fort Benning I managed to keep the wrinkles in my uniform to a minimum. All I had pinned on that uniform that day was my name tag, my brass buttons, my crossed rifle insignia, and my 14 karat gold bars. With my initial clothing allowance of $400.00 I had purchased my uniforms from Lauderstein's of San Antonio, Texas. That purchase included a tan uniform, a flying saucer cap, a pair Florshiem leather shoes, my officer's insignia, and a swagger stick. I was "ready even if I didn't get to go." Upon arriving at Fort Benning and disembarking at the post bus station I secured a taxi to take me to the training company billeting area. The taxi driver was a retired soldier and knew exactly where I needed to go along the row of student officer billets that bordered the airborne training area. I trusted his judgment and went into the building that he told me to go into and to my surprise there stood Billy Washington, the other cadet who had been commissioned in my ceremony two days earlier at West Virginia State College. Billy and I exchanged greetings and he informed me that he already had our room and that he would help me bring in my stuff. Billy was a super nice guy and smart as a whip. He majored in chemistry in college and was a member of Alpha Kappa Mu, a national academic society of smart guys. He had taken a commission in the Chemical Corps but had to spend two years assigned to the Infantry before he would be allowed to transfer to the Chemical Corps. During the next couple of days we were busy with in-processing, getting our initial pay, buying field uniforms, and taking physical examinations for parachutist training. I had no idea how tough it was going to be to get through airborne training.

At the first real formation on Tuesday morning, we lined up in alphabetical order in our platoons. It was at this time that I discovered that all of the second lieutenants commissioned into the Regular Army Infantry, for the year 1962, were present for duty in that formation. That group included graduates from the United States Military Academy at West Point New York, all of the other large and small colleges and universities, and other historically black colleges and universities with ROTC programs from all over the country. I immediately asked myself "What have I gotten myself into?" I was in competition with the very best Infantry lieutenants that this country had to offer, and that made me feel very special. As we started marching to our first classroom location, someone asked for one of us to count cadence. I went to my strength just as I had at Summer Camp. I knew that nobody in that formation could call cadence better than I could. That action alone gained me a modicum of respect right up front. As I remember, there were five black guys in the class of about a thousand officers. There were a couple of guys from Morgan State College. Their names were Miles and Morgan. There was one guy from Tuskegee University whose name I do not recall. And there was Billy Washington and me. That was it for black Regular Army officers at the United States Army Infantry School in 1962. At the end of the morning formation they sent half of our class to the Infantry Officers Basic Course (IOBC) the other half to the United States Army Parachutist School affectionately referred to as "jump school." Billy and I were in the group that went to jump school.

Without any pre-conditioning, a pep talk, or coaching we were sent to the first week (Ground Week) of airborne training. The guys from West Point and some of the other schools knew what to expect. Neither Billy nor I had a clue. I mention this only because I have found that it is sometimes very awkward to go into a new situation or environment even when you have been sufficiently briefed. It is absolutely awful to go into a new situation or environment when you have no idea what to expect. That was the way it was for me during ground week at jump school. I had no idea what was going to happen to me. I remember guys like Joe Rigby, a cross-country runner and Ron Zinn a world-class walker, both from West Point, really ate that physical conditioning stuff up. Ground week in airborne school was all about physical conditioning. It, literally, kicked my butt! I had never run more than a mile, at one time, in my entire life and these guys were talking about running four and five miles at a time two and sometimes three times a day. I knew one thing, I already had orders to be assigned to the 101st Airborne Division and that meant an additional $110.00 supplement to my paycheck of $222.30 each month if I made it through airborne school. Besides I knew that it could not be any worse than being initiated into the Pershing Rifles. So while I was not completely prepared for the rigors of jump school, my basic attitude was – bring it on! I can do this. Somehow we survived Ground Week and we were sent to the second week (Tower Week) of airborne training. Tower week was where we focused on the techniques of landing after jumping from a perfectly good flying airplane. The landing was called a parachute landing fall (PLF). It had five points of contact to ensure that you wouldn't get hurt if you executed it properly. The first point of contact was the balls of your feet. The second was the calf muscle of your leg. The third was your thigh muscle. The fourth and most important was your buttocks and finally you finished on your push up muscle between your waist and shoulder. The idea was to hit, on the balls of your feet with both of your knees bent and your feet together, and while falling shift your weight to your calves and thighs as rapidly as possible, rotate your body so that your buttocks would take the brunt of the impact, and bounce back up to your feet using your pushup muscle on the opposite side. In addition, during tower week you started jumping from the thirty-four foot tower in order to develop a proper airplane door position and proper exit posture. Later in the week we jumped from the famed two hundred and fifty feet towers that were the signature of the airborne training site at Fort Benning. Oh, I almost forgot, you ran about five miles every morning. Billy was having some trouble with the five-mile-runs in the mornings. Because I knew him I would drop back and run with him. That was a mistake! At the end of tower week, they recycled both of us. It was that experience that taught me how to look out for and take care of number one. It's okay to be a nice guy but I found out that they seldom finish first, when it counts. During the first two weeks of airborne school I did not have a car and neither did Billy. So we mooched rides from other classmates who had automobiles. One guy in particular was very kind and gracious to us. His name was Rusty Wilkerson, a West Pointer, from Nashville, Tennessee. Rusty had a little Pontiac Firebird and he was proud of that car. One evening after training, he asked me to take my boots off before getting into his car. That really upset me. Not so much that he asked me to remove my boots but the fact that I allowed myself to get into a predicament where I was not even in control of wearing my boots. That night I went car shopping. Two days later I was the proud owner of an Oldsmobile F85 coupe. I kept my car clean like Rusty did, but I never asked anyone to remove their shoes to ride in it. After being set back a week during Tower Week we went on to (Jump Week) at the airborne school and I got my silver wings…the novice parachutist badge.

Because we were recycled in airborne school, we started the Infantry Officer's Basic Course a week late. I never caught up to the rest of the class. These guys were the cream of the crop from their respective academies, colleges and universities and they all hit the ground running. I struggled to keep myself out of the lower ten percent of the class. I am not offering excuses but I missed all of the important in-processing briefings and assignments. I just started behind the power curve and never hit a successful stride. I was playing catch-up all the way. That was the second time that year that I personally miscalculated a requirement and screwed up. The first mistake occurred back at WVSC, during the spring semester of my senior year.

Before we could graduate from WVSC, in those days, we had to pass certain comprehensive examinations. Since I majored in Education with teaching fields in English and Social Studies, I was required to take three examinations. I made it through the Education and Social Studies examinations without a problem. The English examination was taken from a non–required course, an English curriculum elective entitled English 400 Seminar.

That course was conducted by the English Department Chairperson herself, Dr. Lorna Kemp. Not only was she a terrible teacher, she had an awful disposition that bordered on perpetual arrogance. It was purported that she had a Doctorate degree in Philology. Some people said that she was the first black female to obtain such a degree. She may have been all of that, but in my opinion, that did not give her license to treat students as if they were lesser beings in the order of the species. I did not take English 400 Seminar because I knew I was getting a commission and I would not be teaching school for a living. Also, in my heady state as one of the "big men on campus" I felt that I was smart enough to pass the English Comp. That was my first miscalculation. I was wrong! That's why I received my commission in August instead of June. I had to go to summer school and take English 400 Seminar and retake the English Comprehensive Examination. Early on I went to the cadre leadership in the ROTC Department and complained. My complaint was that there is something wrong with a system that allows an elective course to determine who should graduate and who should not graduate from the English Department. I thought about going in to see the Academic Dean, Dr. Harrison Ferrell and the President, Dr. William Lord Wallace, but LTC Hinkson convinced me that I had made the mistake and that I should live with it. I am proud to say, after taking the class I blew the English Department away. However, the class was not a seminar. We never had one session for class discussions. Dr. Kemp passed out a mimeographed list of four hundred research questions that required answers. Since she was not authorized student assistants for that purpose she had the students in her English 400 Seminar class do research for her. There was one other student who took the summer elective course with me. Her name was Verna Wood. She was tall, attractive and very smart but like me she thought she could pass the English Comp without taking the elective. Verna and I worked in the library doing research every day for eight to ten hours and around six o'clock in the evening we would bring our work to Olivia who would type up our findings in some format that was understandable and catalog them into a loose-leaf binder. We did not have enough money to buy manifold paper and/or make a second copy. Copy machines were very crude in those days and not available for students to do large amounts of reproduction. By the end of the summer session, we had completed all of the assignment and even found some errors that Dr. Kemp and her staff had made. In fact, during the course of retaking the comprehensive examination I went up to the desk where Kemp was sitting as the examination monitor and challenged one of the questions. Verna who was sitting on the other side of the room did the same thing. Kemp became flustered and left the room visibly upset. Olivia was sitting outside of the administration building waiting for me to finish the exam. She told me later that Dr. Kemp came running out of the administration building and headed for the library. Minutes later, she and Dr. Fanning Belcher, another English Professor, came back to the room where we were taking the comprehensive examination with smiles on their faces. From that point on, I never worried, because I knew that Verna and I passed. We had just embarrassed the hell out of them. Quite frankly, I do not think our papers were ever read and evaluated. There were others in that room that had been returning for up to six years and never passed the English Comp. I turned in that notebook that we compiled with all of the answers and Dr. Kemp never returned it. She told me that it was the most comprehensive listing of answers that she had ever received from any student in the past. From that day forward she always referred to me as Mr. Stephens instead of the characteristic and sometimes sarcastic, "young man."

Of course the second miscalculation that year was dropping back with Billy and getting recycled in jump school. It was at that time that I decided that I would not ever get caught short again if I could help it. Since then I have not excelled at everything that I have tried, but I have not failed because of any lack of preparation or focus on my part. I never took another examination or test, of any kind, without preparing and I never fell out of another run unless I was injured. In fact, I vowed that I would not ever fall out of another run unless it was in the direction of the run…puking. About midway into IOBC, I was called in and given a stern talking to by some first lieutenant, acting detachment commander, waiting to attend flight school about being in the lower ten percent of the IOBC class. Actually, I was told that my overall scholastic average was in the mid-eighties. I asked, rather emphatically, perhaps even rudely, what it took to pass. The lieutenant answered that seventy percent was a passing score. Later, I was to find out through the grapevine that only nine points separated the top man from the low man in the class. However, somehow I finished 180 of 180. I didn't believe it then and I don't believe it now; but, I didn't fight it. I found out from talking to my peers that black guys almost always finished in the lower third of the classes. But, I had a diploma, I had airborne wings, and I had an assignment in my hand to the prestigious 101st Airborne Division at Fort Campbell, Kentucky. It does feel kind of good to say now that I was one of the officers who rose to general officer rank out of that IOBC class. Joe Rigby and Phil Browning are the only other ones I know personally that became general officers. There may be others that I do not know about.

I did not like Fort Benning, Georgia. Olivia and I made a conscious decision that she would go to Cleveland, Ohio and teach elementary school that year because we knew it would be tough in the Deep South to get affordable and suitable, temporary housing in Columbus, Georgia. We were to find out later that suitable housing for black folks was difficult to find anywhere in the United States of America at that time, but the difficulty was multiplied several times in the South. What a shocker! Discrimination was alive and well in 1962 and Olivia and I had not had a great deal of prior exposure to it in West Virginia, where we grew up. Oh, we knew that we went to separate schools, we sat in the balcony at the theater, and we couldn't sit down and eat at some lunch counters, even in Charleston, West Virginia. All of these acts were subtle. I guess I was not ready for the blatant display of discrimination that I encountered in Columbus, Georgia, like the signs at public places for restrooms and water. Another example was foreign officers from other countries were welcomed at the lunch counters of Woolworth and other food serving establishments and I, an American Army officer was not. That really struck me as strange and I decided that someday I would do something about it. For the time being there were enough of us from WVSC at Fort Benning to ignore the discrimination and enjoy ourselves and stay amused without socializing with white officers at the local clubs, bars and restaurants. Among the WVSC grads were Rad Robinson, Jimmy Peeler, Thomas (Goody) Goodwin, George Coleman and of course Billy Washington and I. We were not all in the same classes or even assigned to the School Battalion. Yet we sort of hung out together on weekends. Billy and I studied during the week because we were determined not to let our ROTC program at WVSC down by flunking out of IOBC. It was not that uncommon in those days for black officers to flunk out of the basic courses in Army Basic Officer Courses. That was the way it was then and nobody questioned it. Later in life, I asked Major Kelly why he and other members of the cadre at WVSC had not warned us about the degree of blatant discrimination that we would encounter on active duty. His answer was simple and to the point, "We wanted to teach you men about the positive aspects of the military and not start you off on the negatives." I accepted his explanation and never asked him again. I suppose it was also very awkward for them to teach how difficult it would be for black officers to succeed in the Army since half of the students and cadre members at WVSC were white.

Olivia flew into Columbus one weekend from Cleveland, OH to visit me at Fort Benning. It was far and away the best weekend that I had during IOBC. She arrived late on a Friday afternoon and stayed until Sunday afternoon. It cost us an arm and a leg by the dollar standard of the time but we didn't care. It was worth every damn penny. I knew that I could not expect to get decent accommodations at a hotel or motel off post so I got us a room at the main Officers' Club on post. It was clean and very nice. Olivia was pregnant with our first child and I wanted everything to be nice for her. We decided that weekend that we would never voluntarily separate again. From then until now we have remained together unless it was absolutely impossible for her to travel with me.

Billy and I graduated from the IOBC on or about the 16th of November and we headed north in my new car. I dropped him off at the bus station in Bluefield, WV, about ten o'clock and he bought a ticket for Charleston, WV. He offered to pay me for the ride but I refused to accept it. After all I was going that way even if he had not been with me and I was glad to have him along for company. It would be many years before I would see Billy again as a Lieutenant Colonel. An hour after I dropped him off in Bluefield I was at my in-laws' home in Bishop, VA. They got out of bed and we sat and talked for about an hour. Then I headed home to my parents where we sat up until about 3 o'clock in the morning talking. My brother was away at college so I had the spare bedroom all to myself. I slept late the next morning until about eight o'clock. Around noon that day I headed for Cleveland, Ohio to pack up my wife and move her to Fort Campbell, Kentucky. I arrived in Cleveland around midnight and Olivia was glad to see me. She had most of her things packed and she was ready to become a full time officer's wife.

The next day we went by Olivia's school so she could sign out and I met her colleagues. Then we went shopping to get her first maternity outfit. Somehow we ended up in an exclusive maternity boutique that had plush carpeting and nice dressing rooms in which husbands could wait while their spouses tried on the outfits. Well, we did not buy the most expensive frock in the store but we were damn close. If my memory serves me right we spent $249.00 on one dress. That was in 1962, but I didn't care because it was for my lovely wife and our first-born child and nothing was too good for them. After spending a couple of days in Cleveland we headed back to West Virginia for Thanksgiving.

Immediately following the holiday weekend I started driving to Fort Campbell, Kentucky and the World War II famous 101st Airborne Division for my first real Army assignment with the Screaming Eagles.

SIR, REPORTING FOR DUTY

I arrived at Fort Campbell around noon on Tuesday the 27th of November 1962. I reported to the 101st Airborne Division Headquarters in uniform with my novice parachutist wings on my chest and the glider patch on my garrison cap. Major Kelly had impressed upon me the importance to report for duty in uniform. I was about as cocky as I had ever been in my life. I was not afraid of anything or anybody! Somewhere along the training in jump school I had been told that a paratrooper could whip any six men who were not airborne qualified and I guess I believed it. I was directed by the staff duty sergeant in the headquarters building to the Office of the Assistant Chief of Staff for Personnel, G1 (ACofS, G1). The staff duty sergeant blew me away with all of the "yes sir and no sir" answers. And as I walked down the hall other enlisted soldiers braced themselves against the wall and greeted me with "All the way, Sir." I knew enough to reply "Airborne!" Man, I was swept off my feet. So this was the real Army and not the "crap" that I had experienced in IOBC at Fort Benning where you were lucky if an enlisted person spoke to you at all let alone acted alert. I was ready to go to work. After the routine small chatter that I later came to know as regular G1 personnel drivel, i.e., "we've been expecting you and we're so glad you're here." The major with whom I was speaking asked me where I wanted to be assigned. I replied, "The 506th, sir!" Quite frankly, that was the only unit that I knew about, and that was because another lieutenant, Larry Redman, from Seton Hall University, had told me at Fort Benning that he was assigned to the 506th Airborne Battle Group. Redman was a nice, friendly guy who befriended me at Fort Benning when he found out that I had orders to the 101st Airborne Division. He had gone straight from college to the division and gotten his feet firmly on the ground prior to coming to Fort Benning for IOBC. If I had passed my English Comprehensive Examination and not had to attend Summer school to graduate, I would have been on the same tract. Anyway after telling the ACofS, G1 major that I wanted to go the 506th, he smiled and assigned me to the 327th Airborne Battle Group.

According to Wikipedia, The Free Encyclopedia "The 101st Airborne Division (Air Assault)—nicknamed the Screaming Eagles—is an airborne division of the United States Army primarily trained for air assault operations. During the Vietnam War, the 101st was redesignated an airmobile division, and later as an air assault division. For historical reasons, it keeps the identifier "airborne", but does not conduct parachute operations at a division level. Many modern members of the 101st are graduates of the U.S. Army Air Assault School, and wear the Air Assault Badge, but it is not a prerequisite to be assigned to the division. The division is headquartered at Fort Campbell, Kentucky and is currently serving in Iraq." When I arrived there on the 27th of November 1962, it was strictly an airborne infantry division with soldiers jumping out of perfectly good flying airplanes.

I reported to the 327th Battle Group shortly after lunch and met the Assistant Adjutant, Lieutenant Dandridge. He gave me an overall briefing of the battle group headquarters and took me in to meet the Commander, Colonel (COL) Robert Saddler. Saddler was a little guy with a big smile and a firm handshake. He made me feel at ease immediately. The last thing that he said to me that day was "Lieutenant you will make some mistakes. I expect you to make some mistakes. If you don't make mistakes I am going to come looking for you because that means that you won't be doing your job." I left his office feeling pretty good. LT Dandridge took my picture to add to the photographs posted on the wall of the headquarters. As I left the Battle Group headquarters building I met other officers who greeted me with the unit slogan, "Above the Rest." The 327th was steeped in history and tradition. For example I was told that the unit adopted the slogan during World War II when they were surrounded by the Germans at Bastogne and asked to surrender. That's when the acting commander of the 101st Airborne Division, General Anthony C. McAuliffe, replied to the Germans with one word "NUTS." I was ready to become part of all of that. Each officer had his name engraved on a sterling silver cup that was part of the Battle Group's Silver Punch Bowl Service that was used at formal events and unit "prop blasts." That set of silver memorabilia was on display in the headquarters building foyer. I wanted my name on one of those cups. I was further assigned to C Company, the Cold Steel Cobras. Captain John F Sloan was the company commander. He was in the field with the company taking the Annual Training Test (ATT) and I did not have a chance to meet him that day. I did, however, walk over to the company and meet the duty personnel and draw my field gear or as we called it TA21. Again, I was impressed when the enlisted soldiers, some sergeants, braced against the wall when I passed by them in the hallway.

I left the 327th Battle Group area and went back to the division cantonment area to get a room in the Bachelor Officer Quarters (BOQ) and get some supper. After supper I went to bed and slept like a newborn baby. It had been a long day and I was wound tighter than a cheap drum. I had calculated the driving time from my parent's home to Fort Campbell and driven straight through because there were no motels available that accommodated Negroes—that I knew about. When you got tired, you just had to pull over and sleep in the car. The next day I got busy attempting to secure housing for Olivia and me on post. The housing officer, an Army Corps of Engineers captain, did a cursory look at me and told me I'd have to move off post because there was nothing available. I had left Olivia at home with her parents because we anticipated that we would have trouble securing suitable housing in the South. We were determined to be together and so I started calling rental agents for housing immediately. I also called the local United Services Organization (USO). At the USO I spoke with a sergeant who said, "Yes sir, lieutenant, I've got a three bedroom brick ranch for rent in the Fountainbleu subdivision for $120.00 a month." Well my housing allowance was only $110.00 a month but I figured that I could find $10.00 more somewhere and pay the rent. After getting directions to the USO from the sergeant I was elated that I would be able to call Olivia and tell her that she could come to Fort Campbell the next day because I had a house. I went down to Clarksville, TN, to see the sergeant and get the house. I was in civilian clothes and asked for the sergeant at the information desk and approached him. The sergeant turned as red as a beet and apologized profusely. "Sir I did not know that you were a Negro, you have to go to the Negro USO." I was ticked off! And I let everyone in that office know that I was ticked off. They were all embarrassed and very helpful getting me directions to the Negro USO and even offered me a cup of coffee. I refused it. I did not feel like being diplomatic, I wanted to destroy something. Quite frankly, at that moment I wanted to kill something! Here I was a college graduate, a commissioned officer in the Regular U.S. Army, and a working taxpaying citizen and the first thing that I faced was blatant discrimination from a half literate white sargeant who could live anywhere he wanted to live and who was on special duty from the Army that I was a part of sitting on his butt in a plush job in Clarksville, TN. Man was I angry. In fact, I even feel the anger again right now, as I write these words, and that was more than forty-eight years ago.

That was my first taste of real denial because of my skin color. I had gone to a segregated public school, sat in the balcony at local movie theaters and was even denied a seat at the lunch counters in War, West Virginia; but, this incident had a lasting affect on me. I accepted the earlier incidents as a child and a college student but this was different. I had just finished training with the best, most elite male officers from all over the United States of America and I held my own. I was equal to the task. I graduated right along with everyone else. I was a Regular Army officer. That may not appear to be anything special to the reader, but it was sure as hell special to me. Beyond that I was an airborne officer—one of a select group that this country had to offer, and here was this special duty sergeant giving me directions to go across town and inquire about housing at the Negro USO. I went. I did not make waves that day. I just kept thinking, how will I explain this to Olivia? How can I face my wife and tell her that some redneck mouthpiece for the USO had led me down a primrose path. I went over to the Negro USO and met the nicest little black woman (I wish I could remember her name) who gave me a cup of coffee and her undivided attention. She also expressed her pride in me being an officer. Later, I would find that there were no more than two dozen black officers on Fort Campbell at that time and the highest ranking was a major who worked at the airfield. Almost all of us were college graduates with Regular Army commissions.

The nice lady at the Negro USO gave me directions to two places. One was a renovated barracks building that had been moved from the cantonment area of Fort Campbell to downtown Clarksville. The other one was advertised as a two-bedroom apartment with a kitchen nook located in Mrs. Brown's house on 8th Avenue. I left Clarksville and went back to the post to meet my new company commander at 1300 hours.

At the appointed time, the company first sergeant, 1SG Rex Babb, ushered me in to see Captain John Fitzgerald Sloan. Sloan was a tall, shy person from Springfield, MA. After he went through the usual crap of "I was expecting you and I'm really glad that you are finally here." We got down to his true demeanor. He informed me that he was from Massachusetts and that he would not expect any more or any less from me because I was a Negro. I thought "wow, that's the second time today that I have been reminded of my race. Maybe I have picked the wrong profession." Sloan went on to tell me about the company and the platoon that I would get and that my platoon sergeant, Sergeant First Class (SFC) Vincent Rose, would be retiring within thirty days. He stated further that our unit would be going on Initial Ready Force (IRF) duty within two or three weeks and that I needed to be ready for immediate deployment. I do not remember if he even asked if I was married, if my wife was with me, or where I was living. This guy was all business and hell bent on showing me that he was in charge. I was not impressed. I would have even been less impressed if I had known at the time that he graduated in the lower portion of his class West Point class. After all I had been the cadet colonel and commander of my ROTC unit in college, i.e., first in my class. Sloan concluded his interview by telling me that I had the weekend to get settled because we would go on alert on Monday morning, December 10th, 1962. It was at this time that I told him that my wife would be coming in that night. It did not faze him he just continued telling me how I needed to get squared away for next week. I left Sloan's office and went house hunting. I had about ten days before I would be on Division Ready Force alert. It was Thursday, the 29th of November, 1962.

I was a little rushed for time that afternoon because Olivia was coming in that evening and I wanted to have a place to take her besides the temporary BOQ that I was living in at the time. I looked at the two alternatives that the nice woman at the Negro USO had offered. The first place I looked at was a renovated barracks building that had been moved from Fort Campbell and tuned into low rent living space for soldiers. It was awful! The other terrible part was that only black folks lived in this section of the city of Clarksville, TN, and the area was really run down. I just kept saying to myself, "How can I ask Olivia to follow me and live under these conditions." I rejected that option real quick. Then I went down to visit Mrs. Brown on 8th Avenue. She welcomed me into her home and showed me the place that she had advertised as "a two bedroom apartment with a kitchen nook." That's exactly what it was, two rooms with a bed in each room and no other furniture, a kitchen with one chair and a bathroom with a commode and a utility sink to wash the dishes, the floor, your body, and anything else. There was no bathtub or shower. She was nice and I thought that I was desperate at this point so I took it. She asked for two months rent in advance. I gave her $110.00 cash. I left and went back to the BOQ to move my stuff and get ready to meet Olivia at the bus station. Olivia came in around six or seven o'clock. I don't remember the exact time, but it was dark. She was beautiful getting off of that bus and I was embarrassed that I had to take her to the place that I had just rented. She was as great about that situation then, as she has been about similar situations throughout our marriage. She did not complain! We left the bus station and went to dinner at the Officer's "Little Club" which was the annex from the main officers' club. It was late when we arrived at "our apartment." I don't remember, but I think that I had made the bed and we were both exhausted and went directly to bed after "washing up" in the utility sink in the bathroom. Mrs. Brown offered her bathroom, downstairs, if we ever wanted to take a bath. Oh, did I say that this so-called apartment was located in the attic? It had the steepest stairs that I have ever seen in my life and one triangular window in the kitchen for the whole place. The bedrooms were completely dark. The next morning I went to work at 5 o'clock. I left Olivia in bed. She was six months pregnant and she had a long day of travel the day before.

Sloan never asked if I was settled or if my spouse arrived okay. I went into the first sergeant's office and met MSG Rocha, who functioned as the first sergeant most of the time because Rex Babb was always off working an angle and "politicking." Rocha took me into the operations room and introduced me to First Lieutenant Martin and Staff Sergeant Sauder. They ran things for the company. Lieutenant Dale Shipley was also in the office and I met him. There were other sergeants in there and I met them all. Shipley took me down the hall to the "Lieutenants room." We all shared an office that had three or four desks in it. LT Martin was the company executive officer (XO) and had a desk in the operations room. He was also on orders to go to flight school and would be leaving shortly. LT Shipley was going to get promoted soon to first lieutenant and replace LT Martin in operations. I was LT Shipley's replacement in the 2nd Platoon. The company was a typical airborne company of that era that had four rifle platoons and a weapons platoon. One of the rifle platoons was called the "ghost" platoon and would only be filled with personnel in the case of an emergency deployment.

Lieutenant Shipley was assigned to the weapons platoon until LT Martin's departure. Shipley was a fair individual who I served with again on the Army General Staff. He was a military academy graduate from Ohio. He retired as a lieutenant colonel (LTC). SFC Ashby led the 1st platoon. SFC Ashby, even today, remains as one of the premier sergeants that I have known. He knew his job, was courteous to everyone and was immaculately dressed at all times. The truth of the matter was that he did not need an officer to lead in his platoon. He was that good. Second Lieutenant David Bender led the 3rd platoon. LT Bender was a typical rich white boy from New York who never showed any racial prejudice toward me, or anyone else, the entire time that I knew him. I saw him later in my career also when I served on the Army staff. I think that he retired as a colonel. Several excess sergeants first class led the fourth platoon. SFC Long, a Native American and MSG Watts an African American are two that come to mind. All in all we had a good crew in the old Cold Steel Cobra Company. I think that I was fortunate to get SFC Rose as my platoon sergeant. After he met me I think he had second thoughts about retiring right away. In fact, he decided to delay his retirement for six months. This gave him a chance to teach one more second lieutenant how to become an officer. Believe me, I still value some of those lessons that he taught me even today. He was never overbearing and always spoke to me in the third person, i.e., "if I was the lieutenant, I'd do that this way…I cherished our evenings in the field. He taught me well. After SFC Rose retired, my second platoon sergeant was Platoon Sergeant (PSG) Jordan. He was a great guy! He knew that SFC Rose had taught me the right way and that "I had my stuff together." So he and I worked as a team and functioned like a well-oiled watch. Unfortunately, he broke his leg on a parachute jump during Swift Strike III and I lost him. Then I got a slick, drunk by the name of SFC Elkins who was from West Virginia.

He and I never hit it off and I was seasoned enough to tell him to "Go and find a home before I fire you." My relationship with noncommissioned officers (NCO) and other enlisted men was always great. I treated them with decency and respect and would not accept anything less from them. I had learned how to get along well with others at WVSC. I also knew that the key to success was treating everyone fairly.

CPT Sloan was rarely at work before 6:00AM. Revile was always at 5:55AM and was taken by one of the officers every day, usually a second lieutenant. We rotated the duty, weekly, and presented a report to Sloan later in the morning. The cliché, we do more before nine o'clock than civilians do all day was definitely in effect at the 327th Battle Group. The designated company duty officer for the day was supposed to turn off the firelights, check police of the area including the parking lot, and eat breakfast in the mess hall. The duty officer and the mess officer could eat the meal at the reduced rate. CPT Sloan wasted no time assigning me all of the typical "black officer duties." It was customary, however, unstated that black officers would be the company motor officer, the supply officer, the mess officer, and the material readiness officer—all at the same time. In addition, you might also get to be the area beautification officer because they could ride you every day for that or the safety officer, especially during the Christmas holidays. That would guarantee that you spent a minimum of eighteen hours at work during the week and up until about three o'clock in the afternoon on Saturday and at least one or two hours on Sunday. Talk to any black officer of that era and you'll find similar stories. I think that they were trying to make things so unpleasant that we would decide early not to stay on active duty beyond the initial obligation. Do I think there was a concerted conspiracy throughout the Army to do this? Yes!

For doing all of those duties and occasionally doing indebtedness officer duties and during election time serving as the officer who helped soldiers fill out their absentee ballots, I was rated in the lower third of my year group. The highest possible score that one could obtain on an efficiency report, i.e., performance rating, in those days was one hundred twenty points from the rater and one hundred twenty points from the endorser. For my first report I received 75 points from the rater and 75 points from the endorser. My combined score was a measly 150 points out of 240. That was my first report. I think CPT Sloan made some remark with a smirk, about leaving me "room to grow."

When I returned home from that first full day at work in C Company I found Olivia dressed but she had spent the entire day in bed. Early that morning she had seen rats "the size of kittens" roaming around the apartment. I knew that I had to do better by her. She did not deserve that kind of life. Somehow we survived the weekend by essentially staying out of the apartment and riding around in the car. On Monday, the following week I got busy looking for something else. I went back to the post housing office and told the captain that had been so rude to me before that I was going to make two stops when I left his office. The first one was going to be to the Office of the Commanding General of Fort Campbell to inform him of my intentions and the second would be at the Office of the Inspector General in Washington, DC. I was mad as hell and I was not going to accept being a second-class citizen in the South any longer. It must have scared the hell out of everyone in that office because I was offered a one bedroom set of quarters—on post—immediately and put on a list for two bedrooms based upon the fact that Olivia was pregnant. I was given the keys to the quarters, at that moment and I drove to the house before noon. I went and got Olivia and we moved in immediately. I went back to work and she made the place livable by the time I got home that night. The next day I drove to work and left Olivia again to entertain and fend for herself while I tried to get my arms around my job. In the quarters we had a bed, a dining room set that included a table, four chairs and a buffet and everything in the kitchen worked. All of the utilities worked and we even had light bulbs in all the sockets. We survived the rest of the week meeting our neighbors, going to the commissary to buy groceries and shopping at Uncle Bud's a local retail store that sold everything from roofing nails to mink coats. By Saturday afternoon, we had purchased a couch, two occasional chairs, three tables, two lamps and most importantly a television. We had successfully set up our first home. I marvel even today at how meticulous Olivia was about everything and how hard she worked at making our home a comfortable place to live. She is the same way today. Our home is our castle!

Now, this officer stuff was starting to take form. We were special and lots of people worked hard to make sure that we were taken care of, properly. However, we could not get the telephone hooked up for several days so I asked LT Donald Jones and his wife Lillian, another black couple, if we could use their telephone in case of an emergency. They lived three doors down from our apartment in 4744E. We lived in 4744B, in the same building. Our next door neighbor in 4744A was First Lieutenant Ingram, a WVSC graduate who was a junior when I was a freshman. He never came over to welcome us—his wife did and she and Olivia became friends.

I knew that on Monday, the 10th of December, we would become the division's initial ready force (IRF) and I needed to be near a telephone in case an alert was called. Today we would probably call the IRF a first responder. We had to report in on Sunday afternoon for IRF duty. I told CPT Sloan about my arrangement with Don and Lillian Jones and he immediately rejected it. His rational was that he could not be sure that Don or his wife would come and notify me if I had a call and further, Olivia and I might not get up to answer the door. What a crock! I have always wondered if he would have felt that way if Don and I had been West Point graduates and white. His solution was simple. I'd have to move into the barracks with the enlisted soldiers. So, on Sunday night, I moved into the barracks and slept on a cot in the company commander's office. At 5:55 AM, since I was already there, I took revile. After revile, I went home, showered, shaved, and changed clothes and went back to the company. CPT Sloan was so preoccupied and full of himself that he didn't miss me. During that first weekend, I had also showed Olivia how to get around on the post and so I started leaving the car with her so she could move about and get things done. We were on alert for seven days. On Wednesday of the alert week, LT Shipley and his wife Eloise had a party at their home, just around the corner from my quarters. They invited all of the high-ranking officers in the Battle Group headquarters and all of the West Point graduates that were available. LT Shipley was a West Point grad and it might have been a pep party before the annual Army versus Navy football game or maybe he was being promoted. I just do not remember why he threw the party. What I do remember is that Mrs. Dickson, the wife of LTC Dickson the battle group deputy commander, asked Olivia how she liked Fort Campbell. And something happened that I would have to get used to really quick and learn to respect and live with, even today. With Olivia, you don't ask a question unless you really want the answer. She will not lie. She won't even equivocate. She just tells it as she sees it. And that's what she did to LTC Dickson's wife. She told her about the USO situation, about the house that we left down town after four days and didn't get one dime of our deposit back, and she informed her that she was in our home alone because CPT Sloan had me sleeping on a cot in the barracks. LTC Dickson's wife evidently was appalled and went directly to LTC Dickson. About fifteen minutes later CPT Sloan came to me and said, with a crap eating grin on his face "Why don't you go home tonight instead of staying in the company area and take some time off tomorrow to get your wife settled." My guess is that LTC Dickson chewed his butt and brought him to his senses. I went home with Olivia that night and I have never been more proud of her than I was that night.

One more C company story and I'll move on. We went to the field and CPT Sloan told me to stack the sleeping rolls from my platoon at a certain location along side of the road and the company supply personnel would come by and pick them up and transport them back to the company. This incident occurred after we had deployed on a Filed Training Exercise (FTX) called

Cold Eagle. On the afternoon we deployed, the temperature was about 50 degrees Fahrenheit. During the course of the night the January temperatures in Tennessee dropped into the low teens. I called CPT Sloan and requested permission to build fires for my troops. His reply was "permission denied." I waited about an hour until daybreak, and I called again. This time when he denied it I already had a five to ten feet high bonfire going before I called. My troops thought that I was a stud because I didn't put up with the stupidity that the company commander engaged in. My platoon was the only one in the company that did not have one single case of frostbite during that FTX. Later in a field exercise he directed me to stack our sleeping rolls along side of the road as we moved out on a forced road march. Two of the sleeping rolls disappeared. Sloan called me in and told me that he was going to recommend that I be held liable for the loss on a Report of Survey. I was really angry. I told my platoon sergeant, and he "arranged" to have two bedrolls delivered to the platoon for a fifth of Old Grandad whiskey. I bought the booze at the post package store. In retrospect, I believe now that the NCO's worked a scam on me. That's okay though, I learned a very important lesson and that was never to trust blindly another commanding officer as long as I remained on active duty.

CPT Sloan left the company after about a year and was replaced briefly by LT Shipley who gave me another mediocre performance evaluation with a numerical value of 150 out of 240 possible points. Shipley was followed by an officer named CPT "Jumping Jim" Damron. This guy was called up during the Cuban Crisis and remained on active duty for as long as he possibly could after that. I think he was liked by his peers and the Battle Group staff for the comic relief that he provided. All he wanted to do was jump out of airplanes and lead the "aggressor forces" during training exercises. When we went to field training with him, we ate from the officers' mess kit service, played bridge in his tent during the afternoon, and had an opportunity to sleep in his tent at night. I always declined sleeping in his tent. For some reason I never wanted to get too close to him. My guess is that he did not have a Bachelor's degree and probably would have been more comfortable pumping gas at a service station back home. I think he was from the Midwest. How he became an officer was a mystery to me. He was awful! On a typical workday he would call the company at about 0830 and tell the first sergeant to "Send one of them lieutenants over to my quarters to pick me up." He only had one car and his wife kept it at home most of the time for her use. One of us would drive over to Werner Park, the company grade housing area, and he would run out of the house in his boxer shorts, a tee shirt, and a field jacket with his pants on a clothes hanger. We would drive him to the company area and he would dismount as close to the front door of the company as possible and run inside carrying his starched fatigue pants. He would go into his office and finish dressing. His driver or one of the soldiers on work detail was responsible for shining his boots during the night. He would put on his Louisville pop-up hat, which had a large cardboard pair of master parachutist wings on the front, and yell out to the first sergeant, "Bring the guilty bastards in here and let's try them." In those days there were Articles 15 of the Uniform Code of Military Justice and other forms of non judicial punishments, i.e., the first sergeant's punishment given almost every day. He lasted about three months and then he disappeared. Thank God he was not in command long enough to rate me. Damron was followed in command, by CPT Leslie G. Gibbins another West Pointer, who was coming to us from Europe where he had been an aide de camp to a general officer. To say the least, he was a little stiff. On his first night in the field he gave me an objective that was a benchmark on the map. I said to him, "you know that this is a metal marking on the ground, sir" he replied, "of course, I want you to find it." I went back and briefed my platoon sergeant and squad leaders and SSG McGlory, the first squad leader, said "Don't worry Lieutenant I know exactly where that is." What Gibbins didn't know was that the sergeants in the 101st Airborne Division had served only in the 101st and the 82nd Airborne Divisions when they were stateside. Some of these guys had been at Campbell for five consecutive years and they knew the terrain like the back of their hand. During their free time they hunted in the same areas. We took him directly to the spot that he was looking for and he tripped over it stepping out of the wood line. From that point on, my stuff was golden with CPT Gibbins. He trusted me to get everything done. I was still the motor officer, the supply officer, the mess officer, and the material readiness officer. The difference now was that I had done those jobs for so long that I was good at them and everyone knew it. And that's what gave me my first big break.

In February of 1964, the 101st Airborne Division switched to the Reorganization Army Division (ROAD) and we were no longer in Battle Groups. We were battalions under the command of tactical brigade headquarters. The 327th Battle Group became the First Brigade that was the tactical headquarters for the 1st Battalion, 327th Infantry, the 2nd Battalion, 327th Infantry, and the 2nd Battalion, 502nd Infantry. Upon reorganization, I was made the Supply Officer, (S-4) of the 1st Battalion. LT Salvatore Pagliario was the S-4 of the 2nd Battalion. He was my competition. In my mind, all I had to do was beat Sal at the logistics game and I would win. We were co-located for the turnover under Major Mark Hanson, the hardest working person I had met to that point in my career. I learned a lot from MAJ Hanson. I think the most important thing that I learned was that there are some jobs where you never finish. At some point you just have to stop and get a fresh start the next day. I hired SSG Bleman the supply sergeant from C Company as my assistant since I knew his capabilities and trusted him. Our Battalion Commander was LTC Ritchie. Ritchie was an older guy—easy going and he let me do my job. Sometimes I remember and say to myself how fortunate I was to work for LTC Ritchie. He was a great old guy. He must have been at least forty years old. The Brigade Commander was none other than the flamboyant thirty-something-year-old Colonel Herbert G. Wolfe. He had very high standards and demanded a great deal from everyone. While he was very stern and strutted around like a peacock, he was not abusive and did not appear to have any racial prejudices. I was the first officer promoted in the 1st Brigade and Colonel Wolfe had a picture taken of the ceremony along with me and LTC Ritchie and published it in the post newspaper. When I left that job I scored 230 out of 240 on my performance appraisal. Not a maximum score but people were starting to notice and reward my hard work. LTC Ritchie never exhibited any racial prejudices.

Olivia and I were stationed at Fort Campbell slightly less than three years. All in all, my first years with the Screaming Eagles were challenging, fun, and fast paced. Our son was born there on the 11th of February 1963. About three months after I signed into C Company. When we woke that morning Olivia said she wasn't feeling well so I drove her to the hospital emergency room, left her there and went on to work. The company was scheduled for its Annual Inspector General Inspection (AGI) that day. Since I was the motor officer, mess officer, supply officer, voting officer, indebtedness officer and the material readiness officer I knew that CPT Sloan would never forgive me if I called in because Olivia was sick. There was no family sick leave policy in those days. I told Olivia to call me after she saw a doctor and I would come and pick her up and take her home. At about 0930 she left a message with the first sergeant; "My water has broken and I am in labor at the hospital." The first sergeant very cleverly told me that in front of the Inspector General and Captain Sloan. The Inspector General did not give Sloan a chance to speak…He said to me "You get out of here and go see about your wife, now!" Bob was born that evening, one month premature and with yellow jaundice. He had to have three complete blood transfusions within the first week of his life. I was proud to name him Robert Louis Stephens, III. He was the first grandchild for both pairs of grandparents and was nicknamed "Bobby." Needless to say, everyone dearly loved him.

About a year after Bobby was born I received a call from the Infantry officer's assignment branch in Washington, DC. Apparently during the course of signing papers in the basic officer's course at Fort Benning, Georgia, I signed up for Special

Forces training. LTC Lewellan, an assignment officer, wanted to know if I was still interested. I told him that I wanted to talk it over with my wife and I also called my mother. I don't know even today why I felt that I had to call my mother except that she always seemed to make wise decisions and I respected her input. Olivia and I discussed it and we decided that we would give it a try. LTC Lewellan told me that I had to take a language examination. He also said that if I accepted his offer that I had a choice of assignments between the Special Forces Groups in Germany and Panama. We chose Germany because both of us wanted to see Europe. At the language exam, LT Don Jones said to me "If you want to go Germany, don't make a high score on this test." My reply was that I had never deliberately scored low on anything and I was not about to start now. I made a high score. We were sent to the Defense Language Institute (DLI) in Monterey, CA, to study Spanish, and subsequently sent to the 8th Special Action Force in the Canal Zone (CZ), Panama. I would later just accept this as the Army way…That is to tell you one thing and do another. I learned over the years to make the best of the Army's arbitrary personnel decisions and make them work the best for my family and me. Because of that foul up I am fluent in Spanish. Later in my career, when I became a Colonel, it was the Spanish language capability that got me a brigade command in Panama. So things worked out for the best.

I remember LTC Richie being quite upset with me for accepting that assignment without consulting him. That was my first lesson in "who is in control of your future." Richie in an attempt to dissuade me said, "You will become a highly skilled Soldier wearing officer's brass." He indicated that I had a much greater capability than would be shown in a Special Forces outfit and that I should stay with him in the 327th Infantry Battalion. Although I felt bad about not informing my chain of command about my decision, but I had given my word to Infantry branch and I would not go back on it, even if it was a mistake. As it turned out, Richie's intentions were not all altruistic. The brigade had been tapped to participate in Operation

Delawar in Iran in the spring of 1964, and he didn't want to break-in a new battalion logistics officer before that Exercise. So my departure from the battalion was delayed and I not only jumped into Iran in April 1964 with the battalion, but I was also extended a second time to participate in Operation Desert Strike in late May. Olivia and I finally left Fort Campbell during the first week of July. Olivia was pregnant with our second child and decided to fly from West Virginia to California after I secured housing. Upon my arrival in Monterey, CA, I went to the housing office at Fort Ord, CA, the first day and upon telling them that my wife was expecting another baby they gave me a house right away. Little did I know until I called to relay the good news to Olivia, our first daughter was born on the day before I went to secure the quarters. This was all during the time before people carried cell telephones everywhere. Now I was the father of two children, a boy and a girl. Stephanie Lyn was born in Bluefield, WV, on the 8th of July 1964. We thought we had the perfect family.

I breezed through language school with a 90 plus average and finished number three in the class. Of course nobody cared where I finished except me. It was important to me to do well in everything in light of my screw up with the comprehensive exam in college and the low finish in OBC. While I was at the language school the Commandant called me in. I had no idea why I was being called into his office but was pleasantly surprised when he presented me with a certificate of appreciation from the 327th Battalion, 1st Brigade, 101st Airborne Division for "a job well done." I never expected that LTC Richie would do that. I felt like I had earned something special. It was not until later that I found out that white officers in similar jobs, in other divisions, received Army Commendation medals for their service. I just chalked it up to "that's the way they treated black officers in those days." After the six-month language course at the Presidio of Monterey, I was sent to Fort Bragg, NC, to study unconventional warfare, specifically to attend the Guerrilla Warfare Course.

Man, did I have fun at Fort Bragg. The course requirements were not stiff at all and I had a lot of free time to just goof off. Because it was another temporary duty assignment in the South, we didn't even consider moving our family down there. Olivia and the children moved in with her parents, which worked out good for a host of reasons. The first was that I never worried about their security. Second, they were close enough that I could visit almost every weekend. Finally, I had no distractions and was free to study and do well in the course. And I did do well! We did not have a class ranking, as I remember, but everyone knew that I had my stuff together. I could plan and execute patrols as well as anyone in the class. During the course I met and became good friends with three Marine Corps Lieutenants, J.J. Carroll, Lenny Nisisen and one other whose name I can't recall off hand. They were great and I gained far more than a modicum of respect for "the Corps" after going to school with those guys. I carry the admiration and respect for them with me even until today. Olivia came down during graduation week and we went shopping for shoes for her before I was off to Panama in the Canal Zone and the 8th Special Forces Group. She wore a size four shoe and they were hard to find.

THE HOOK ASSIGNMENT

Landing at the airport in Panama was like stepping into an oven. I had never experienced stifling heat like that before in my life. We were met by the Special Forces Group liaison officer, a Captain, and taken to a BOQ for the night. The next morning, bright and early, we were picked up and taken to the train station in Balboa, CZ and we rode the train to the station in Colon, CZ on the Atlantic side of the Panama Canal. We were met by some more liaison types who loaded our baggage onto pick up trucks and we were transported, in the back of the trucks, to Fort Gulick, CZ. I do not remember everyone who was with me but I do remember that LT John Gorely and CPT Arthur Williams were two of the folks that arrived in "Group" with me. I was assigned to B Company, more specifically A Team number 21. What I did not know was that there was a major build up of special operating forces going on in Latin America and I was told by the rumor mill the Organization of American States (OAS) had specifically asked for more officers of color to be assigned to the 8th Special Forces Group.

I arrived in Panama as a geographical bachelor. Families had a four to six month wait, depending on rank, before they acquired living quarters. I moved into the BOQ and met an interesting group of guys, most of whom were in Special Forces. They were absolutely crazy. There was nothing that they wouldn't try, nothing they wouldn't drink, and nothing they wouldn't say. They were complete nuts! I remember Captains Ralph "Pappie" Shelton, Dale Ritter, and others whose names I don't remember. I knew these guys from my Spanish language class at Monterey, California. Then there were the Lieutenants: Fred Peters, Robie Robinson, and Steve Perry. What a great group we were in that BOQ. We raised holy hell all the time...CPT Shelton was the old guy of the group. CPT Ritter was also an old guy and kind of lack luster except when he was drinking heavily. I had known LT John R. Robinson at WVSC except that we called him Rad. Two of the other guys ended up living in my neighborhood in the Fort Sherman Officer's Housing Area when we finally got quarters. They were LT Steve Perry and LT Fred Peters. All of us made Captain in about six months to a year.

One afternoon I was in the BOQ early for some reason and I heard a taxi pull up outside. I forgot to mention that this building did not have air conditioning and was screened in to save us from the mosquitoes. As I looked out of the screened opening I was shocked and surprised to see none other than CPT Jack Sloan, my first company commander, getting out of a taxi. Of course, I helped him with his bags and tried not to show any sign of dislike for him. However, I never forgot that he screwed me on my performance rating and he tried to stick me with paying for the bedrolls in my platoon that were lost by the company supply folks who worked for him. I just kept my distance and decided that I did not need him and, therefore, did not associate with him. I was a First Lieutenant on the promotion list for Captain, wearing a green beret with an authorized unit tab, and commanding an A Team. At that time in my life, it just didn't get any better than that. The best way for him to get into a quick hand-to-hand brawl would have been to mess with me just a little bit. I was top drawer Army material and by that time, even I knew it.

Panama and the 8th Special Forces were good to me and Olivia, and our children, Bobby and Stephanie. We secured quarters initially at Fort Sherman, CZ which was on the north side of the Isthmus at Gatun Lake. That meant that we were either early or late for every event that we attended across the canal locks. We chose to be early and that trait has remained with us even until today. The reason we were early or late depended on whether or not there was a ship in the Gatun Locks, the north entrance into the Panama Canal. It normally took 30 to 45 minutes for a ship to clear the Locks and invariably we would get caught at the most inopportune time. After a year we were able to move across the canal to some really nice quarters on Fort Randolph, CZ which was closer to the post where I worked and the school where Olivia taught. I worked on Fort Gulick, CZ and she taught at Coco Solo Elementary School. On Fort Randolph our family enjoyed prosperity that we had never dreamed was possible. We had a full-time, live-in maid, two cars, and money coming in from two workers. We were doing well!

I kept my job as an A Team Leader but was placed out on "special duty" at the United States Army South (USARSO) Parachute School, the Jungle School, and finally the Noncommissioned Officer Academy where my final job was Commandant. I worked with some fine soldiers in the 8th Special Forces Group. We had more fun at work than should have been legal. Best of all, I learned to value the friendship and professionalism of the men in the noncommissioned officer corps. Men like Master Sergeants Hoss Mason, Jessie Shifflet, and Billy Toston were A Team, Team Sergeants. Sergeants First Class Bob Hines and Pappy Grant were Operations and Intelligence Specialists. Sergeant First Class Ralph Lampkins was a Medical Specialist. Staff Sergeants Dailey, Colson, and Porter were all young NCO's at that time and served as Demolition Specialist, Communications Specialist and Operations Specialist, respectively. I learned a lot from those guys. The most important thing that I learned was: to never quit until the job was done no matter how long it takes. They made me "a highly skilled Soldier wearing officers' brass."

During the first month or so that I was in Panama, the 8th Group was conducting a field training exercise on Zora Island on the north side of the Isthmus. Although I was only a lieutenant, I was assigned to perform as an A Team Leader. Some of the sergeants of the team were Doc Lampkins, Gogo Gomez, Perez, Trotter and Hines. These were all Sergeants who could kill in several ways and had the brains, guts, and patience to be as deliberate as necessary to accomplish any mission. Within the first twenty-four hours of the operation, I was cutting myself a "hooch pole" for my poncho liner when SFC Gogo Gomez called to me. I turned to answer and cut a sliver off of the end of my left forefinger. I was using Doc Lampkins' "K bar" knife that was razor sharp and all it took was a slight bit of pressure for me to receive a bad cut. The immediate reaction of the team was for me to go in and get medical treatment. Doc Lampkins called me aside and said, "If you go in now you will never gain the respect of this team and you'll suffer for the rest of your tour here." I took him at his word and trusted him to treat my infected finger until the end of the exercise some fourteen days later.

During that little exercise I learned a lot about military exercises in the special operations area. The exercise controllers and referees were members of the original group of folks who came to Panama. They had written the scenarios and phased the exercise and determined the out come. At the After Action Review they made some statements that were patently untrue and I called their hand on it. It resulted in a small confrontation in front of the Group Commander and the USARSO Operations Officer. I stood my ground and the group commander moved on without resolution to the confrontation. That incident, however, drew me a great deal of visibility and respect from the noncommissioned officer corps and the junior officers who were present from other "A" Teams. From that point forward I was accepted as a leader in B Company and subsequently the 8th Special Forces Group.

I went on training missions in Panama that had the same degree of realism as doing it for real. We trained hard and long and we were constantly on alert for some reason or another. In fact, I spent every one of my wedding anniversaries in Panama on alert sitting in the Team room with my rucksack ready to go. I also played unit level football and softball. I could fly in those days and all the quarterback, CPT Dave Decker, had to do was put it up and I could run under it. The other wide receiver was CPT Joe Almaguer who had set the record at West Point, in the

100-yard dash. With our speed and Decker's accuracy our football team was virtually unbeatable. We also had an opportunity to jump out of all kinds of military aircraft, i.e., the C 46, C47, C119, the L19 and L20, and the C123, and C130 in the Canal Zone. We had night jumps, water jumps and sometimes, by mistake of course, jungle jumps. Panama was a period of growing up for me, and a period of becoming a family man. Bob and Stephanie were preschoolers and I could spend a lot of time at home with them when I was not away on temporary duty.

While I was in Panama I learned to play golf. On Wednesday afternoon in B Company, we had physical training (PT). The activity always appeared on the training schedule as organized athletics. That meant that teams would be formed by A Teams and B Teams for minor competition. The NCO's affectionately referred to the training time as "organized grab ass." Sometimes a group of senior sergeants would go to the golf course at Fort Davis and play golf. On one such Wednesday I was enticed by the B Team Sergeant Major to go with them and play golf. I was reluctant to go but they talked me into it. I actually played well shooting 120 for the first time out. I had never held a golf club before that day. There were no real lessons just a demonstration of how to grip the clubs and away we went. They cut me no slack! About a week after, I was at the Fort Gulick Officers' Club for lunch and got into a discussion with LT Ed Lesegne. LT Lesegne bet me that the difference between a C46 and a C47 aircraft was that one had two engines and the other one had four engines. I knew the difference. The C46 had two jump doors for paratroopers and the C47 only had one. We had a pretty good argument and I finally bet him forty dollars that I was right. He said that he did not have forty dollars but would bet me his golf clubs. I took the bet, golf clubs sight unseen. I knew that I was right. I won and he paid off. The golf clubs were not that good but he kicked in the bag, a glove and several shag balls. I started to play regularly on Saturday mornings after that and the rest is history. Today I am an eleven handicap. I saw Mr. Lesegne later in my career and thanked him for getting me started in golf.

My last job during that tour in Panama was Commandant of the USARSO Noncommissioned Officer Academy. I was only a Captain, but I was a Captain with superb leadership skills and excellent public speaking abilities. I was sitting in Panama as we used to say "fat, dumb, and happy" when I was struck with sudden case of brain cramps. All of a sudden I wanted to go to the Vietnam War. In fact, I was so afraid that I would not get there in time that I volunteered to go. Somehow I believed that I needed to get there and get a chest full of medals in order to succeed in the Army. Olivia thought I was crazy and said as much but I put in my DA Form 1049 anyway. Subsequently, I got orders to report in June or July of 1966. My report date had to be adjusted though because I would experience one of the great tragedies of my life…the death of my Mother.

As was noted earlier, I played football for B Company. It was right after a game on Wednesday night, when Olivia, the kids and I got home and Major James, a friend, and B Team Leader from B Company came up on my backdoor steps. He asked if he could come in and of course I invited him in and offered him a drink. He declined the drink and asked me to sit down. He said, "Has your mother been ill?" I replied, "yes, she's been ill with some nagging ailment all of her life." And like a salvo from a 155mm Howitzer, he said, "she died this morning." Olivia immediately screamed out, "Oh no!" I was momentarily paralyzed. I couldn't speak or move for a few seconds. I was devastated.

My mother and I were very close. She was one of the strongest women that I have ever known. However, with my brother and me she was the most tender the softest, and the most loving person in the world. I was never afraid of anything as long as she was alive. She always supported everything that I ever thought I wanted to do. As I remember her, it's always the same scenario…she is taking me to school on my first day, back in September, 1946. As I left home, she asked if I wanted her to walk a little ways with me. My Dad worked on the night shift at the mines and was at home to look after my two-year old younger brother. Mom and I walked about a quarter of a mile and she said goodbye to me again and started to turn around and go back home. I paused for a second, and she was by my side again and stayed there until she released me to the care of Ms. Wright, my first teacher. The next day she walked me all the way to the school yard but did not go into the building. The third day she told me that I should know the way by now and she stayed at home. That's the way that I remember her the most!

ROOTS

Mom was a stout woman of about 5 feet and three inches in height who was fond of saying, "I cover the ground that I stand on." She absolutely took no crap from anybody. She spoke her mind, took no quarter and gave no quarter. She took me to school that first day and expected me to find my way there from the third day forward. She acted tough, but her biggest problem was that her body cavity was not large enough to hold her heart. However, everyone loved her because she was consistent. You could predict her behavior in 99 percent of the situations that she faced. She was morally correct all the time. She would not lie, even for her children. She was a God fearing Christian. She loved her children, loved her snuff (tobacco) and she dearly loved my Daddy. She was not a learned women but she had the common sense and wisdom of a highly educated scholar. She could out cook, out sew, and out wash and iron any woman in our community. She always took pride in her accomplishments and the accomplishments of her children.

Mom and Daddy were from Alabama. She was from Choctaw County and he was from neighboring Sumter County. These counties are co-located so they knew each from church. As the story goes, Dad left Alabama in 1936 and headed for West Virginia. Before he left he asked my mother to wait for him to return and marry him. He returned in December (Christmas) 1938 and they were married in January 1939. My mother always had a reputation among her peers at home for staying faithful to my Dad and not dating anyone else. In her own words, she would often brag about being a virgin when she married him. She had some interesting tales about her childhood in rural Alabama and working in homes that had white males in them. Upon being married they moved to Court Street in Welch, WV, where I was born on September 21, 1940. I was born in a one bedroom house that my parents rented from Mr. Ganaway. Ms. Lettie Ganaway was my unofficial Godmother. We remained in Welch until I was about three years old and my parents bought a house and we moved to Warrior Mines, WV, which was my official home of record for the entire time I was in the Army.

Estella Ward Stephens, my mother, was the oldest living child of Moses (Papa) and Annie (Mama) Ward's nine offspring. Estella had an older sister whose name was Mamie Kate. My mother's family called her Sister. Sister died as a child. My mother's nickname was Lil' Sis. That's logical because she was the little sister to Mamie Kate. The next child was a boy called Buddy (Oliver). Now my conjecture is that Mama had two girls that she referred to as Sister and Little Sister and Papa finally got his buddy when Oliver was born. The next child to be born was named Willie and was called Lil. Of course he was the little brother to Oliver. Next came, Mary who was called Tutter an Ebonics spin on the word Sister. To this point, the nicknames were used exclusively and signified that the Wards had a cozy little family. Later Callie, Lucille, and Dora, were born in that order. None of them had nicknames. The final child born to the union of Moses and Annie Ward was a baby girl named Annie Louise, but what was she called? You guessed it, "Baby." There appears to be something finite about calling Annie Louise, "Baby." I think that was a signal that she would be the last one. She is only six years older than I am and therefore, she was very close to me growing up. Again, my mother, Lil Sis, was the undisputed leader and self proclaimed matriarch of the family. Everybody looked up to her for advice, counsel, and occasionally a couple of dollars. She always ensured that my brother and I went "down home" to Choctaw County Alabama, about once a year so that we could know our grandparents, uncles and aunts, and our cousins. We were always glad to go and see them but equally as glad to leave the "country" and return to West

Virginia. It was always so rural for us compared to Southern West Virginia. There was no running water, no electricity, and some of the time no outhouse. You had your daily constitutionals in the cotton fields and cleaned yourself on the leaves from the cotton plants. Of course that would make you chafe and get a rash. There were always ticks and other bugs everywhere.

My grandfather, Moses Ward, was one of the most remarkable men I have known. He was the son of a slave, Jacob Ward. Legend has it that Jacob often told the story of how he came to the shores of South Carolina in a ship. Allegedly Jacob had a brother who remained in South Carolina when he was sold as a slave and brought to Alabama. My guess is Moses had no formal schooling, yet he was a wizard at figuring things out. He could read, write and do numbers. Because of those skills he was a Steward in the local AME Zion Methodist Church, Wards Chapel. He treated all of his grandchildren like special angels. Today, there is not one of us who does not believe that we were his favorite among his grandchildren. I only saw him about ten days a year but my memories of him are as large as life. Sometime during our stay in the summer, he would come and get me up out of bed at about five o'clock in the morning and take me out to his old beat-up truck and we would head out to Mr. Walter Drinkard's store. On the way to Mr. Drinkard's store he would always ask if I had any money. I usually had a few cents and he would say "Give that to Papa son?" At Drinkard's store we would encounter men, many of whom were very young, going to work as loggers. Papa would strike up conversations with them and Mr. Drinkard. He would always introduce me as "my grandbaby from Virginia." It was not until I became a man myself that I realized that many southerners did not know the difference between the states of Virginia and West Virginia. Anyway, Papa's favorite trick was to lift a cane bottom chair by the front rungs. He would then challenge the young men to do the same thing. Most of the time, the men could not do it. He would then say, "I'll bet a dollar that my grand son can lift it." Of course this would always threaten the manhood of the young loggers and they would take the bet. What they did not know was that he had drilled me for hours the night before showing me how to stiffen my wrists and lift the chair. Of course we would win the bets and he would buy my breakfast—a gingerbread cake and an RC Cola. Oh, he would also return my money that I had loaned him earlier. We would then put a few gallons of gas in the old truck and head out to visit relatives and friends. Gas was no more than fifteen cents a gallon. We would return about noon in time for lunch. As I tell these stories to my cousins they have similar yet, different stories about him but none of them can top my experiences with him. He was a remarkable man.

On one of those summer visits I had the opportunity to meet my great grandmother, Minerva Ward. She was in her late eighties when I met her. She was stern and didn't have much time for her great grandchildren. She had been a slave as a child.

I don't have much to say about Mama, Annie Ward, Papa's spouse, except that she was always busy trying to make us comfortable. Her maiden name was a Jordan pronounced the southern way i.e., Jourdan. She was a very thin beautiful woman with Native American features. Her straight hair hung almost to her waist. It was rumored that her family also came from South Carolina. Once Papa and I were playing in a hayloft and I got hurt, she was there to soothe the pain when we got back home. Another time Papa and I were riding horses bareback and I got chafed really bad, Mama put some talcum powder on it and made it all better. Papa also took me hunting one time and I shot a Partridge. Mama cooked it, but I could not eat it. They were great grandparents during the short periods I saw them.

Those summer visits were all done by car from Warrior Mines, West Virginia. We would leave late in the evening after Daddy got off from work. We left around six o'clock in the evening, and drove all night to Birmingham, Alabama. We drove on U.S. Highway 11 and the task was to clear Birmingham without having to stop at a traffic light. There were no places we could stop en route to eat or rest—not even to use a restroom. We would stop normally in Bristol, Tennessee, and gas up and stop again in Chattanooga, Tennessee. One time, when I was about eight years old, we stopped in Chattanooga and my Mother needed to use the restroom. All of the restrooms were locked and you had to ask an attendant for the key. When Daddy asked for a key the attendant said, "We don't have a restroom for you." My Dad got so angry he told the guy to stop filling the gas tank and I thought that he was going to hit him. I had never seen him angry before. He was almost crying he was so angry. I found out later, my mother was pregnant at the time and really needed to use the privy. We left the service station and drove back out on U.S. Highway 11 and pulled over and my mother squatted in the sagebrush along side of the road. When I was older and heard the incident again I wanted to go and find the service station and kick the attendant's butt. Of course my Dad had already forgiven the attendant. That's the way he was.

Mother and Daddy had five sons and no daughters. Only two of us lived. The others either died at birth or only lived a short time. I was so glad to have a little brother when Booker was born. In fact my parents allowed me to give him his name. I knew that my Daddy's brother, that I had met, was named Booker, and I thought that would be a good name for my brother. I had heard of Booker T. Washington through my parents, so I named him Booker T. Of course the dumb folks at the hospital took it literally and did not bother to find out Washington's middle name. So my brother's middle name is T, a phenomenon that really upsets him at times.

My Daddy's family was not quite as animated as my mother's. They were predominantly men. There was Jake, Eugene, Lee, Booker, and Henry. There were also two sisters: Ardillia and Lora. Henry, who was the youngest, was shot and killed by the local Sheriff, in Sumter County, long before I was born. Jake was a logger and lived in Whitfield all of his life. He probably never traveled more than fifty miles from where he was born throughout his entire life. Eugene was a farmer. However, legend has it that he served in the U.S. Merchant Marines for a short period and was quite worldly. Lee was a mechanic in York, Alabama, and around 1950 moved to West Virginia and worked in my Daddy's garage for a while. He eventually settled on the south side of Chicago. Booker worked in the West Virginia coalmines until the mid 1950's and he moved to Chicago also. Upon retirement from the steel mills he moved back to Tuscaloosa, Alabama, where he eventually expired. Both of my grandparents on my Daddy's side were deceased before I was born so I never had the pleasure of knowing them.

My grandfather, Thomas Stephens, was a good businessman. He and my grandmother, Mary Marshall Stephens owned their own home and the property around it. They were married and apparently combined their "40 acres and mules" after Reconstruction and set up housekeeping in Whitfield, Alabama, a little cotton farming town just south of the town of York, in Sumter County. I should point out that the town of York, Alabama, is only 27 miles east of Meridian, Mississippi. My grandfather Thomas owned a store in York. I don't know what kind of store a black man could have owned in southern Alabama in those days, but lore has it that he owned a store. I do know that he had the good sense and presence of mind to put the property that he and my grandmother owned in perpetuity in 1907. Since that time the property has been passed down to the legal heirs of Thomas and Mary Stephens. Of course, as members of the immediate family have died the property has been parceled out to surviving spouses who sold it off to the point where only about half of it remains today. However, that is a Stephens legacy that I will always fight to keep intact—as long as I live. Currently, my brother and I are the largest shareholders and we have no plans to sell our shares.

Judge Booker T. Stephens, my brother, is the Chief Judge in the 8th Judicial District of West Virginia. A graduate of West Virginia State College and Howard University Law School, he represents 500% of my parent's perfect record for raising two perfect off springs. I was overjoyed when he was born and I am extremely proud of him today. He chose to remain in West Virginia and pursue his dream of becoming an outstanding member of the judiciary. He has done that! He is in his fourth or fifth term as a consummate elected politician in southern West Virginia. He is married to a lawyer and they have raised two children who are successful in their own right. He is a God fearing Christian who stands up for what is right no matter what the consequences may be. He is a true tribute to the forthrightness of Estella Ward Stephens.

Mom was our matriarch, our leader, our defender and our role model. We are who we are today because of her sterling example of leadership, courage, and dedication. She treated all people with decency and respect as long as there was reciprocity. However, if you ever got on her bad side it was hell coming back to the good side. What I admired most was that she did not take a backseat to white folks at a time when it was not popular to speak up and act. That's what she taught my brother and me. And we are the way we are today because of her teaching. She died on the 8th of June 1966. She was 52 years old. Daddy passed in July of 1984. He was 73 years old.

OFF TO WAR

We buried my mother at Ward's Chapel, an AME Zion Methodist Church, back at her home in Choctaw County, Alabama. I did not have a long time to grieve because I was on orders for deployment to the Republic of Vietnam, as an individual replacement. I arrived in Vietnam in late July and met Major Bean who was the Deputy Assistant Chief of Staff, G1, (ACofS, G1) of the 1st Cavalry Division. My airplane trip to Vietnam had been uneventful yet exciting because I was traveling with a close friend, Captain Walter Gunn, who I had known in Panama. We landed at Tan Sanut Airbase and immediately picked up the smell of burning feces. That is still one of the most distinctive things that I remember about Vietnam…It stunk!

MAJ Bean told me that he was sending me forward for an interview with the Assistant Chief of Staff, G5, (ACofS,G5) LTC Joseph Wasiak. LTC Wasiak was a West Point graduate from New York City who had six kids. He was a good Catholic. He said to me "So you want to go to work for me, huh?" I answered him as only a cocky former Special Forces "A Team" Leader knew how—"You see these crossed rifles on my collar sir, I want to command a combat company. I want to kill something." He laughed and said, "This collar staff insignia that I am wearing is misleading. I am also an Infantryman and I am going to get a battalion and if you sign on with me and do a good job, I'll give you a company." I was cocky but not stupid, so I signed on with LTC Wasiak as a Deputy to the ACof S, G5. I knew that this guy was a member of the West Point Protective Association (WPPA) and that those guys always looked out for each other and that my chances were pretty good that he would get a battalion. Since the members of the WPPA take pride in not lying, cheating, or stealing nor tolerating those who do, I knew he would keep his word and give me a command. Now all I had to do was impress him enough to hire me. I felt confident that I could do that. We chatted for a little while and agreed that I would go back to the rear area and go to the local 1st Cavalry Orientation Course and return to work for him. I was told to report to CPT James Lamont who ran the ACofS, G5 (Rear) Office.

CPT Lamont was one of the craziest guys I have known. He was, or acted like he was, filthy rich. He said that his mother was a Spanish Contessa, whatever that is. He never talked about his father. Anyway he was just crazy as hell. He would say, "Let's go downtown for lunch" and off we would go to lunch in downtown An Khe, Republic of Vietnam. An Khe was where the 1st Cavalry Division set up its main command post although we referred to it as the "Rear." The 1st Cavalry had its main headquarters set up in the central highlands just north of Qui Nhon. After my in-country indoctrination class was over I went to Landing Zone (LZ) Two Bits on the Bong Song Plains, the forward command post of the 1st Cavalry Division, to work with LTC Wasiak.

I went on several combat assaults and even joined in on some defoliation missions with a Chemical Corps officer, Captain Peter D. Hidalgo. Most of my work was done during the day and I thought I was relatively safe. Sometimes, very rare times, I had the chance to observe soldiers in a firefight, watch an interrogation, or drop leaflets, from a helicopter or small airplane, on suspected enemy locations. When CPT Lamont was selected for a Company Commander position I was sent back to the Rear as his replacement in the ACofS, G5 (REAR) office. I felt completely safe there and became involved in the civic action projects that were going on in the 1st Cavalry Area of Operations (AO).

An Khe, was our town. It was wide open from 0900 in the morning until 1630 in the afternoon. Aside from the main street there was a side area that was shaped like a wagon wheel. Some say there were approximately 200 bars and 2000 prostitutes in that area. I went down on one occasion to observe our medics giving periodic penicillin shots to the girls that worked in the bars. They would arrive on motor bikes and go into a general purpose (GP) medium size tent and get a shot in the buttocks and ride out, back to the bar area where they worked. I also had to visit several Montagard refugee camps, almost daily. The Montagards were an ethnic mixture of dark-skinned Asian people who inhabited the highlands of South Vietnam. They had been uprooted and moved from the "free fire zones" that had been established on their homelands. It was with them that I learned to eat almost anything as food and drink rice wine through a bamboo straw. They were some of the nicest people I have met in my entire life. They were always smiling and eager to do whatever we asked them to do. Sometimes I would get blown away on that rice wine and of course get sicker than hell with diarrhea for a week. However, I enjoyed going out to see them and I went almost every day. Besides it gave me something to do. Working in the division rear area was boring. I got up at 0600, for some reason, and went to breakfast at the General's Mess. Officers lived in three bedroom house trailers in An Khe. Because I was the ACofS, G5 principal in the Rear, I had an option to belong to the Commanding General's Mess for about $12.00 a month. I would leave the Mess and go to the office where my assistants, three enlisted men, were already at work typing reports and answering inquiries about civic action projects. One of the enlisted men was named James Whittaker. He was from St. Albans, West Virginia, and so we bonded right away as men from the Mountain state. He was primarily my driver, although I enjoyed driving myself most of the time and he would carry the rifle and ride as my passenger, a.k.a. "The Shotgun." We would go downtown and check on our schoolhouse project, or go to one of the Montagard villages. Usually we had lunch downtown. Sometimes, I could get a helicopter ride and go forward and visit the guys at Two Bits Landing Zone. However, I had to make sure that I was available for questions when the Commanding General (Rear), Brigadier General Oscar Davis, had them.

The officers in the Rear played volleyball in the late afternoon as our physical training (PT) program. We called it combat volleyball and it was not unusual for someone to lose a tooth or get a broken leg or arm while playing. I was absolutely an expert at the game. Of course, I had played a hell of a lot of it with noncommissioned officers in Special Forces. I could climb the net and spike an opponent in the top of the head with one hand and still block his shot with my other hand. We would finish PT around 1700 and go and get cleaned up for supper. That usually meant that we would take a shower and put on a clean, starched, battle dress uniform and fresh spit shined jungle boots. Of course everyone paid a houseboy to clean their trailer, take care of their uniforms, and polish their boots. The evening meal was served daily by the Generals' Mess support staff. We ate on white linen tablecloths, with silver flatware, and good stemware. Sometimes, we invited Doughnut Six and the Red Cross girls as our guests and occasionally, we also invited Nurse Six and a bevy of nurses from the hospital to eat with us. There was Italian night, seafood night, and other special evenings if we could get the ingredients. We had dinner with guests such as the television star Leif Erickson from *High Chapparal*, Joe DeMaggio and others. I also met two of the finest black officers that I encountered throughout my career in the General's Mess. They were Lieutenant Colonel Roscoe Robinson and Major Mahatha Oliver. LTC Robinson went on to become the first black four-star general in the Army. He was quite an officer and I looked up to him like a big brother. He was so polished, well mannered and intelligent that the other officers always paid attention when he spoke. He never raised his voice, used profanity, and he never showed anger or disgust. He was the officer that I wanted to become. He always had his stuff together. He was also the first black lieutenant colonel that I had known up close. Serving with him on that staff was a great experience and a pleasure for me. I remember that at the daily staff briefing, which took place at

1800 just before dinner, the Deputy, ACofS G1, would announce something like we were expecting 25 Lieutenants, 10 Captains, 5 Majors, and two Lieutenant Colonels in the next days distribution of officers. General Davis would ask "Who are the Lieutenant Colonels?" The Deputy G1 would call their names and Davis would ask "Does anyone know these guys?" If the answer was yes, a discussion would ensue about whether they were "good guys or duds." It was in those meetings that I began to realize that white guys did not only discriminate against Negroes, Hispanics and Asians, they discriminated against each other too. Not one time did I ever hear anyone ask about an incoming lieutenant colonel's ethnicity or credentials? If the "(expletive deleted) new guy (FNG)" was perceived to be a good guy he was placed in a position where he could rotate into a battalion commander position. If someone said that the FNG was arrogant or not trust worthy he was placed on the staff to work his way up to a better position, but probably no prospect of command. I consider that to be one of the greatest lessons of my life. I was in An Khe when the first Tet Offensive began. I had just been notified that I was going to get a Company Commander position in the 1-7 Cavalry.

LTC Wasiak was selected for battalion command around the late January early February timeframe. His call sign was Red Baron 6. LTC Robinson was also selected for battalion command at about the same time. His call sign was White Cloud 6. I was scheduled to go on rest and recuperation (R&R) in February. LTC Wasiak had not yet delivered on his word to give me a command. About two or three days before I left for R&R White Cloud 6 (LTC Robinson) sent a guy down to replace me. He was offering to give me a company. He and I had never discussed the possibility of me working for him before. I believe he was just looking out for my best interest. He knew that I needed a command in order to move ahead in the Army and he was going to help me get it. I have attempted to pass that attitude on to many young officers that I have encountered since that time. I left Vietnam to meet Olivia in Hawaii, for R&R.

Upon returning to Vietnam I was told that I was not going to get a command in White Cloud's battalion, 5-7 Cavalry. However, I was also informed that I should go to Red Baron's battalion for an interview. I went to see LTC Wasiak and he offered me B Company, 1-7 Cavalry. My call sign was Crazy Horse 6. Wasiak kept his word and I kept mine. I went to work for him.

I was the third Company Commander for that Company within about a six-week period. I was told that all of the pervious commanders had been killed. I took over the outfit on a firebase in the northern highlands of South Vietnam near Quang Tri Province. On the morning that I assumed command the troops were in stand down mode waiting for me to arrive. I met with LTC Wasiak on the way over to the firebase and he said that he would give me a week to get the company ready to go on missions. The situation was really bad. They were all scared to death. After all they had lost three commanders in a very short period of time. One of the ways you can assess morale and discipline in an outfit is to check how they dispose of body waste. These guys were crapping, on top of the ground, just outside of their foxholes and not covering it up. I discovered this on my initial walk around the perimeter. I was furious. I called all of the leaders to my bunker immediately. I laid down the law. First, I wanted to be saluted by the soldiers when they recognized me. The reply was that we were in combat and they had been told not to salute the officers. I told them, "That's bullshit I want 'Charlie' to know who I am. Salute me!" Second I wanted a complete police call of the area. I was very specific about cleaning up the fecal matter from around the tops of the foxholes. In fact, I said that I would be all over the person whose pile I stepped in if it occurred. I also mandated that platoon leaders were required to walk their portion of the perimeter regularly at least four times a day. I told the company headquarters radio telephone operators that their jobs depended upon me having constant communications with Red Baron 6. If for some reason they lost it for an appreciable amount of time they would be replaced.

It was about noon and I told them to eat lunch and get ready for training in the afternoon. I wanted training in terrain appreciation, not map reading. I wanted everyone to clean their weapons and test fire them. Finally, I wanted every one on the firebase to get cleaned up. I had made arrangements for clean jungle fatigue uniforms to be brought out with the evening meal. This was my first conventional company. I was a seasoned ex-Special Forces Captain and I knew how to take charge and lead. I had learned early in my career that being a good leader oftentimes meant being a good actor. So I acted like their leader. I strapped on a pistol and got rid of the fancy CAR 15 rifle with a folding stock that had a "yeady strap" made of parachute strings that the previous commander had carried. I wanted no fancy trappings. We were in real combat and the basics applied…no Hollywood!

I will admit that I learned a lot from the troopers in B Company. They had been in the forward battle area for several months and had learned the survival techniques necessary to make life better in the field. For example, they knew how to make the best pizza that I have eaten anywhere using the ingredients in C rations. They knew how to find the meal they wanted in a box of rations that had been turned upside down so that the labels were not visible. They didn't have anything on me though SFC Vincent Rose had taught me that as a Lieutenant. They knew how to lighten their load and take only the food that was necessary on an operation. For example a can of pork and beans, a can of cookies, and a canteen of water was good for about 1400 meters in the wait-a-minute vines. These guys were not always the most intelligent guys in the world but they were jungle smart and battle hardened about combat, and that's what they were being paid to do. I learned, in time, to appreciate and love every one of them. I spent time walking around talking to them, that first day, about anything they wanted to talk about. You have to understand that in those days we had a lot of draftees in the field and their jargon was entirely different than soldiers today. I had been an A Team leader in Special Forces and I could talk soldier "street talk" with the best of them. I think they appreciated that more than anything else…I sounded like one of the guys. However, I knew the limits. I had learned as a young lieutenant, sometimes the hard way, "east is east and west is west and never the twain shall meet." An officer could not afford to let his guard down completely with enlisted men. I was the Captain. They called me "Six." I was in charge and I took charge. Strangely enough that first day was a total success. That was good because early the next day LTC Wasiak sent his helicopter for me to come to a meeting at his bunker. Although he had told me that I had a week to train these guys he gave me a mission for that very afternoon.

I left LTC Wasiak's field headquarters and started to formulate plans for the very first air assault mission in my whole life. I had started when I was a lieutenant to rewrite my notes and deliver them to subordinates in the five paragraph field order format. I was going to take my company into combat. I was also apprehensive because I didn't think that they were ready. I was wrong! These guys were seasoned veterans in the art of air assaults and they proceeded to show me their stuff. They swaggered as they were getting ready to board the "choppers." We boarded the helicopters just as I had planned and moved toward the landing zone (LZ). I was excited! This was what I had trained for every day of my adult life and now it was about to happen. I had done a hundred of these operations on paper and at least a dozen in my mind but never a live one. We landed in a perfect "V" formation. That's when I began to appreciate the guys holding the joysticks in the cockpits of those helicopters. The gun ships were flying around in a counter clockwise formation and laying down suppressing fire; while the field artillery was firing and preparing the LZ, and my troops, MY TROOPS, were as cool as cucumbers waiting to land and leave the helicopters. It was like reading a movie script except this time I had the starring role in it. We landed and fanned out just like I had planned with the weapons pointed to the outer perimeter of the LZ. It was not a "hot" LZ, thank God, and I was able to assemble my gaggle and move out without incident. That little drill gave me a chance to look at my troops and I was proud of them. They just needed to have the proper guidance and leadership and they would be topnotch. I also knew that I could provide that to them.

We proceeded up a draw and started to climb up a hill. It was not very steep and there was a footpath that was available to ease our movement. It appeared that the locals used the path regularly. That was fine, except there should not have been any local folks in the area. This was a free fire zone. I got organized with my most experienced platoon leader's platoon leading the company. I was in the second echelon with my radio operators, the medic and a couple of other straphangers. We were moving okay when all of a sudden, shots rang out up ahead. This was the first time that I had seen real bullets bouncing off of the trees and the ground in live combat. It scared the crap out of me but I was cool. I started to go forward and my radio telephone operator (RTO), tackled me and said; "Where the hell are you going six?" I said that I was going forward to see what was happening. He said, rather emphatically, "That's why I am here, sir. If you go forward I have to go with you and that sucks, sir. Let me get those guys on the radio and we'll find out what's going on up there." His field name was Red. I do not remember his real name. He was a savvy, seasoned Soldier who was on the down side of his year in Vietnam for his country. He taught me a lot about how to relax and take things easy in combat. He could do things with a PRC10 radio that I have never seen anyone else do. He could "get commo!" My other radio operator was named John Boloslavski. We called him "Ski." He was from the Minneapolis/Saint Paul area. He was a great guy too. The Medic was named "Doc." I am sure all of these men had given names but I do not remember ever hearing them. By the way, we did not wear nametags in the field. I had a great time with these guys. We shared everything...food, water, socks, cigarettes and a lot of tall tales.

That first firefight was a real experience. Red asked what was going on up front and was told that the platoon RTO had somehow gotten out in front of the platoon and had taken a round in the head. The platoon leader, who was from the same hometown as the RTO, went forward to check out the situation and also took a round in the head. The third person to go forward was a sergeant. He took a round in the helmet that went all the way around between the helmet and the helmet liner and exited the same hole that it entered. He was not killed but had a helluva headache. It was complete pandemonium up there. Rounds were flying all over the place and people were yelling and running around. There was a complete letdown in discipline and many of the soldiers were on the verge of breaking and running. I was cool. I started getting things organized and made an assessment and a decision to continue moving up the hill. We retrieved our dead and got them evacuated out of the area of operations (AO). We started moving again. All of a sudden the platoon sergeant from the weapons platoon called me and asked if I could come to his location. I was annoyed because we had just started to move again and because the situation had been so tense, I was now very close to the front of the column. This meant that I had to turn my attention to something else. When I got to his location, he was standing with a big strapping blond haired boy who said that he was so scared that he wanted to be evacuated. My first inclination was to tear into his butt like a buzz saw. Everyone in the platoon was standing around watching the new company commander handle his first personnel crisis. I decided to talk softly to this soldier and say "Stay out here with me tonight, son. If you are still scared tomorrow, I'll reconsider and maybe let you go in." However, I was emphatic about him staying out there with me that night. Had I been with my Special Forces NCOs I would have ripped his butt open verbally but I decided that I needed a different approach with these younger guys. I was 27 years old and he was probably eighteen. I went back to the front and made sure that I had flank security out and we began to move again. We only moved a short distance and the guys on point, started to complain about the wait-a-minute vines. We had reached a little plateau and I decided that we would stop for the day and set up a perimeter. We set up for the night and the artillery forward observer (FO) and I started putting in the defensive fires for the night. I don't remember his name but the FO was a great guy. Above all he could read a map. I found that I had so many ancillary things to do as a commander that I didn't have time to keep up with where we were on the ground all the time. I relied on the FO and his RTO to do that. I was constantly on the radio to Red Baron 6 (Wasiak) and others. If the situation became tense enough, the Brigade Commander would be flying above you, and when the situation really got interesting you would hear, "This is Tarhill 6. What's going on down there?" That would be MG John J. Tolson, the 1st Cavalry Division Commander.

We made it through the first night without incident. Everybody was down though because we had lost the best platoon leader in the company and one of the best RTO's. The next morning we brought in hot chow. There is nothing like a hot meal to improve troop morale. That's when I found out how smart the troops were about logistics. If they fooled around long enough it would take forever to get the "backhaul" out on the helicopters. That meant that you wouldn't get started on your daily mission until late morning—0900–1000 hours. You'd only work a couple of hours before you had to stop for lunch and of course you had to backhaul that out too. It would be 1400 hours before we could start afternoon operations and we would quit for supper around five o'clock. They pulled that crap on me the first day but after that the schedule would be different. From that day forward we had C rations for breakfast. Eat 'em on your own time! We had C rations for lunch. Eat 'em on your own time! Finally, we had a hot supper with beer when we could get it and ice cream on Fridays. In retrospect the beer was not a good idea. What I found out, the hard way, was that some Soldiers did not drink beer so they either gave their ration away, or worse, they sold them to the other Soldiers. I would find out very soon that Soldiers and alcohol do not mix in combat.

On the second day out, LTC Wasiak was above me in his helicopter and wanted to know how far we had moved. Apparently my answer was not good enough for him and he said, "Am I going to have to come down there and move that gaggle for you?" I asked Red for a smoke grenade and popped smoke as a signal and said, "If you want this outfit, come and get it." That was the closet thing that he and I ever had to an unpleasant encounter. He was a great commander who after that left me alone to run my outfit as I wanted. Of course he knew and I knew that my goal was to be the best troop commander in the 1-7 Cavalry. Crazy Horse Company may not have been the best outfit on the second day of my command tour but it didn't take us long to become the best. We got good at doing everything right, the first time, very quickly. The way you know that you are the best is when the commander calls on you to be the lead company in battalion combat operations. After a short while, B Company was leading all of the time. We were good and we were cocky about it. Part of the reason we were so good was I received an outstanding lieutenant out of the Ranger Department at Fort Benning, Georgia. His name was Douglas Fournet. He was outstanding! I also received two more lieutenants. Their names were Rod Rodriguez and Jack Delustro. Rodriguez was returning from the hospital. He was very good and had already received three purple hearts. I didn't keep him long. I felt that he had paid his dues and the first chance I got to send him to the rear I gave it to him. Delustro was a different story. He was the first real coward that I ever met wearing officer's brass. He came to me whimpering about how scared he was and said that he really wanted to be in the Medical Service Corps because he planned to go to medical school. I remember saying to him, "You are here as a 'grunt,' and you are going to get missions just like everyone else. Get over your fear of combat because I don't want you to get anyone hurt."

During the first week of April 1967, we went into Khe San as part of Operation Pegasus, the largest air armada that had been attempted at that time. The 1st Cavalry Division was the tip of spear to liberate the Marines at Khe San. What an operation! I was so excited that I could barely sit still. We were going to ride helicopters for several thousand kilometers and conduct the mother of all air assaults. We landed on top of a hill. I had a chance to see White Cloud 6 (LTC Robinson) on top of that hill and thank him for his help in getting me a command. He was gracious and accepted no credit, but I knew better. I put LT Rodriguez in the lead that afternoon and we moved out to our night location. We had to cross a rather wide stream. I told LT Rodriguez to find a fording site and get us across the river. He fooled around, looking for a fording site, for what I determined to be an excessive amount of time, so I went forward. When I got to his location he and a bunch of troops were trying to figure out who would go in the water first. I was so ticked off that I proceeded to enter the water immediately and yelled back at them, to follow me! I went across to the other side without security or any far side reconnaissance. When I reached the other side I came to my senses and damn near passed out. That was the dumbest thing that I had done in a long time. It had an effect on the troops though. From that day forth they knew that I wouldn't ask them to do anything that I wouldn't do also. For their money I was fearless. Once we set up on the hilltop for the night, I started to walk my perimeter and a couple of the black soldiers approached me and said, "Six, the (expletive deleted) done killed Martin Luther King!" They had heard it on a portable radio that someone had in the field. I sat with them for a little while and we talked about different things. They were saddened and in shock. I was also saddened but I had work to do so there was not a lot of time available for grief or reflection.

I had met Martin Luther King, Jr. as a college student at WVSC. He came to Charleston, WV, when I was a junior and spoke at the African American First Baptist Church. Dr. Moses Newsome was the pastor. Dr. King was a member of Alpha Phi Alpha, Inc. and Dr. Newsome asked members of the undergraduate chapter, Alpha Zeta, to participate. I read one of the morning scriptures. Before the service I had a chance to talk with Dr.

King in the pastor's study. He was so ordinary and easy to talk with that morning. I remember that he was a smoker and that he wanted to smoke a cigarette before we walked out to the pulpit. That was my only encounter with him and I do not remember what we discussed but I remember the encounter as if it were today.

The next morning we moved back into the valley around Khe San on or about the 5th of April and started patrolling the area. I remember that LT Fournet had called in and told me that he found some fresh graves. I had just given a lecture to leaders the night before about padding the body count. I questioned LT Fournet about how fresh the graves were; if they actually had bodies in them; and finally, that I would not tolerate needless padding of the body count for that morning. After about an hour, when I had spread out my cookies and hot chocolate for breakfast, he rode up on a bicycle that someone had found and dumped the head of a corpse right in the middle of my meal. I was furious. I chewed his butt for twenty minutes. He replied, "Sir, I don't lie. When I say that I have a body in a fresh grave, I am not lying." From that point on he and I had a great relationship. We developed a level of mutual trust that only exists between professional soldiers. Later, he would distinguish himself by earning the Congressional Medal of Honor. Unfortunately, he gave his life while earning it. Later that day, we were standing down for a while and getting a change of clothes and I allowed the troops to go swimming in the river. That was my second dumb mistake on that operation. A soldier drowned because he apparently did not know how to swim. They recovered his body and brought it to me for evacuation to the rear. That was really a sad time for me. I knew that I would lose some soldiers to combat but that death seemed so needless to me. It took me a little while to get over that one.

Time has no meaning when you are in combat. I don't know how long we spent on that operation. I just remember that it was not fun. At some point around Easter, we went back to a firebase and stood down to prepare for another operation in the

Ashau Valley. The Ashau Valley was home to a large portion of the main force North Vietnamese Army and it sat astride the Ho Chi Minh Trail. We began planning on a Sunday afternoon and boarded helicopters the next morning. We had to ride for several thousand kilometers to get there. However, you knew when you entered the AO. There was 37mm anti-aircraft fire, i.e., flak bursting all over the place. Crazy Horse had the third helicopter lift in. Each company had been allocated 40 UH1 helicopters to move into the Ashau Valley. When they came to pick up my company they were down to thirty-one helicopters. So I had to hastily reconfigure my loads and board 'em for the air assault. As we were flying along, over the LZ, the flak was bursting just outside of the helicopter. Everyone on my helicopter was scared to death including me. It was one of the times when you are not in control of your destiny. You couldn't fire back because you couldn't see anything except the shells bursting in air. I couldn't think of anything to do to loosen people up except to say to one of the troopers, give me your camera and I'll take some pictures. That seemed to relieve the pressure and they started to smile a little. We landed on an uneven LZ, which made it dangerous to get out of the helicopters. One of the worst things that can happen to a soldier is to receive a blade strike as you jump off of a helicopter. If you survive you will have, at the very least, a severe headache. However, I saw crew chiefs literally throwing soldiers off of the helicopters that day because the pilots wanted to get the hell out of there. As we were setting up we had a CH 47 (Chinook) helicopter crash just outside of our perimeter. What a sight to see that big chopper being shot down. Fortunately, there were only three crewmembers on board. They all survived but had severe burns on their hands and faces. We backhauled them out with our logistics helicopters as they were coming in to resupply us. It took us a while to get organized that day. We had never gone into a hot LZ like that before. The North Vietnamese soldiers had mortar and anti-aircraft fire flying all over the place. That was my first encounter with disciplined, main force North Vietnamese regular troops. They were pretty good.

The next day we moved into the valley and started to go after designated objectives that had been assigned before the air assault. Quite frankly, I was disappointed that there was not more resistance. We encountered an occasional sniper but not much action from any large concentration of troops. After two days of encountering snipers and a few ambushes we came upon a few dug in enemy soldiers in spider holes. LT Fournet took his platoon and went across a little stream and personally dropped hand grenades into the spider holes. I thought to myself, what a great leader this guy is going to be some day. That same day we heard what sounded like a tank. I thought, oh no, we didn't plan on this. Well the enemy abandoned the single tank and we discovered that it had Russian markings on the data plate. We had not gotten any supplies for about 48 hours because of bad weather. Right after our encounter with the tank we found a stream and got some water for our canteens. It was not difficult to carry enough rations for a couple of days but it was almost impossible to carry enough water to last more than a day. Water was heavy, bulky and cumbersome.

The Troop Commanders had a meeting at LTC Wasiak's command post and planned our next moves throughout the valley. LTC Wasiak finished his briefing and said, '"Who wants to lead?" That's when all of the other commanders started looking out into space and up into the air as if they are looking for the right answer. I stepped up and volunteered "Crazy Horse will lead sir!" My feeling was, when the going gets tough, the tough takes the lead. As we moved out we had to pass through another company and I heard their soldiers say "That's them bad asses from Crazy Horse. Their Six is a bad (expletive deleted). That's him! He don't even carry a gun." My soldiers were proud that the other guys looked up to us. However, one thing that my troops knew that the others did not know was that I did carry a gun. It was a .45 caliber pistol hidden under my backpack. The reason that I didn't carry a rifle was, I figured if it ever came down to me having to fire a rifle there would be enough lying around for me to use from the dead and wounded. I was cocky and rather full of myself. After all I had been out there, in command, about 90 days at that time. As we moved forward, either that day or the next day, we found a communications line with poles, insulators and copper wire. This was evidently a line to something very important. After I informed Red Baron 6 and got permission we started to follow the line. As we started up a little hill we encountered sniper gunfire. Since we were on a path without a lot of flank security out we were moving extremely slow. Darkness caught us and we literally had a fight with snipers all night.

Early the next morning I spread out my cookies and hot chocolate for breakfast. I started to communicate with Red Baron 6 at battalion headquarters, my platoons, and the forward air controller (FAC) that was bringing in napalm and other big armament. All of a sudden one small arms round came in and hit me in the upper thigh. It felt like someone had hit me with a two by four. It hurt like hell. I started scrambling around trying to make it difficult for a second shot to hit me. All hell broke loose on the perimeter. I finally got the firing turned off and called Red Baron 6. I informed him that I had been hit and that I was going to be evacuated as soon as I could get things under control at my location. I reached into my backpack and got my bottle of Chivas Regal and took a big pull on it. I then called for LT Fournet to come to my location. LT Delusto was the senior officer left but I was not about to leave him in charge. After I briefed LT Fournet and got everybody situated, and called for a medical evacuation helicopter, I told Doc to give me a shot of morphine. As I left LT Fournet was already organizing for an assault on that hill. It is my understanding that Red Baron 6 sent another lieutenant from his headquarters to take over the Company instead.

I was evacuated to a division aide station and later transported to a surgical hospital in Chu Lai. They operated on me there and sewed me up with wire and transported me to a general hospital in Cam Ranh Bay. I was in the hospital system for about thirty days. My most vivid memories are of the first night right after my surgery in Chu Lai when I went to the out house and we had a couple of mortar rounds come into the hospital area. I remember screaming to the top of my voice because I couldn't move without crutches and I did not have a weapon. Again, I was in a situation over which I had no control. The second vivid memory was when a Captain, male nurse, told me it was my turn to sweep out the ward. I said to him, "I am going to do that right after you do it." I was a Combat Arms Captain and I sure as hell was not going to take orders from some "hospital puke." The third memory was when I woke up in intensive care in the Cam Ranh Bay Convalescent Center and found that I still had my BDU shirt with about five hundred dollars in cash in the side pocket. When I could get up and walk with a cane I went to the PX and asked the counter clerk to turn to the page that had silver tea service sets on it. I ordered one of everything on that page including bread trays and serving pieces and had them sent to Olivia. I had money left so I bought a complete set of China with all of the serving pieces. That left me with less than twenty dollars. I was happy and felt that I would not be robbed of that small mount.

When I returned from Cam Ranh Bay I went to see LTC Wasiak. He had saved my Company for me and offered it back to me. I told him that I didn't feel well enough to go back to the field at that time and I thought that the troops deserved a Commander that was a hundred percent healthy. He had sent me a purple heart and a bronze star for meritorious service while I was in the hospital. He agreed with me and hired the Commanding General's Aide de Camp, Captain George Fisher as my replacement. I went to the Office of the Brigade S3 as the night tactical operations center (TOC) officer. That meant that I worked from about three o'clock in the afternoon until about six o'clock in the morning. I was the guy who prepared and presented the evening briefing to the Brigade Commander and his staff. That job lasted about three weeks. Subsequently, I was given the job of Headquarters and Headquarters Company (HHC) Commander 3rd Brigade. I reported to the Brigade

Executive Officer, Lieutenant Colonel Johnson. Johnson was the quintessential Brigade Executive Officer. He was the second in command, but everyone knew he was in charge. LTC Johnson was a great man with whom to work. The brigade commander was a blustering buffoon who had been taken from a desk in Washington and sent to Vietnam to get promoted. I do not remember his name. He was terrible and he did not get promoted.

As Commander of the HHC, I was in charge of the Brigade rear area, all meals and supplies, and security. It was a good job but not very demanding. Every morning LTC Johnson stood in front of the mess hall and handed out tasks for everyone to complete during the day. In that regard he acted more like a sergeant major than a lieutenant colonel. I decided that I would turn his game around on him. I started asking him questions and giving him little incidents to check out and he subsequently started avoiding me. Except for the day that he asked me to get wine for the Colonel's Table. The brigade commander had a little corner of the mess cordoned off where the officers ate. He wanted wine served with the evening meal. Johnson gave me the duty of securing the wine. I took a helicopter and went south to Hue, where there was a Class VI store and bought a pallet of wine. The wine that I purchased was a very dry red wine (Claret) and tasted like hell. However, the Colonel was happy. The way he drank, my guess is he would have been happy even with a cheap bottle of Port. One day I was called in by LTC Johnson and informed that my son was sick back in the states and the Red Cross had requested that I come home immediately. LTC Johnson put together a quick ceremony and gave me my awards, a bronze star w/ V device and an air metal and the bevy of "been there medals" that went with them and sent me home one month short of a full tour. The adjutant, Major Scales handed me a packet of evaluations to drop in the mail in the states. I did so at the post office in Newhall, WV.

Olivia was at the airport to meet me. However, the most dangerous part of going back and forth to Vietnam was landing at the airport in Bluefield, WV. On that trip, the Piedmont Airlines DC 3 that flew in and out of Bluefield had a flat tire upon trying to land and immediately took off before running over the edge of the mountain that served as the runway. We went on to land in Roanoke, VA. I called Olivia and told her that I was going to rent a car and drive home. I rented a car and drove back to Bluefield instead of flying back. I also wanted to test the system since I had tried to rent a car a year earlier in that area and had been turned down. I was going to throw a real fit if I was denied a car coming back from fighting in the Vietnam War. Fortunately, there were no problems. I drove back to Bluefield and went directly to the hospital to see Bob. He was through the crisis and said to me, "You need a shave." I knew then that he was going to be okay. He was discharged that day. I had orders for Fort Benning, Georgia, as a student in the Advance Course for Infantry officers. Olivia and the children had stayed in a little house that we rented in Newhall, WV, while I was away in Vietnam.

OLIVIA

When I entered the seventh grade at Excelsior High School I met an entirely new group of kids that came from all around our school district. One of the people I met was a diminutive little girl from Bishop, WV, who was neat and stood out as something special. It was not until I was in about the ninth grade that I determined that I was going to approach her. That year at the ninth grade prom, her mother and my mother were chaperons and they talked. The result was my mother speaking very favorably to me about Olivia, and her mother speaking very favorably to her about me. The following year we started to date and as they say, "the rest is history." We were almost inseparable from the tenth grade, through college and we were married as soon as she completed college in June of 1962. We were married in her hometown of Bishop, WV, in Little Zion Baptist Church. My dad, Reverend Robert L. Stephens, Sr., officiated, and Olivia's sister, Mina, was the maid of honor. My brother, Booker, was the best man. The wedding reception was held at her parent's house on Stoney Ridge, about a mile from the church, and the event was attended by all of the prominent Negro families in Big Creek District. Ours was the first real wedding to take place in that little church and certainly we were the most well educated couple to get married there at that time. Everybody wanted to be invited. In fact, there was a fair amount of scrambling around by the local black educators when some were not invited. Somehow all who wanted to come were accommodated. When the reception was over Olivia's uncle Boots drove us to Institute, WV, where I had to complete my studies and graduate from college. Uncle Boots' real name was Alonzo Lambright. Over the ensuing years he and I would become very close friends and confidants to each other. He often said that Olivia was his favorite niece and he volunteered to take us to our home Charleston, WV, on our wedding day. We had eleven dollars in the Dunbar Bank at Dunbar, WV. My dad gave me two $20.00 dollar bills. I had a student labor check of $30.00 and an ROTC cadet check of $27.90. That was all of the money that we had in the world, that day. Our guests had given us a lot of gifts but no cash. Olivia's Dad walked to the bottom of the driveway with me and said, "Steve, take care of my girl." I took that as a charge to keep and I hope that I have not let him down.

Delores Olivia Bennett Stephens is small in stature, soft spoken and fragile. However, under the right circumstances, she is one of the strongest people I have ever known. I left her in charge of everything in a little rented house in Newhall, WV, when I went to Vietnam the first time and never worried one minute that there would be anything that would not go well. She managed the household alone with two small children. That was the first time that we had a separation for more than sixty days since the tenth grade. When Bob, our son, became ill with what she and the doctors thought was encephalitis she wanted me home. I came home immediately! Otherwise, she handled everything extremely well.

At heart, Olivia, as she is called, is a teacher par excellence who has taught in Georgia, Kentucky, Ohio, Virginia, Washington, and West Virginia. In addition, she has taught in Panama (the Canal Zone and the Republic) at separate times and in The Kingdom of Thailand. I believe if chimpanzees could pronounce words she could teach them to read. She preferred working with first graders and kindergartners throughout her career because that's when children learn to read. She often says that her passion is teaching reading and her results all over the world bear her out. She knows how to teach children to read! She recently retired from teaching first grade in a little elementary school south of Atlanta. The school had three grades and she consistently had the top reader in the entire school for the last three years that she taught. It is her belief that if one cannot read they cannot excel in life.

She is the oldest of four children born to Frank and Ethel Bennett. Olivia was the first person in her family, to go to college. Both of her parents were high school graduates. Her father was a coal miner and her mother was a practical nurse for the local company doctor. On the side they ran a little roadhouse juke joint called The Rockhouse. None of the children ever had an association with The Rockhouse except that Olivia's brothers Bill and Rod may have gone there and danced in the room that had the jukebox when they were teenagers. The girls, Olivia and her sister, Mina, did not frequent the place. Olivia was very studious and graduated from high school with honors when she was only sixteen years old. The Bennetts lived in a brick house on Stoney Ridge that was built by Mr. Bennett. Frank studied at a local trade school and obtained certifications in plumbing, masonry, and carpentry. Then he set out to build his family a home. He can tell you how many board feet of lumber are in the house, how many pounds of nails that were used, and the number of bricks that were laid. It is a fine house and Olivia's parents still live in it today.

Over the years Olivia has grown along with me first as a military wife and later as a woman of stature in the communities in which we have lived. She has served on numerous boards and commissions including being a member of the Vestry at our church. From the beginning of our military career, she worked hard to measure up to the other wives in the units in which we served. However because she had a degree and was a teacher, she had special status among the spouses of other officers. I have always been proud of the way she presents herself to others. At home the children and I affectionately call her "goodie two shoes" because she never breaks the rules and she does everything by the book. She just never makes mistakes. That makes her special in everyone's eyes. She speaks perfect English all of the time. She won spelling bees in middle school and her grammar is impeccable. She always dresses just right, almost never overdoing it. She is elegant without being overbearing and when she walks into a room everyone takes notice. She is beautiful inside and outside.

She came into her own, as an Army wife when we moved to Panama the first time. She taught school and yet found the time to participate in unit functions with the other spouses. We had started going out for dinner regularly when I was in language school at Monterey, CA. So we continued to do so when she arrived in Panama. She is a non-alcohol drinker at social events so she almost never sticks her foot in her mouth. Over the years she became a good dancer and an easy person with whom most people could talk. When I became a battalion commander she led the women's club of about 35 in the battalion and kept a full time job in a Fort Lewis Elementary School. When I became a brigade commander she led the women's club of about 100 in the brigade and kept a full time job in the Department of Defense Schools (DODS), Panama. By the way, with her working a full time job I was never in fear of not having enough money to do the things we wanted to do. We always had the normal parties and social events associated with command positions at our home that were required. She is a superb organizer and she would assign specific jobs to our children for those functions and the events always came off perfectly. When I became a general she was the model Army wife and everyone knew it. Her mannerisms and demeanor were modeled after the classic senior officers' wives that we had known in the past. For example, she resisted getting a full-length mink coat because she did not want to be accused of being insensitive to those people who love animals. She always puts other people first.

During our tour in Thailand she was absolutely outstanding as the wife of the senior ranking foreign military officer in the country. When we arrived she had to ride taxis everywhere because we were without our private automobile for about forty-five days. She never complained. She had lunch meetings in our quarters to which she invited the Thai ladies who worked on our JUSMAG compound. Incidentally, she personally prepared the entire meal. The highlight in Thailand was a New Year's Day Reception in our home to which we invited the American Ambassador among other guests. He and his spouse attended. We also invited the Thai general and flag officers and their spouses to our quarters along with many Thai civilian families. She taught in an international private school in which she had diplomat's children from Brazil, France, Canada, Thailand, and the United States. She was able to handle the language barriers and taught all of them to read English. It was during this tour that her elegant behavior and superb social skills were refined. On one occasion, when I was away at a Senior Managers in Government Course at Harvard University, she met the Commander in Chief, Pacific (CINCPAC) and his wife and escorted them until I arrived back from the United States the following day. I felt very comfortable with her doing that because she is always at ease with everyone.

During times of crises Olivia always shines. She has taught me so much over the years, especially about forgiving others and moving on. She does not harbor ill feelings or animosities against anyone for very long. I have seen her forgive folks and genuinely accept them in amazingly short periods of time. I am not even close to her in that regard but she has shown me the way to forgiveness on numerous occasions. One incident, in particular, stands out in my mind. When we moved to West Virginia after my retirement from the Army, Olivia became a real estate agent. A friend of ours, who was also a real estate agent, mistreated her. For a short time Olivia did not speak to that person and refused to have anything to do with her. As fate would have it, we bumped into that person and her husband at a social event and Olivia was genuinely gracious to her. That lady later remarked to me that night, "Olivia is a helluva woman. I thought she would never associate with me again." That's the way she is; a class act all the time. Just recently she stopped one morning on the way to work, in the dark, to help two Hispanic men who were having car trouble along the highway. I chewed her out for stopping in the dark to help two unknown men. She just smiled and I knew that she would do it again if the occasion arose.

In the summer of 2004 I had a complete hip replacement. She was there by my side the whole time. She is a remarkable woman. I am extremely proud that I was smart enough to marry her. She is literally the wind beneath my wings and the impetus behind any modicum of success that I have attained. Obviously, I love her dearly! Her personal growth started during that first tour in Vietnam when she was left to run the household and make decisions without me interfering or having any influence. She took charge and has never completely given up the reins. She is heard to say sometimes, "I started running things and doing the books when we didn't have a lot of money. When Steve took over the books again we were out of the red and into the black. Now he runs things and acts like there never was a concern."

I dearly love that woman!

After the Vietnam tour our next station was Fort Benning, Georgia, Home of the Infantry, and the Infantry Officer Advanced Course (IOAC).

OFF TO FORT BENNING, AGAIN

I really enjoyed my thirty-day leave with Olivia and the children in Newhall, WV, after the Vietnam tour. We prepared to move to Fort Benning, Georgia, The Home of the Infantry, to attend the Officers Advance Course (AOC). The course length exceeded twenty-four weeks and, therefore, the move was classified by the Army as a permanent change of station (PCS) which authorized us to request on-post living quarters. We arrived at Fort Benning in late August because I had left Vietnam early for Bob's illness. That meant that I would be given a "snowbird" job to keep me busy until my AOC started in October. I was given the position of Senior Evaluator for one of the Infantry Officer Basic Courses. I had two other Captains helping me. One was named Julius Frank Johnson (JJ) who would become a life-long friend. We worked with the basic course students primarily as role models, mentors and leaders getting them to class at the right location and on time. It was a good job except that we worked for a battalion commander in the Infantry School Brigade, an item that was not explained to me when I took the job. This guy was my rater and I never ever had a conversation with him. He never even visited a training site where I was located. He gave me a mediocre performance report. I was furious! I went to see him and was stiff-armed by his executive officer, saying that he was not available to see me. I am certain the executive officer wrote the report and the jackass lieutenant colonel just signed it without reading it. The battalion commander's last name was Theil. I fought the report on the grounds that I was not under his supervision for a sufficient amount of time to be rated. Somehow that two-month report was later removed from my file. I felt that lieutenant colonel was out to ruin me and I was not about to take it lying down. After all, I had just returned from Vietnam where I had given up a pound of flesh to an AK47 round in my right thigh. It was about this time that I resolved to never, never accept discrimination ever again. Not only was I not going to accept it for myself but also I was not going to accept it for Olivia or my children.

The AOC began in October and I saw the largest collection of black Captains and Majors in one location that I had ever seen in my life. We were all students in the Infantry School. Most of the classes were held in Building Four, the new Infantry Center Headquarters building. I don't remember the name of the Infantry School Commandant, but the Deputy Commandant was named Brigadier General (BG) Sidney B. Berry. He was impressive! Above all, he appeared to treat all of us with the same degree of dignity and respect. He even stopped and talked to black officers in the hallways. That was a real novel action in those days. In my previous experiences senior white officers had scant time for black officers and invariably we were given short shrift. General Berry was everywhere during the day. He visited classes, attended physical fitness drills and was at social events in the evening. This was the first general that I had met who seemed to have enough energy for the job he was assigned to do.

At the beginning of the Advance Course we had to take diagnostic examinations in map reading, communications, and physical fitness. Nobody wanted to fail any of these examinations because the remedial classes were held on Saturday. It was at this time that I hit a low point in my career. The cribs for these exams were all over the place. The West Point graduates had a study group, the Officer Candidate School (OCS) graduates had a study group, and the black officers had a study group. Every study group had the crib sheets of all of the former examinations. We met in small cells and studied the old examinations. I remember that we had codes to remember the sequences and some people even went to the extent of inscribing the codes on a pencil and literally copying the answers for the true/false or multiple choice questions. It appeared that everyone was cheating on one level or another. I will admit that I studied from the old examinations for the diagnostic tests. J.J. Johnson and I lived very close in the housing area and we studied together. I sat beside Captain Timothy Smith, an Armor branch officer in the branch exchange program with the Infantry school. Tim and I determined that if we put the same energy into studying our notes that we put into trying to remember what was on the crib sheets we would probably do very well in addition to actually knowing the material. So at some point I regained my dignity and integrity and stopped studying from the crib sheets. By the way, Captain Smith was a Southern University, in Baton Rouge, LA, graduate.

Early on in the course, like the second week, a promotion list for major was posted in the hallway of Building Four. Now you have to understand the mentality of the Infantry School staff to comprehend the way they displayed the list. First, they posted it right outside of the bookstore and snack bar area, in the direct path of everyone walking from the administrative area to the academic part of the building. Second, they placed the list of names of everyone selected for promotion on the wall on the right side of the hallway. Likewise, they posted the names of the officers that were not selected on the left side of the hallway. I know, Infantrymen are not considered to be very smart but we are sure as hell direct. Olivia was at the beauty parlor that day and the women were talking about the selection list. I was home watching the children while she went to have her hair done. She came home and said to me, "You're on the major's list." I had only been in the Army six years and I had no expectation of being promoted to major that fast. I ignored her. When she realized that I had not paid her any attention she said again, and this time with emphasis, "You're on the majors list" she added, "Go over and get your number." I still did not believe but now I was curious so I made the five-minute trip from the housing area to Building Four to look at the promotion list for major.

The hallway was full of folks looking at the lists. I looked and did not see my name and started to leave when someone came up and congratulated me. I thanked him and said that I did not see my name so they must be mistaken. The person asked where I had looked and I pointed and said, over there. That's when I was informed that there were two lists posted. A list of the ones that made it, and another list of the ones who failed to make it. Later in my career I would think about that day and hope that I would not ever be that insensitive. There were a lot of us on that list because it was in the middle of the Vietnam War and one of the incentives for people staying on active duty was the possibility of being promoted. I do not remember my promotion list number. That list lasted almost four years. I was promoted to Major on the 27th of June 1969. About three months later, I was called to the office of the same student battalion commander, the lieutenant colonel with a German name, by a note left in my student mailbox. Upon arrival in LTC Theil's office I was informed by his executive officer, a major, I was going to be promoted that afternoon when the colonel finished promoting another officer to major. Of course they had invited the other officer's family there and they had refreshments after the ceremony. I did not have an opportunity to call my family. Remember, this was before the days when everyone had a cell phone. I remained a major until March 1979. There were 226 people in my advance class and 225 of them had already served in Vietnam. The one guy who had not gone to Vietnam was an officer of Cuban decent who was a member of the 2506 Brigade that had gone to Cuba as part of La Invasion en la Bahia de los Cochinos. We were a class of veterans.

As part of the advance course we were required to take some elective courses. Because some of my previous raters had rated me as average in writing and oral presentation I chose to take advanced writing and public speaking. I knew that the stereotypical thinking about black officers, at that time, included a belief that most of us could neither write well nor speak well in public. I was an Education major in college with a specialization in teaching English and I knew that I did not fit that stereotype. Again I will admit, however, that I learned a lot in the public speaking class. It was the first time that I had observed myself on videotape and I immediately started to correct some of the mannerisms and guttural pauses that I had developed. Toward the end of the course we were called in and briefed on how we would be rated by our faculty advisers. Sure enough, my rater, an officer who probably did not have a college degree, had given me an average grade in writing and an average grade in oral communications. I opened my shirt and pulled out my grade cards from my electives. I had a score of 95% on both. I asked the rater how he interrupted the 95 percentile score. He agreed that it was outstanding and after a little prodding on my part (I actually threatened to go and see General Berry) he changed that portion of my rating from average to outstanding. I guess one could say I went into the rating session mad as hell and I wasn't going to take it anymore.

Except for the daily routine of attending class, that year went by rather fast and uneventful. Our two children started preschool and Olivia informed me that she was looking for work outside of the home. I objected saying that I wanted her to stay home and take care of our children. She replied, "I'd rather work and pay someone else to do that." I was flabbergasted. Of course she won the argument and the question about her working has never come up again.

We became close friends with some folks that have remained our friends for life. J.J. Johnson and his family became our closest friends. We also became closer friends with Joe and Wenefred Left, and Rad and Ros Robinson, couples we had known in Panama. We also met David and Betty Foy. We are still friends with all of them by mail today. It was about this time that I realized how small the Army can be. One usually associated with people who were about the same age and commissioning year group. As time went on I began to recognize that our friends and acquaintances were confined to folks who were about three years younger or three years older than we were.

The Advance Course graduation ceremony was unique. General William E. Depuy addressed the class. He asked us to go home and take a lined tablet and place the year of our Lord

1989 on the top line. "Using a pencil with a good eraser, go down the page in descending order until you reach the year of our Lord 1969." The graduation was happening in August 1969. He said "over the next six months, in collaboration with your spouse, all children over age six, and anyone else that you considered significant, fill in the empty lines." General Depuy also said that the following year we should do the same thing but this time place 1990 at the top of the page. In fact he said to do it every year thereafter. He emphasized that it was okay to use the eraser and change anything that you had planned, because it was your life, your marriage and your future and you could plan it any way you wanted. Olivia and I went home and we did it. We planned for me to become a brigadier general in 1989. I was selected for promotion to general rank in 1987.

While we were at Fort Benning I also met with the Infantry officer's branch representative from Washington, DC on his trip to the Infantry School and I expressed a desire to go to a fully funded graduate school program and to helicopter flight school. He said that flight school was definitely out of the question. However, he did not count out fully funded graduate school. Well the compromise was that they gave me a ROTC assignment. That was great except that they sent me to a college that very few people had heard of, Alfred University, in Alfred, New York.

SECTION II

THE FIELD GRADE YEARS

Operations Officer and Assistant Professor of Military Science at Alfred University circa 1970.

Official Army Photo as a LTC assigned to the Pentagon in 1977.

Official Army photograph of Colonel Stephens—1984.

General Joe Palastra and Olivia promoting me to Lieutenant Colonel in the Joint Chiefs of Staff—12 September 1978.

Official photo, Brigade Commander, Task Force Bayonet later 193rd Infantry Brigade (LT)—Republic of Panama—1986.

14—The Welch Daily News Monday Eve., Oct. 17, 1983

Major General J.R. Curry, Col. Robert L. Stephens Jr. And Olivia Stephens

Stevens Promoted To Colonel In U.S. Army

Robert L. Stephens Jr., son of Rev. Robert L. Stephens of War, was promoted to Colonel in the U.S. Army on Oct. 3. Major Gen. Jerry R. Curry, the Commanding General of the Military District of Washington, performed the honors in a special ceremony at Fort McNair in Washington, D.C. attended by dozens of relatives, [illegible]

Chiefs of Staff in the Pentagon; and battalion commander of the 2nd Battalion, 39th Infantry at Fort Lewis, Washington. He is currently Inspector General of the U.S. Army Military District of Washington.

Col. Stephens has attended the Infantry Basic and Advanced courses at Fort Benning, GA; the Defense Language Institute [illegible]

MG Jerry Curry and Olivia promoting me to Colonel with full narrative on 01 October 1983.

Waiting to board a Vietnamese Air Force (VNAF) helicopter to start the day's missions in Truc Yang Province, Republic of Vietnam—1973.

Being promoted to Major in Fort Benning, GA, on 27 June 1969.

Completing the Marine Corps Marathon in 1984.

Entry number in the U.S. Marine Corps Marathon, 1984.

SỐ KIỂM SOÁT: 738 CONTROL NR. 738

ỦY-NHIỆM-TRẠNG
BAN LIÊN-HỢP
QUÂN-SỰ BỐN BÊN

CREDENTIALS
FOUR-PARTY
JOINT MILITARY
COMMISSION

STEPHENS, ROBERT L. JR.
(Tên Name)

Major 0-4
(Cấp bậc Rank)

UNITED STATES DELEGATION
(Phái Party)

Member JMT/Region 7
(Bổ nhiệm Assignment)

Xác nhận
Authentication:

G.H. Woodward
Thiếu Tướng LQHK
Trưởng Phái-Đoàn Hoa-Kỳ

G.H. WOODWARD
Major General, USA
Chief, US Delegation

Credentials for the Four Party Joint Military Commission, Republic of Vietnam—1971.

Military District of Washington (MDW) Staff in 1984.

Stephens as a Major in the 3rd BN,
187th Infantry circa 1973.

Veteran's Day wreath laying in Panama, 1986.

Commandant of the USARSO NCO Academy Staff in Coco Solo, Panama, Canal Zone in 1966.

THE FIELD GRADE YEARS

A field grade officer is an army or marine commissioned officer senior in rank to a company officer but junior to a general officer. Field officers, also referred to "field-grade officers" or "senior officers," are officers who typically command units that can be expected to operate independently for short periods of time (infantry battalions, cavalry or artillery regiments, large warships, air squadrons). Field officers also commonly fill brigade, division corps, and army level staff positions both as principals and assistants.

At the time I became a field grade officer the general thought amongst my contemporaries was that if you could become a Major you had the potential to become a Colonel. I was promoted to Major in June of 1969 almost seven years after being commissioned. Most people believe that becoming a field grade officer distinguishes one from the "pack." I suppose that a promotion to major clearly shows that an officer has displayed the potential to be given greater duties of responsibility. For the most part I spent my years as a major in secondary staff roles completing actions for more senior officers. I remember that one of my proudest moments came when I was called in for my Advance Course evaluation from another major. He acted officially and started to tell me that he was going to cut me for written and oral communications. I displayed my scores from my classes in those subjects and demanded that he change the evaluations. My worst day as a major was the day that I was promoted. The lieutenant colonel that promoted me called me over from class in the Advance Course and had me to wait outside his office until he was ready to call me in for a two to five minute ceremony. The other officer promoted that day, had his wife, children and his parents present. My wife and children were only minutes away but were not invited.

For my promotion to lieutenant colonel I asked a person that I considered a friend to promote me. BG Joseph T. Palastra had been my brigade commander and mentor as a major and I was proud for him and his wife Anne to assist Olivia in promoting me to lieutenant colonel (LTC). As a LTC I worked in a very high level staff position in the Joint Chiefs of Staff, commanded an Infantry battalion, and attended the National War College.

Becoming a full colonel was more than I had ever dreamed of accomplishing in the Army. It was the one rank that I always thought gave leaders autonomy. As a colonel there were always people around you that wanted guidance and direction and almost never enough general or flag officers around to give you a ration of crap. You were literally "the man" or "the woman" as the case may be. Being a colonel afforded me the opportunity to command a one-of-kind forward deployed brigade in the Republic of Panama. I loved being a brigade commander! At the time I became a colonel a transformation was taking place in the Army which gave colonels the privilege of being called "senior officers." Everyone knew that it was not true technically but it felt good.

Right after graduation from the AOC my brother, who was a lawyer and a legislator at the time, and I made a trip to Alfred, New York, to look the place over. We arrived late in the evening and got a room in The Squirrel's Nest, the only motel in town. We went to a little package store nearby and bought a bottle of gin. We had driven through a part of the town of Alfred, NY, and quite frankly I needed a drink. At first glance, I was really angry at Infantry branch for even suggesting that I be assigned to the university in this little town. I remember my brother asking me if I had ticked someone off at Infantry branch and if this was the proper treatment for a purple heart wearing Vietnam War veteran. We had a couple of drinks and bought some chicken dinners at the local fried chicken place. I was upset but I would never let anyone know. Not even my brother.

We were up bright and early the next day and I went to the Alfred University ROTC building. The ROTC building was a World War II Quonset Hut that had been converted to an office building with a couple of classrooms. From the outside it looked like the pits. I went inside and met the secretary, Helen Clark. She was a middle-aged woman who appeared to have arrived on campus at about the same time that the building had been built. She was ex-military. She got me a cup of coffee and started showing me around. None of the officers were at work. The sergeants, with the exception of the supply sergeant, were at Summer Camp with the cadets at Indiantown Gap, PA. It was after 9:00 AM.

At about 9:30 a.m. LTC Seip arrived. George Seip was a 1943 graduate of the U.S. Military Academy at West Point, NY. He was promoted to Lieutenant Colonel in 1952. It was 1969, so he had somewhere around seventeen years in grade. We talked briefly and the Professor of Military Science (PMS), Colonel Robert Schumacher arrived. Both of these gentlemen were dressed in civilian clothes. Helen had already informed me that we would only wear uniforms when we were teaching classes. Schumacher was on his third ROTC assignment during the course of his career. After a brief exchange of pleasantries he informed me that I was going to be the operations officer for the Detachment. He had no guidance for me. He just sort of talked in circles which let me know immediately that he did not have a clue about what was going on at the University. I had come to that conclusion much earlier with LTC Seip. They turned out to be a good guys who stayed out of my way and let me run the place. Neither one of these guys taught classes, attended ROTC Summer Camp, or sat on any faculty committees. So one might ask, what did they do? Over time I found that the answer would be that they showed up and read the New York Times everyday and waited for phone calls from our headquarters, First United States Army in Fort Meade, Maryland.

I was the replacement for Major Robert Deshler, the previous operations officer. He apparently ran the place. There was present also Major Peter Doak. Coming into the assignment with me were Captains Jerry Cosey and David Porreca. Apparently COL Schumacher and Major Doak did not hit it off and COL Schumacher chose me to be the Operations Officer over him, sight unseen. I left Schumacher's office and went house hunting. I wound up with the town real estate agent whose name was Manny. Manny owned a series of properties in town that he rented out to students. He had just built a new apartment building on Jericho Hill and was trying to fill it with occupants. Compared to his other properties, this complex was upscale. I paid him a deposit and took a two-bedroom apartment in the new building. My brother and I left Alfred early the next day and headed back to Bishop, WV, to get my family. We moved to Alfred, New York the following week and stayed a couple of days in the Squirrel's Nest Motel until our furniture arrived. It was not the ideal situation but Olivia did not complain. In the meantime, Captains Porreca and Cosey arrived with their families and we all got acquainted. We were in the middle of the summer term ending and the fall term beginning so nothing was going on at the University. Olivia and I got the household goods unpacked and put everything away. It was the first time during my career that I had time to spend with my family without a lot of outside interference.

It was not long before we were settled in our apartment and enrolling our children in Alfred-Almond Elementary School. I am not certain but I would make a large wager that they were the first full blooded black children to attend that school. Olivia took care of enrolling them and looking after their well being. I went to work in the ROTC building with the other staff members. I do not remember a lot about them except that they were all friendly and cordial. I do remember that Helen was our main secretary and Deana Polson was my secretary. There was one other black member on the staff. His name was Sergeant First Class Paul Manuel. Paul was my assistant as the Operations

Sergeant and we became almost inseparable at work. He preceded me by a year at Alfred University and knew his way around. He was the gap between what I did not know about the academic side of the business and what students thought and expected. He was a member of one of the student fraternities and spent a lot of time with students as the varsity rifle team coach. Together, we ran the ROTC operation and did it extremely well. The truth of the matter is that no one else wanted to work the hours that Paul and I worked including Colonel Shumacher. LTC Seip was only marking time. He taught no classes, made no trips to recruit students, and did not perform funeral details. He was just there in the office from about 0915 to about 1130 at which time he went and played badminton for about an hour and returned to read novels tucked inside of the New York Times while eating his ham sandwich. Helen was the person who told us about it and we would take turns going in to interrupt him and watch him scramble around and try to hide his novels. Master Sergeant Green was our Administrative Sergeant. He was a great guy with a Japanese wife and a great family. He kept us sane for the most part, because of his sense of humor and flexible personality. He worked with me on next of kin (NOK) notifications and funeral details. I am certain that between the two of us we could write a bestseller about those experiences.

The first year at Alfred University went by pretty fast. It snowed around the first week of October and it didn't thaw completely until the first week in May. I was busy trying to learn my new job and make a good impression on everyone in Alfred. Because I was the Operations Officer for the ROTC program I was automatically placed on several university committees. That turned out to be both hard work and a lot of fun. It also meant instant recognition and in most cases acceptance from the university faculty and staff. Although COL Shumacher told me not to enroll in any University classes, I enrolled in two graduate level courses in January of 1970. I was really busy. Aside from being the Operations Officer, I taught classes to two sections of seniors, advised the rifle team and the drill team, and did some of the funeral details. The colonels did absolutely nothing. So the first year sped by like lightening. Before the year ended COL Shumacher announced his retirement and LTC Seip was involuntarily retired at the end of the year. Watching LTC Seip leave the only life that he had known since he was about sixteen years old was a real eye opener for me. He left unwillingly, in tears, and bitter. For a short period, during the summer, I was actually on the books as the Alfred University Professor of Military Science. I was the ranking person in charge until LTC Robert Hetz the newly assigned PMS arrived.

LTC Hetz was a different kind of guy. He was also a Military Academy graduate like LTC Seip. He wanted to teach classes and got all of us involved as a unit. He invited all of us to his house for a party in September and set the tone for what turned out to be an enjoyable year. Rather than keep us from attending classes as students he encouraged all of us to get our Master's degrees. In fact he started working on his advanced degree as well. The main thing was he carried his own load and served on many of the university committees and took some of the funeral details. Soon, it was clear to me that I was within striking distance of obtaining a Master's degree. In fact, it looked to me like at the end of the second year I would be only nine semester credit hours away from obtaining my Master's degree. So, I went down to Infantry Branch in Washington, DC, at Fort McNair in the fall of 1970 to request an extension at Alfred University for two months to finish my degree. Infantry Branch was housed in something called Tempo A, a wooden Quonset hut area. I was told by an insensitive major, at Infantry Branch, that I would have to go back to Vietnam before I could finish my degree. I got so angry and raised such a ruckus that the lieutenant colonel in the office across the hall came over to see what was going on. I had actually asked for paper and pen to offer my resignation from the Army. I had completed my initial obligation and I was not about to be pushed around by some assignment officer in Washington. Oh, and I was not attending Alfred University under any Army programs. I was receiving the G.I. Bill but there was no obligation attached to it. I did not have any educational obligations to pay back to the Army. In fact, because I was a member of the faculty I was allowed to attend the university free. The lieutenant colonel at Infantry Branch was a lot smarter than the dumb, major with which I was arguing and immediately gave me my two month deferment. It really became a moot point by December, 1970, because I was selected to attend the United States Army Command and General Staff College (CGSC) in Fort Leavenworth, KS, the falling year. So I left Washington and went on back to Alfred for a successful second year. As the summer began, I sent Olivia and the children home to her mother's house, packed up our household goods and moved them to Fort Leavenworth, KS, for storage, and I moved into the dormitory to take nine graduate credits in summer school. I enrolled in a psychological test and measurements class, a clinical practicum counseling class and an elective course administered by the university track coach. For the elective I actually mapped out and constructed an orienteering course at the top of Jericho Hill. I wonder if it is still being used?

Our daughter, Christa, was born while we were at Alfred. She was actually born in Hornell, New York, about 10 miles north of Alfred. The day that we brought her home the local temperature was minus 26 degrees. Olivia told the doctor that she did not want to bring our baby home in that weather. The doctor laughed and told her that the baby would be fine in the weather. Our neighbors were absolutely marvelous about our baby. At the time, we thought that everybody just wanted to see the "little black baby" in Alfred because folks came from miles around bringing food and gifts. Now that we are older it is clear that people were just being nice. Alfred will always be, in my mind, one of the best places that we ever lived!

I lost weight that last summer and left Alfred totally exhausted. But I left with a Master's degree in Guidance and Counseling. I had administered, scored, and interpreted about forty-five psychological tests; made several trips to observe the operation of Leroy State Hospital, a mental institution; finished the orienteering course and acquired three A's for my grade point average. I left Alfred with my old Thunderbird loaded to the brim on a Friday afternoon, headed to Bishop, WV, to pick up Olivia and the children to go to Leavenworth, Kansas. Upon arriving in Bishop, WV, I could tell that Olivia and the children were ready to move. We packed the car, rented a U-Haul trailer and planned to leave for Kansas on Sunday afternoon. The brake lights on the U-Haul trailer would not work so I went to Bluefield, WV, to get someone to work on them. It was Sunday and almost every place that we stopped was either closed or had reduced staff and no mechanic. Finally, I got frustrated and asked my father-in-law if he knew where I could buy another car. He said that he knew Mr. Bledsoe, a car salesman, who lived about three miles from him. I asked him to take me to him. Bledsoe went and opened the dealership, showed me a few cars including a station wagon that I liked and I bought it. Because it was Sunday we could not complete the transaction and had to wait until Monday morning to leave. If my memory serves me right we had an extra travel day built into our schedule anyway so we were okay for the reporting time to CGSC. As it turned out we packed everything in the station wagon on Sunday night and we left bright and early on Monday morning with a quick stop in Bluefield, WV, to complete the paperwork for the purchase of the vehicle. We did the loan by telephone with Mr. Beavers the manager at Tazewell National Bank in Tazewell, VA, and switched the insurance by telephone with United Services Automobile Association. We were on the road by ten o'clock. We stopped at the post office in Institute, WV, to mail an application transfer letter to United Services Automobile Association (USAA) and ran into Dr. Lorna Kemp, the woman who had been my nemesis many years earlier when I didn't graduate on time from West Virginia State College. I tried to ignore her but she recognized me and wanted to talk. I disliked that woman and I was in no mood to be cordial with her. She followed me out of the post office to my car and wanted to meet my children. She was very cordial and respectful to my wife and children and told my children how much she admired me. She told them what a good student that I had been and, in general, she sang my praises to them. I was surprised and forgave her, to a certain extent, for treating me the way she did earlier.

We arrived at Fort Leavenworth, Kansas, late in the evening on the following day. I do not remember where we spent the night but I am almost certain that we did not try to travel a thousand miles in one day. We probably spent the night at Scott Air Force Base in East Saint Louis, IL. Upon arriving at Fort Leavenworth we were given a set of keys and told that we had been assigned to a townhouse in a government sponsored housing complex in Kansas City, Kansas. In-processing at CGSC was the most efficient report and sign-in procedure that I had experienced to that point in my career. The first night in our quarters, we slept on the floor with blankets because we did not have our household goods. Olivia did not complain. Our furniture and household goods were delivered the next day. I did something very stupid that day. Instead of getting all of our things unpacked and settled I decided to go downtown with J.J. Johnson and drink booze. When I returned home Olivia made it very clear to me that I was wrong and that she was not going to tolerate that kind of treatment from me in the future. I was remorseful, admitted my mistake and proceeded to clean up my act. I got everything unpacked and set up a study area in the basement. An area, in which, I very rarely studied for a year. I had just spent two years in graduate school and I was not in the mood for trying to be the honor graduate of my CGSC class. In retrospect that was a mistake.

After we were settled I had a couple of days off before classes started and so we set out to meet our neighbors. There were more than thirty housing units in our complex and each one was occupied. I later found out the quarters were allocated based on our dates-of-rank. Since I was so junior in grade we were not even assigned in the city of Leavenworth, Kansas. We were thirty minutes away from class by carpool. Because most of us only had one car we did commute by carpools. That was quite an experience. The first thing that one has to realize about the students at CGSG is that all of them think they have made the first cut toward becoming a successful military officer. By being selected for the field grade rank, i.e., major, one has just demonstrated that there is the potential to become a full bird colonel. To be selected to attend CGSC means that you have made the first cut in that process. That's the reason I bought that car on a Sunday afternoon without any fear. I was Regular Army and had no fear of losing my military job before my twentieth year. So we had neighbors who had new cars, boats and one even had an airplane. Everyone's ego was sky high and we were all Vietnam veterans. There were approximately 1480 students in my class including the foreign students. Most of the foreign officers knew that they were going to become generals in the armies of their countries and most of the Americans thought that they would become, at least, full bird colonels. We were placed in class sections of sixty officers, in most cases, according to housing areas in order to facilitate carpooling and studying.

We became friends with some couples with whom we remain friends until today. Bill and Merlyn Edwards became our best friends and we visited with them regularly. They had a daughter and a son that were close in age to our children. Unfortunately Bill passed away a few years ago but Olivia and Merlyn still remain very close. We were unique in our little enclave in Kansas City, KS. We had our own Boy and Girl Scout Troops, our own children's athletic teams and we rotated happy hour at each other's quarters every week. The egomania was such that all of our kids excelled in the local school because we all had time to attend Parent Teacher Organization meetings, demanded the best for them and visited their classrooms regularly. The local school board officials loved us. In addition we were in close proximity to the Indian Hills Shopping Mall which made the local vendors happy. The year at CGSC was very enjoyable and relaxing. Because the Vietnam War was still going on we knew that no one would be dismissed for academic reasons. We had a saying when something came up that we did not want to do. It was: "What are they going to do? Send me to Vietnam?"

We had a few female officers in the class. Major Evelyn Patricia Foote, went on to become a general officer. In fact, my daughter Stephanie became Pat Foote's aide de camp when she commanded Fort Belvoir, Virginia. Upon Pat's departure from the service she arranged for Stephanie to become the commanding officer of the Headquarters and Headquarters Company at Fort Belvoir. Other officers who went on to general officer rank were John Stanford who became the Superintendent of the Seattle City School System, Charles Otstott who retired as a Lieutenant General, Joe Stringham, a Special Operations expert and several others.

Upon graduating from CGSC I received orders to return to the Republic of Vietnam. I did not want to go and tried every legal maneuver that I could think of to get out of it. Nothing worked so I resigned myself to the fact that I would be going back. The officer with whom I dealt for the assignment was Lieutenant Colonel John McLeod in Infantry Branch at the new U.S. Army Military Personnel Center (MILPERCEN) at Alexandria, Virginia. McLeod was, to say the least, insensitive and rude. I later found out that he had put a derogatory note in my file. I felt that I should have had some priority of assignment since I had served one tour and earned a purple heart. Obviously to him I was just another square peg to pound into a round hole. As he finally said to me, "You're going back to Vietnam and that's it major." What I didn't know was that he was also on orders for Vietnam. So I graduated from CGSC and moved my family back to West Virginia again. This time we bought the house next door to my wife's parents for my family to live in while I was away. Olivia got a job teaching in one of the local elementary schools in War, WV.

WE'VE GOT TO GET OUT OF THIS PLACE

Sergeant First Class Paul Manuel had met and started dating a coed at Alfred University, named Evelyn. They fell in love and decided to get married. Ordinarily, this would not have been a big deal. However, there were several disparities that did not indicate that this was a good decision. First was the age factor. Paul was, at least, ten years older than Evelyn. Second, she was receiving a Master's degree from Alfred and Paul did not have a degree. Finally, she was white and he was black. All of this was happening in 1972. However, they declared their love for each other and asked me to be Paul's best man. I said yes and flew off to New York to participate in their wedding. I got back home and planned to take a day with my family and depart for Vietnam. I had looked at my orders wrong and ended up a day late getting to Oakland, CA, for movement to the Republic of Vietnam. I thought that someone in the Army would be upset because missing movement is a serious offense. Instead, I was just put on a later flight as if nothing had happened. If I had known that nobody cared about the time I would have taken that extra day. This time my trip to Vietnam was dead serious. I was not off on an adventure like I was for the first tour. There was no hard drinking in Hawaii or Guam this time. I just wanted to get there and get it over.

I landed at Tan Sanut Airbase to the same smell of burning feces and was processed for assignment to the Delta Regional Area Command (DRAC). DRAC was under the command of a retired colonel named Wilbur Wilson. Mr. Wilson who had been given the name "Coal Bin Willie" when he was on active duty at Fort Bragg, NC, because he had a fetish for having all of the lumps of coal in the coal bins lined up in straight lines. Wilson had retired from the active Army and was hired by the Military Assistance Command Vietnam (MACV) as a civilian in charge of the Delta Regional Area. He was not alone. There were a lot of these guys who could not get promoted to the next rank while they were on active duty but could and did assume the role of the next higher rank in retirement. Some of them were pretty good at it and others were just collecting a paycheck. One of the better ones I was told was John Paul Van. I never met him, never saw anything that he did but everyone talked about his accomplishments. When I arrived Coal Bin Willie was in charge of the entire Delta Region, of the Republic of Vietnam.

Upon arriving in the Delta Region, one of the first persons that I saw was a former associate by the name of Major Robert Manning. I met Manning when I was in language school at Monterey, CA, in 1964 when we were lieutenants. He was an Intelligence Corps officer and was studying Vietnamese. He and another African American officer, LT John Carter, were en route to the 1st Special Forces Group in Okinawa, Japan.

At this time he was assigned to the DRAC Headquarters in Can Tho as one of the Intelligence Officers. I told him how I hated the idea of going back to the field in a place called Truc Yang. He said that he would introduce me to the Deputy Chief of Staff, a black lieutenant colonel, who would probably be able to keep me at DRAC Headquarters. He told me to meet him at the club around five o'clock that evening. I arrived at five o'clock and met LTC John McLeod, the same jackass that had put me on orders. I was cordial to him and even was prepared to suck-up a bit. So, I asked him to reassign me to the DRAC Headquarters. I will always remember what he said, "Major, if you think that assignment in Truc Yang is bad now, you (expletive deleted) up the efficiency report, and it will be bad." I did not answer him or offer to buy him a drink as I had planned to do. I disliked that jackass and I resolved to never forget him. The next day, I drew my gear, got a briefing from Colonel Rogers, the military deputy in charge at DRAC, and headed for Team 88 with the helicopter mail run. I never saw Mcleod again, ever. It was June 1972.

I arrived at Team 88 in Truc Yang, Province on the mail run and proceeded to see most of the province before I arrived at the Military Assistance Command, Team 88 Headquarters. The headquarters was a little compound that housed about fifty Americans. They were being led by the three stooges, Mr. Katzubu, a retired lieutenant colonel, the province senior advisor, LTC William Tausch, an aviator, the deputy province senior advisor, and LTC Eric Christensen, the Team 88 chief of staff. What a trio! All three of these guys were full of themselves. Mr. Katzubu had been a prodigy of John Paul Van. LTC Tausch was from Arkansas and thought that he should be promoted to Colonel. I hope he made it. LTC Christensen was a mediocre officer who graduated from the military academy and had spent about seven years in Vietnam. By the way, he kept the same live-in staff the whole time. Tausch also had a live-in staff. None of the Team 88 leaders lived on the Military Assistance Command, Vietnam (MACV) compound. They lived downtown with their house staffs in private quarters. All of these guys were marking time. Ironically, I replaced LTC Robert Deshler again. Believe it or not I have never met this guy but I was his replacement twice in a period of about five years. I also inherited his maid/English student who cleaned my room, washed my clothes, and polished my shoes for about $20.00 a month. However, as team members we did not pay these ladies directly. They were paid by an American Master Sergeant who "ran" the compound. This guy collected the money from us and paid the compound staff. He also collected and distributed the mail and sold us items from the military sundry packets that we received from the military distribution system. I couldn't believe what I saw in MACV Team 88 in 1971. As far as I am concerned the entire bunch were a collection of misfits. I never wore that patch on any of my uniforms after I left Vietnam.

Most of the American troops had gone home when I arrived back in Vietnam the second time. The MACV system was running on autopilot and civilians were in charge everywhere. As I said before, these province and district advisors were people who could not get promoted on active duty so they retired and took the civilian leadership jobs. That was the first time that I experienced outsourcing. Think about it? We were outsourcing command positions. I was designated as the Province S-3 Operations Advisor. I was the newest field grade officer to arrive in Team 88. Another major had preceded my arrival by about a week. He had a German name that I cannot remember at the moment. He was assigned as the Regional Forces/Province Forces (RF/PF) Advisor.

I was the principal counterpart to Major Nguyen Van No. Major No was a classic Vietnamese officer who had been the Truc Yang Province Operations Officer, S-3 for seven years. He knew what he was doing! I just tagged along with him to provide an American presence and sanction for his plans. The first time I met Major No, we talked for about 30 minutes and he asked me to get him a flight helmet. I got ticked off at him right away but I got the helmet more to shut him up than to accommodate him. I felt that if I procrastinated on the requirement to get him "something" the first time, the next "ask" would be greater. I had worked with Vietnamese military officials during my first tour and I knew that they always had their hands out. As a group, Katzubu, Colonel Than the Vietnamese Province Chief, Major No, and I would meet every afternoon to plan the next day's operation. This was part of an overall strategy that came from an American general named Oliver Dillard. I met Dillard one day when he visited our team. According to what I was told by the province deputy senior advisor and the chief of staff, we were supposed to have a "daily personal objective, everyday." That was Dillard's guidance. When I met him he asked me what my objective was for that day and I said to get home alive. That ticked him off and he turned to Tausch and said, "This guy doesn't know what he is doing." Then he stormed off. What he didn't know was that the entire leadership team at Team 88 considered him a buffoon and talked badly about him before he arrived at our headquarters and behind his back while he was there. As near as I could tell we were engaged in day-to-day activities in Vietnam with no long range objectives. We had constant visitors because the war was winding down and everyone was desperately trying to justify being there. The peace talks were going on in Paris and the civilian strap hangers sensed an end coming to their little fiefdoms around the country. At the time I arrived for my second tour we had been in Vietnam ten years. There was a lot of hanky panky and some outright corruption going down on both sides, Vietnamese and American.

My normal day at Truc Yang Province during this tour usually began with breakfast in our air conditioned dining facility that was staffed and run by a bevy of Vietnamese women. They were hired, fired and courted by the compound sergeant that I mentioned earlier. To his credit, he was a bachelor. They were attired in white uniforms, always neat and clean and had been taught to cook American food fairly well. After breakfast, I would generally meet Major No at the My Tho river helipad and we would mount a Vietnamese Air Force (VNAF) helicopter and fly around either putting in air assaults or visiting Vietnamese District Headquarters. Generally at noon we would land and eat lunch at one of the District Chief's home/compound. I remember one incident that occurred in Ham Long District. The Vietnamese Lieutenant Colonel who was the District Chief, Major No, and I we were seated under a parachute canopy that had been fashioned into a tent, for lunch. The district chief spoke very good English and was serving lunch. He took chop sticks and reached into a bowl that had a broth that had a green hue and plucked the head off of an eel and plopped it onto my plate. Without hesitating I picked it up chewed it and swallowed it. I then picked up part of a chicken from a plate and ripped the head off of it and put it in his plate. He did not eat it. However, I think that he respected me for it and treated me differently from then on. On another occasion we landed in another district at about 12 o'clock one afternoon and I watched a Vietnamese lady kill, pluck, and cook a turkey that we ate in about an hour. I have got to tell you though that I drank about a half of a fifth of cognac to get enough nerve to eat that raw turkey. I had some good times flying around with Major No and I had some times that were not too good.

One day we were in Tan Phu District and we were putting in a Vietnamese Air Assault. Flying with us that day was the American District Senior Advisor, the Vietnamese District Chief, and the Truc Yang Province Deputy Province Chief. We were boring holes in the sky flying clockwise and putting in the troops. We had put in two lifts of troops and we were scheduled to put in five. All of a sudden, we were being fired upon. If you have never seen antiaircraft fire from a helicopter you have missed some great fire works. Usually gunfire from an automatic weapon is laced with one tracer in every four rounds and from an aircraft it looks like they are all tracer. Anyway the Vietnamese deputy province chief was leaning over looking out of the helicopter. I signaled to him that we should be flying higher but he ignored me. Suddenly, the red, basketball size, tracers started coming up at us and we were hit. The Vietnamese lieutenant colonel slumped over in the seat after catching two rounds in the butt and one in the gut. The pilot was hit in the toe and the helicopter was smoking and losing altitude. My means of communicating with the Province Headquarters was by PRC 25 radio with an antenna. I had my helmet off and under my seat so I could use the attached headset. My helmet caught two rounds that ricocheted someplace else. I felt myself all over and could not believe that I was not hit. I called in the incident immediately and let the tactical operations center (TOC) know that we were going down. We crash landed in Ba Tri Province, a province that was "pacified." Since our helicopter was damaged we immediately changed to another one. We delivered the Vietnamese lieutenant colonel to a Vietnamese hospital in My Tho. Major No and I reloaded the helicopter and at the behest of LTC Tausch flew for another three hours until we finished putting in the Air Assault. For that action I was awarded the Air Medal with "V" device for valor. LTC Tausch ordered me back into that fight. In retrospect I probably should have told Tausch to go to hell but I didn't think about it at the time.

There was also another officer from West Virginia State College in the Province at that time. His name was LTC Otis Saunders. The name we gave him at college was "Turkey Breast." Turkey Breast was a District Senior Advisor in Mo Cay District. Many people believe that Mo Cay District was the birthplace of the Viet Cong and consequently even the children were not friendly. They wouldn't even take candy from Americans. LTC Saunders had nice quarters with a compliment of Vietnamese help dressed in miniskirts and knee high boots. I had lunch at his headquarters one day and vowed that darkness would never catch me in that district, if I could avoid it. I remember sitting off in a helicopter, at a forty-five degree angle and watching a B-52 air strike go into that district one afternoon. When it was over we were flying in for a bomb damage assessment (BDA) and those little insurgent warriors came up out of their spider holes bleeding from their ears and noses firing at our helicopters. That was the day that I knew we couldn't win that war. I figured that if a person believed that strongly in a cause and if there were tens of thousands like them, we may as well pack up and leave. LTC Saunders was a very close friend with LTC Tausch and he was well liked by everyone. In fact, Major Bone, the American Province Intelligence Adviser, told me that Mr. Wilson told him that LTC Saunders was the best "colored officer" that he had ever seen. Major Bone and I had words over that little revelation. I kind of half heartily did not believe him but I made an issue of it just to establish that I was not going to sit by and listen to what I determined was a racial slur.

On payday Team 88 would have a monthly meeting/briefing. I soon found out that of the MACV leaders would come in from the districts. We would have a cookout at the mess hall, and serve 25 cent drinks at the compound bar. Late in the afternoon the officers would go to LTC Tausch's house to play poker. It soon became apparent to me that the name of the game was: let Tausch win. I chose not to cooperate. I remember that he had words with me one time about my lack of friendliness to the other officers. Although he never said it directly, he hinted about my failure to be a team player in the poker game. I won every hand that I could and I always quit a winner, went home early, and never worried about it.

The routine at the province headquarters was about the same everyday. Believe me nobody wanted to upset that "apple cart." These folks were routinely serving and extending their tours in an area that had relatively low Viet Cong (VC) activity and virtually no North Vietnamese Army (NVA) activity. We received mortar rounds only one night during my five or six months there and we only had one officer killed on patrol. Otherwise we had to leave the safety of the provincial capitol to find a fight. After all it was 1971 and everyone including the VC was eager to end the conflict and get on with their lives. In fact I was flying at the time the war ended. I also won the pool for guessing the time and the day that the announcement would be made. If my memory is correct we put in $5.00–$10.00 a piece in the pot and selected a day and a time from a chart that someone made up. Anyway I won the money. I do not remember how much it was but it must have been about a hundred dollars or so. Anyway, the message came over the radio, "Cease Fire! Cease Fire! Cease Fire! Hostilities are now terminated. The war is over." I was with Major No putting in another air assault in one of the districts. LTC Tausch came up on the net immediately and told me to complete that operation before returning to Truc Yang Province headquarters. I have often wondered how the VC disseminated their message. My guess is it probably took weeks to get the word out to everyone.

Shortly after my last combat air assault mission I went to Saigon for a little rest and recuperation (R and R). When I returned to Truc Yang at about 1500 hours, the symbolic "short timer stilts" were outside of my room. The stilts were used as a symbol to let everyone know that you were "short." In fact, the real story was that you were so short that your feet would not touch the ground. Anyway the stilts were leaning against my hooch. Nobody was talking! A message was tacked on the door for me to "contact LTC Tausch immediately."

I went to Tausch's office and he was all smiles. He explained to me that they had just gotten a requirement while I was away to fill a vacancy on the upcoming Joint Military Commission (JMC) that was being formed to oversee the transitioning of property and equipment at the end of the war. He further explained that I was picked because I was a CGSC graduate. He was all smiles and warm like a thief. His actions at the time made me want to check and insure that my wallet was still in my pocket. We were soon joined by LTC Christensen who was also very warm and friendly. I knew that I was being screwed, but I also knew that this was my ticket out from that pile of human excrement called Team 88. Finally, we went in to see Mr. Katzubu. He too was friendly for a change. These guys had never treated me with decency and respect and all of a sudden they were very cordial and friendly. Katzubu told me that I was being reassigned to Vinh Long Province and that I would be leaving in about two hours by helicopter. That was the catch. Those guys had found a way to get rid of me and do it very fast. I was hurt and confused. Why had they not tried to contact me in Saigon and get the word to me? Why was I picked over others who acted like they wanted the transfer to the JMC and stay in Vietnam? Why was everyone so happy? Well the bottom line was I was the only major on the Truc Yang compound with the proper credentials, i.e., a GCSC diploma. Second, that transfer also meant that I would automatically be extended in Vietnam until all of the Americans were sent home. In other words, the JMC members were to stay in The Republic of Vietnam for an additional sixty days. Finally, and most important, I was a burr in everyone's saddle in Truc Yang and they could finally get rid of me. I really only had two friends in Truc Yang. They were the Team Medic, SFC Richards and the major with the German name that I am not able to remember. Oh, I almost forgot, Katzubu offered to buy my television for $30.00 and others bought out the other things that I had accumulated. My first inclination was to smash my television set and leave it in the trash but I took the $30.00 bucks and gave it up. After all, I had bought it for $30.00 when I arrived. I left Team 88 on the helicopter mail run at about 1900 hours and arrived in Vinh Long Province about thirty minutes later. It was dusk dark in the evening. Just before I left a black NCO, Sergeant First Class Hudson, came up to me and gave me his sterling silver master parachutist wings as a going away gift. I still wear them on my uniforms today. SFC Hudson had been in Vietnam more than five continuous years. He was the only American in Team 88 that would go on patrol with the Vietnamese, alone. He was one of the bravest soldiers I have ever known.

My arrival at Vinh Long Province was done very well. There were people to meet me, help with my luggage, and take me to my new quarters and there was a nice dining facility and bar. It seemed to be more pacified than Truc Yang and the team leader, Lieutenant Colonel Putnam, was a lot friendlier than the folks I had just left. In fact, he was really a nice person who said up front, "I don't want any of you to be the last person killed in Vietnam so take the proper precautions and be careful at all times." I was settled in my new quarters in about an hour. There were Vietnamese maids to help make beds, clean, and do chores. There was also a compound sergeant who collected the fees and paid them. I guess that was pretty standard throughout MACV. Anyway he was both helpful and accessible. So I was in and settled pretty quickly. LTC Putnam said he would brief me the following morning. I went to the bar on the third floor of the living quarters and observed a lot of the same activity that went on in Truc Yang, i.e., straphangers from different United States Agencies with their Vietnamese spouses and girlfriends enjoying the comforts of a relatively quiet city. Most of the assigned personnel were about to leave and go back to the United States and their Vietnamese families were very uncertain about their future. What I observed most was that a helluva lot of people were in denial about the war actually ending. The next day, I received my briefing from LTC Putnam. He said that we were to wear an orange armband on our uniforms at all times. We also had to get diplomatic identification papers and badges. We were to fly in helicopters that had large orange stripes painted on them. That very day one of those helicopters was shot down and the pilot was killed. I was assigned duties as the administration and logistics officer. My job was to redistribute the United States equipment in Vinh Long Province to the South Vietnamese Army members stationed there.

The City of Vinh Long was a lot different than Truc Yang. It was more developed and urbane and the people were more relaxed and routinely going about their business. There were several shops and venders that did not appear to be afraid to operate their stores. There was more vehicular traffic and I do not remember a curfew at night although there may have been one. I stayed, for the most part on the MACV compound. The compound was large compared to the one I left and the sleeping quarters was a hotel configuration with multiple floors. As with all U.S. installations it had a main gate that was staffed by the Vietnamese Armed Forces. Most of the first floor was office space and the sleeping area was on the second floor. The third floor was used for sleeping also at an earlier time and was now mostly storage. There was a dining area and bar on the ground floor and another bar on the third floor. The first thing I did was get rid of the third floor bar and subsequently shut down all activity on that floor. Eventually, we got down to only six people on our team. There was the lieutenant colonel, two other majors besides me, and two enlisted men.

One day, I received a telephone call from a Sergeant in the DRAC personnel section at Can Tho and he asked if I had seen my efficiency report, i.e., performance appraisal from Truc Yang. I told him no. He said, "Sir I don't know who you are but you are getting screwed by those guys up in Truc Yang." He asked if I could come down to Can Tho and get the report before it was forwarded to Washington. I went down and picked it up and I was appalled. LTC Tausch was my endorser and he had really marked me low. I guess, in retrospect, I should have expected a low rating from that bunch of cowards. It was the way that they looked at me when I left that led me to believe that I was in for some low numbers. What I resent even until today was their lack of guts in the matter. They waited until I left and did it behind my back. As I remember, Christensen was the rater, Tausch was the endorser and Katzubu was the senior rater. Katzubu's comments were not that bad. He was smart enough to let Christensen and Tausch do most of the dirty work. I spoke with the sergeant and asked his advice on what I should do. He told me to bring it to the attention of Colonel Rogers, the Deputy Commander of DRAC. I got an appointment that afternoon and went to see Colonel Rogers. He took the report from me and said he would take care of it. The next time I saw it was after I came back to the United States. Someone, maybe it was Rogers or maybe they sent it back to that gutless bunch in Truc Yang, but somebody had upgraded the numbers and signed their initials after each change. The narrative was not that bad so there were few changes there. It may have been the great staff sergeant that made the initial call to me, but somebody, a guardian angel maybe at the time took care of me. There is no way that I can find that noncommissioned officer and personally thank him but I know that I owe him. That is one of the greatest human interactions that I have had in my entire life and I am grateful to him for it. The irony of all of this is that I believed, at the time, Tausch and Katzubu were doing this to me because I was a black officer. The sergeant that called me and helped me was Caucasian. That may have been my first step toward accepting the fact that not all white people were out to get me. Obviously neither the sergeant nor I knew the ethnicity of the other person until we met.

A typical day at the Vinh Long MACV Compound began with breakfast from 0700 to 0900. After breakfast I would either finish the novel that I started reading the day before or start a new one. Lunch was from 1100 to 1330. At about 1300 a couple of us would team up and go to Can Tho to pick up the mail. It was the highlight of the day. It took about an hour to drive there and we could always waste another hour which put us back at Vinh Long around suppertime, 1630 to 1800. We took turns going back and forth because it was so boring just sitting around waiting for time to pass. It reminded me of a similar duty that I had in the Dominican Republic in 1966 during the so called Dominican War. Captains Walter Nelms and Joe Almaguer, and I just sat around for days with nothing to do. I remember Major Lumbranja, a member of the Dominican Republic Military Advisory Group saying that we were filling a void…whatever that meant. There I was again filling a void in the Republic of Vietnam. The trip to Can Tho was generally, usually, normally, almost always uneventful. I remember that we had to ride a ferry across the Mekong River to get to Can Tho. That was always a scary time for me. We always had to wait on one side or the other of the ferry and I was always suspicious of the Vietnamese people. I did not have any animosity, I was just being very cautious. You never knew if someone had a hidden grenade or something. Of course my little orange armband shield would have been worthless. We were not supposed to carry weapons but I always had a .45 caliber pistol hidden in a shoulder holster under my battle dress uniform ready for use.

Most of the time, we returned to the Vinh Long Compound early in the afternoon and got ready to play volley ball with the other JMC members. The other Commission members were from Canada, Indonesia and Poland. We were very friendly with the Canucks and played volley ball with them almost every day. The Poles and the Indonesians took some time to warm up to us and we didn't really invite a lot of interchange. The volley ball was the typical combat version that soldiers play and did not have a lot of rules. It took more than a good sense of humor to play it. Antics like pulling on the net to ensure that a volley cleared the net were normal. Also, climbing on the net to spike a volley was allowed. The day usually ended with a movie back at the MACV Compound bar, after supper. We were still able to get movies through the Army Air Force Exchange Service (AAFES). The JMC duty was not very exciting, to say the least. I remember that we were invited to the Vinh Long Province American Senior Advisor's home for dinner one evening. That was quite an experience. He had a typical Vietnamese home with the proper staff including his chief cook and hostesses serving us throughout the evening.

On or about the 30th of March 1971 the United States contingent of the JMC began our retrograde from Vinh Long through Can Tho to Tan Sanut Air Force Base for departure to the United States of America. We spent one night in Can Tho and moved on to Saigon to catch an airplane back to "the world." We also referred to it as going back to "the land of the big PX." We departed Tan Sanut around noon. Now there has always been a bit of a debate between me and a Lieutenant Colonel by the name of John D. Putnam a CGSC classmate on who left Vietnam last. He claims to have been on the last airplane out and I make the same claim. I do not really know which airplane left the ground last but I was on one of them. We stopped in Alaska for refueling and had some maintenance problems so the chances are great that I was on the last plane to land in San Francisco, CA, not that it is significant at this time. We landed, I went into the nearest rest room and changed into civilian clothes and headed for Bishop, VA, and my family. I was authorized thirty days of leave and I was going to take every minute of it.

I had taken leave the week after Christmas during that second tour in Vietnam. Olivia and the children delayed their Christmas Day celebrations until I came home around the first week of January 1973. Although they were in school at War Elementary School, we kept them out for a couple of days and I spent time with them. Olivia was teaching at the same school and she took a couple days off also. The assistant principal, Ms. Hatcher, docked her pay for taking off. In retrospect, that was a rather harsh move on her part but it signified the tenor of the times and the strong American sentiments against the Vietnam

War. While I was on leave I called the Military Personnel Center in Alexandria, VA, and talked to my assignment officer. During those years the Army had a dual job specialty system and my two specialties were Infantry and Personnel Management. The idea was that an officer would rotate in and out his specialties on alternating permanent change of station assignments. Since the Vietnam tour was considered an Infantry assignment I had to speak to an adjutant general personnel assignment manager. I called and spoke with LTC John Sherburn, a CGSC classmate who asked me "What do you want to do Steve?" This was a real contrasting difference in the experience that I had with LTC John McCleod the guy that I dealt with before going over to Vietnam. I told John Sherburn that I wanted to return to Fort Campbell and the 101st Airborne Division. Without hesitation that is what he did. I should point out that this was the first time that I would experience a result based on my friendship with a classmate from the U.S. Army Command and General Staff College. To say the least, the connections that I made at CGSC and the National War College have assisted me greatly over the years. Incidentally, John Sherburn retired as a full bird Colonel. He deserved it. He was a great guy!

So the long and short of this story is I knew where my next assignment was going to be months in advance for the first time in my career.

RETURN TO FORT CAMPBELL

While I was on leave between my second Vietnam tour and reporting to Fort Campbell, Kentucky my father gave me a 1964 Thunderbird automobile as a gift. At the time he was part owner in a used car dealership in War, WV. They didn't sell many cars and this was one that he liked and he wanted to do something nice for me. One of the great lessons that my Dad taught was to always give someone a gift that you really would like to have yourself. That is what he did by giving me that car. Around the 1st of April, 1971 I packed my personal belongings in the car and headed west to Fort Campbell, KY. Olivia was under contract to the McDowell County School System in West Virginia and stayed to honor her commitment. I think that it surprised old lady Hatcher that Olivia had that kind of integrity. We were also a bit apprehensive about moving back to the Clarksville, TN, area without a firm commitment for housing. It was about this time that I confirmed, in concrete, my decision to never accept discrimination again. I did not know if housing would be bad or good at Fort Campbell. I knew that I would not subject my children to the racism that Olivia and I had experienced there in 1962.

The trip to Fort Campbell was about eleven hours if you exceeded the local speed limits. I was driving that old thunderbird and I did not want to push it. The trip was uneventful and I arrived late in the evening. I checked in at the in-processing station and got a room at the bachelor officer quarters at the hospital area. These quarters were temporary and, therefore free. This meant that I could continue to draw my regular housing allowance while living on post in government housing. It was not great! It was not even air conditioned and you had to do your own cleaning The next day I signed in and went to the Office of the Assistant Chief of Staff for Personnel, G1 (ACofS, G1) for an assignment. The ACofS, G1 was named LTC John Crosby. Crosby was a nice guy with a friendly smile and an easygoing manner. He offered me the position of Race Relations and Equal Opportunity Officer (RREO) for the entire post. At that time the Army had just completed a study that concluded that the 101st Airborne Division and the Garrison of Fort Campbell, Kentucky should have separate general staffs. The division side would have a General Staff and the post side would have a Directorate Staff. For example, the personnel staff officer for the division was the ACofS, G1 and the post side had the Directorate of Personnel and Community Affairs (DPCA). Crosby's position was dual-hatted as the ACofS, G1/DPCA. The guy who did the DPCA duties was LTC Thomas Kehoe. I decided to refuse the position. The odd thing is that I had never tried that before and to my surprise no one opposed me. I told them that I wanted to be a Battalion Executive Officer (XO) in the 101st Airborne Division, and not "a 'staff puke' in a Directorate." Remember, I had just come from Vietnam and the bad experience with MACV Team 88. I didn't even know if I wanted to stay in the Army or not, at that point, and so I just said no. LTC Crosby was cool. He did not argue with me, but rather, asked me to go and talk to the division Chief of Staff, Colonel George Viney. Colonel Viney decided to impress me with some cockamamie story about him climbing up the wall at Corregidor, during World War II (WWII). I was not impressed. I respected his service but it was not relevant that day. I had earned to date, the Purple Heart Medal among other medals including the Bronze Star Medal with three oak leaf clusters and a "V" device. I had been shot down in a helicopter in Than Phu District. I was one of the few non aviator Infantry officers wearing an Air Medal with the number four on it and a "V" device. I also told him that I did not want the job. Now it appears that the Army had pulled my personnel file in MILPERCEN and wrote the job description right out of my profile. I know that is not true but it really appeared that way at the time. The job called for a major, preferably of African American descent, someone with a Spanish language capability, a desired Appalachian familiarity and combat experience. I was from West Virginia, black, spoke Spanish and I was coming in from Vietnam. I was perfect for the job. After the interview with Colonel Viney, they sent me to see the Assistant Division Commander for Support (ADC-S), BG Clyde Spence. He was also a very nice man. All of a sudden I was meeting all of these white guys that were decent people who were treating me with decency and respect. General Spence was the smartest of all and asked me to go and meet Mr. Perry Barrington, the Fort Campbell civilian Equal Employment Opportunity Officer (EEOO). Mr. Barrington and I hit it off from the very beginning.

At the time I met him, Perry Barrington was a forty-six year old African American male in charge of ensuring that the civilian workforce at Fort Campbell received fair and equitable treatment. He was mild mannered, well educated with a Master's degree, and he was a staunch member of Alpha Phi Alpha Fraternity, Inc. He welcomed me into his office with the Alpha Phi Alpha handshake and referred to me as Brother from the beginning. He said, "I knew you were an Alpha. You can just tell 'em. You can't tell 'em much but you can tell 'em." He began immediately talking to me about what he was doing and the missing military piece that I could provide if I took the job. He was married to Ruby and they had a two year old son, Michael. After spending about a half hour or so with Perry I partially decided that I would enjoy working with a nice counterpart for a change. The real story is: I had been on the ground at Campbell for more than a week and had not put on my uniform. I was determined that I was not going to be pushed around by the military or anyone else again. I was an angry young man after dealing with the likes of McLeod, Tausch, and Katzubu for the last year. I figured that the worst that could happen would be that I would resign from the Army and go somewhere in West Virginia and teach school. After all, I had a Master's degree in Education from a pretty good northern school, Alfred University. Going to meet with Perry Barrington also gave me an opportunity to see where I would be working. He and I would share a building that was the first building that everyone saw as they entered Fort Campbell through Gate Number 4. I even had dinner with Mr. Barrington and his wife that weekend. She was a superb cook and their home was very hospitable. He was really a cool guy and I felt extremely comfortable with him. The next week I was scheduled to meet with the commanding general (CG). The CG was MG John H. Cushman. I did put on a fresh starched set of fatigues and spit shined my boots before I went to see him. Mrs. Warren, the Commanding General's secretary, ushered me into his office. When I entered his office he used a technique that has worked many times for me since then. He took the initiative and said, "So I hear you want to be my Race Relations Officer." I did not answer him. He sensed that I was not enthusiastic and quickly followed up with "Have you ever been discriminated against Stephens?" I replied that I had and that I was determined not to let it happen again. He smiled and said "I don't know what I'd do if someone discriminated against me. I know I wouldn't take it." As he said that he had a far off look in his face that made me think that he was sincere. This guy's frank and open manner disarmed me completely and I found myself beginning to like the conversation. He finally said "Okay you're my man. How can I support you?" I began to tell him that I wanted to be assigned to the division and not the garrison and wear the Screaming Eagle patch, he said "Okay, what else?" I told him that I wanted to have his assurance that he would back me up on sensitive matters, he said, "Okay, what else?" I said to him that I would go and think about what I needed and come back. Before he dismissed me he called a young black noncommissioned officer in and introduced him as his Post Ombudsman. Somehow I got the feeling that this was going to be a great job for me if Cushman delivered. I saluted him and left his office. I went back to the Office of the ACof S, G1 and told LTC Crosby that I would take the job. He immediately announced that I would report to Major Regina Long in DPCA. We talked a bit and I was changed to report to LTC Kehoe the Director, however, I was allowed to wear the screaming eagle patch. For some reason that was important to me and I would not let it go.

The 101st Airborne Division had just returned from Vietnam and was just getting things back into focus. The colonels in charge were a bunch of insensitive veterans who were used to having their way with racial and discrimination matters. I decided that I was going to "take them on" but first I needed to get the lay of the land. We were in the midst of a transition in the Army and I or my position would be one of the pivotal points on that installation. MG Cushman was a workaholic who had his office to deliver the last round of distribution at his quarters at 2100 every night. He worked that staff as if they were pack horses. His deputy commanders could not keep up with him and the staff was barely hanging on. He supported me with his attendance at installation town meetings in which he personally fielded questions. He was true to his word regarding support for my office. He gave me everything that I asked for in the way of personnel and equipment. All I had to do was threaten to go and see him and everyone fell into line. The rumor was MG Cushman and his guys were about to be replaced by a group of younger leaders that were going places in the Army and I determined that I was going places with them. What I remember most about MG Cushman though was his support for me as I tackled one of the most difficult tasks that I had encountered to that point in my life. Specifically, he wanted me to plan a first ever installation wide leaders conference on race relations.

Part of my job was addressing the troops of the division about race relations during battalion meetings. During one such meeting I told a joke about a person with a cleft lip. I had learned a lot of soldier jokes while I was in Special Forces and could probably go for about three or four hours telling jokes without telling the same one twice. I was a pretty good comedian. Well when I finished this particular joke I looked out into the audience and the troops were howling, except for one soldier on the front row. He had a cleft lip. I was so embarrassed that I wanted to go through the floor. I vowed that day that I would never tell another ethnic joke or another disability oriented joke. I have not done so until today. However, those troop conferences during that time were worth their weight in gold.

To that end Perry Barrington was a Godsend for me. He knew how to organize, plan and execute conferences. I knew how to get difficult decisions made at the headquarters building. I was a CGSC graduate and knew how to organize for victory. It was never a matter of having a dog in the fight. For me, it was the fight in the dog that counted and I was a pit bull. Together Perry and I were virtually unbeatable. At the opening session of the installation conference on race relations, General Cushman was present. Now I had learned somewhere that everybody wants to be seen by the boss. So, my task was to get Cushman there. I didn't go to any staff person and get them to go and ask. I went directly to his personal secretary, Ms. Warren, and she put it on his calendar. The word got out and everybody showed. I guess I had learned that from CGSC. Anyway MG Cushman came to the opening session. All of the battalion commanders and all of the brigade equivalent commanders were there and most of the division and directorate supporting staff members were present. The room was full. Perry Barrington was elated. He had never seen that kind of installation support for our programs. After I thanked everyone for coming I asked General Cushman if he wanted to say a few words before the first presenter spoke. He and I had discussed the fact that I wanted him to set the tone for the meeting. He was wonderful! I have always felt that one of the greatest things that a leader can do is stand in front of his or her workgroup and declare that they will not tolerate discrimination, in any form. At one point in his remarks, MG Cushman casually asked, "How many of you think that we have a race problem on this post?" No one raised their hand. He then said, "I believe that I have a race problem on this installation. Now how many of you believe we have a problem?" Everyone in the room raised their hand. Some of the weasels even raised both hands. It was impressive to see those sniveling cowards suck up to him that fast. I was overjoyed and felt like I had an ally in him if I ever needed him. MG Cushman left Fort Campbell shortly after I took the race relations job and he was replaced by MG Sidney B. Berry, a forty-five-year-old major general with outstanding credentials. I had met MG Berry when he was the Assistant Commandant of the Infantry School and I had a great deal of confidence in him. MG Cushman moved on to a three star billet and became the Commandant at the U.S. Army Command and General Staff College and Fort Leavenworth, Kansas.

General Berry was a unique individual. I had actually talked to him in the hallway when I was a student in the Advance Course at Fort Benning, GA. At that time, he wore all of the right skill badges, was a West Point graduate, and was physically fit. He actually visited the classes and talked with the black officers in the hallway at Fort Benning. That was a very unusual trait for senior white officers at that time. General Berry was from Mississippi. Most important to a bunch of young Infantry captains, he had been mentioned in Secretary of Defense McNamara's book *The Essence of Security.* I really looked forward to seeing him at Fort Campbell, because I trusted him. Ironically, he chose my office to be the first place that he would visit after his assumption of command. I was both excited and honored. During the course of the transition of command, the Office of the Chief of Staff for the Division also changed. The new Chief of Staff was a Louisiana State University graduate named Colonel Edward Basonez. I had visited him when he commanded the 101st Airborne Division Artillery (DIVARTY). He appeared to be a good guy when I visited him. With some folks you can just get a warm and fuzzy feeling talking to them. You can feel their fairness. COL Basonez was that kind of guy.

On Monday, during his first week of command, General Berry along with Colonel Basonez came to our office at 1300 hours for a half hour visit. They stayed for almost two hours. I knew how to brief. I had learned while teaching at Alfred University that trying to brief without visual aids was disastrous. In fact, I attended a ROTC workshop at The Virginia

Polytechnic Institute that was put on by an Army Reserve Captain who was a wizard on how to deliver your message in a briefing. Our text book for the course was *Understanding Media* by Marshall McLuhan. Perry Barrington yielded to my expertise for setting up and delivering the briefing. He handled getting the place cleaned up and ready to receive the CG. I remember that Perry and I went in on Sunday and cut the grass around the building and I even raked the dirt under the building so that it looked fresh and clean. MG Berry was absolutely smooth in his approach to getting briefed. Instead of letting me take charge and go right into my briefing, he asked if we could "just talk and get to know a little bit about each other first." I still use that technique today to relax presenters. He started with asking Mr. Barrington questions first. He just did small talk and finally he asked Perry's age. When Perry said forty-six, he answered "you are one year older than I am." He then asked me a few questions and told me to proceed with the briefing. I think that it is important to point out here that he deferred to the civilian and oldest guy in the office for questions first. He also put us at ease and ensured that we would give him truthful facts and data and not the regular crap, i.e., we treat everyone the same; all soldiers are green, there are no black or white soldiers; that the military was spreading after the Vietnam War. I had my facts and figures together and I laid out my case. The major problem at Fort Campbell at that time was we did not have any black leaders beyond company commanders. MG Berry turned to COL Basonez and asked him if that was true. COL Basonez reluctantly acknowledged that there were no black field grade officers in command positions at Fort Campbell. As only I know how to do it I interrupted them without being threatening, and said that Major (P) Willie Wright was ready for command.

Willie Wright had invited me to play golf, early on, when I arrived at Fort Campbell and afterwards he and his wife Maxine had me over for lunch one Saturday. I knew him, respected him and liked him. Therefore, I felt comfortable recommending him to MG Berry. I never told Willie about that conversation with the CG, even until today. I have told other people so he may well know about it but I never discussed it with him, personally. MG Sid Berry turned to Colonel Basonez and said words to the effect, "Ed, can we make this happen?" Old Colonel Basonez appeared to be flustered but answered in the affirmative and later LTC Willie Wright was designated as the commander of the 1st Battalion, 327th Infantry. I would like to think that my recommendation had a lot to do with that, suffice it to say that Willie was an outstanding officer and probably would have been picked without my interference anyway. The selection procedure in those days was more internal than the external system that is in effect now. As I remember it, the CG and division staff would submit a list of officers that they felt were worthy and/or ready for command to MILPERCEN. The lists were reviewed at MILPERCEN and officers were subsequently "placed in command by MILPERCEN usually at the local installation to which they were assigned." That's how selected officers were able to remain at the location where they were already serving. Willie Wright assumed command of 1-327 Infantry and did a good job. At that time command tours were only eighteen months long.

Shortly after General Berry became the CG I was called to the Chief of Staff's office and offered the job of Headquarters Commandant for the 101st Airborne Division. I accepted the position partly because I really did not enjoy being the race relations officer. I kept the RREO job about three months and established it as an important position to the command. However, I think that everyone realized that I had a lot more capability than that position demanded. One of the highlights of that short period was a visit from the Department of the Army RREO, Colonel Frasier. The U.S Army Office of Race Relations and Equal Opportunity was located in the Office of the Deputy Chief of Staff for Personnel (DCSPER) at the Department of the Army, in the pentagon. COL Frasier, the Army's first RREO at Department level was visiting Fort Knox and Fort Campbell during the same trip. He was supposed to arrive at Fort Campbell at about four o'clock in the afternoon and later that evening he, Mr. Barrington and I along with our spouses were invited to General Berry's quarters for dinner. At about 1500 hours we received a call from COL Frasier saying that his aircraft was having trouble and he would probably arrive late. I figured no problem. I'd just cancel the evening briefing that was scheduled for 1630 hours and take him directly to the installation Very Important Person (VIP) Quarters and we would still be at the CG's home for dinner at 1800. At about 1600 hours Frasier called again and requested that the 101st Airborne Division send an aircraft down to Fort Knox to pick him up. I went directly to the Chief of Staff and he made it happen. However, we were now past any reasonable window of time to have dinner with the CG at six o'clock. Frasier arrived at about six o'clock and I had a sedan waiting to take him to the VIP quarters where he could change clothes and walk around the corner to General Berry's house. I figured he could arrive by 1830 hours. COL Frasier informed me that he had a long day and he was tired. He emphatically refused to go to the CG's house. I said to him, "What should I tell the general?' to which he replied, "I don't give a damn what you tell him I am not going." I took him to the VIP guest house and went to the commanding general's house totally embarrassed. The Berry's were wonderfully gracious and passed it off without comment. Colonel Basonez was ticked off and let me and Perry Barrington know it. We didn't miss Frasier that evening and we got to meet Ms. Anne Berry and their daughter.

In all of my travel and going to functions, that sometimes included royalty, I have never met a more gracious lady than Ms. Anne Berry. She was what Olivia aspired to be when I became a general officer. We were invited to their home for other functions again and we learned something different about protocol every time. Almost every function that has happened in our quarters has been modeled after the Berry's brand of hospitality. Of special note was their New Year's Day affair that was billed as an "AT HOME." At the behest of COL Basonez, I had the protocol office to prepare three guest lists for visitors to the Berry's quarters that day. We organized the visits in forty-five minute segments commencing at 1200. We had groups to park in the officers' club parking lot in different time blocks and mount buses to the CG's home. We scheduled 15 minutes between groups so the aides and volunteers, including my spouse, cleaned and replenished the serving areas. This also gave the Berry's time to look over the next guest list of visitors before they arrived. As a matter of fact one major crashed the affair and General Berry simply said, "Well Major I did not expect to see you today." The guy was embarrassed and turned crimson. The menu was simple yet elegant. It was ham biscuits and hot apple cider. There were no funds to pay for the affair and so the Berry's had to carve it out of their personal money. There must have been 150 guests at that event. What a learning experience for me and Olivia.

I kept the Headquarters Commandant position for about ninety days. During that time I had the complete cooperation of Major Thomas Denny, the Secretary to the General Staff (SGS), Captain Rick Breslin who was the Division Protocol Officer and Ms Marie Warren, the commanding General's Secretary In the meantime, LTC Crosby left the ACofS, G1 position and he was replaced by another lieutenant colonel. I remember that he asked me one Saturday morning how I would feel if I, and my spouse, were invited to the Hopkinsville Country Club in Hopkinsville, Kentucky, for a social event. I said to him that I was okay with it but I would be reluctant to subject Olivia to possible racial insensitivities or other embarrassing situations that may make her feel uncomfortable. He reminded me that "Jackie Robinson didn't have a problem with those kinds of situations." To which I replied rather angrily and enthusiastically, "Do I look like Jackie Robinson to you?" I was ready to take him on at that time. In those days I was a real "hothead" and would fight at the drop of a hat. He sensed that he had ticked me off and didn't say anything else. As the Headquarters Commandant, I was scheduled to be rated by him and endorsed by the Chief of Staff. I had been given low marks by my raters in Vietnam. I was well aware of the consequences of working for an insensitive rater. My chance to escape from him came about a month later, before he had a chance to put the quietus on me.

One of my primary duties as the 101st Airborne Division Headquarters Commandant was also serving as the officer in charge of protocol for the division. Captain Rick Bressnan was the Division Protocol Officer but I had the responsibility and accountability for the office. However, the duty that I liked most as the Headquarters Commandant was being the defacto mayor of the Division Main Command Post (DIV MAIN CP) in the field. That meant that I was responsible for finding the site, establishing security, and running the CGs Mess. Immediately upon assuming the duties of the Division Headquarters Commandant Colonel Basonez called me in and told me to "Take a chopper and find a suitable site for the DIV MAIN CP and make it ready for the division's upcoming command post exercise (CPX)." He gave me a list of requirements. They were in part: the CG's helipad must not be located more than two and a half minutes from the Tactical Operations Center (TOC); the CG wants to see everyone within the perimeter from the front of his tent; the CGs messing facility must be tactical at all times and serve the same food that the troops eat; and finally, there were to be no cots for sleeping within the headquarters area. This was my forte. Upon getting the place ready for display I reported to the Chief of Staff that we were "good to go" and he said "I want a 'tactical walk' of it before I show it to the CG." We went to the site by helicopter so he could gauge the time it would take to dismount and walk to the TOC. I remember saying to him, "This is probably not what you wanted but it is the best that I could do." He replied with a phrase that I have used over and over throughout my life. He said "Don't tell me that crap! Your professional career depends on how well you did this project." From that day forward I have never made another excuse for my work. If I do not think that it is up to par I do not bring visitors to see it until it meets my standard...and that is pretty damn high! Needless to say, the tactical walk was perfect. I even had the barbed wire in place and coffee cooking in the CG's Mess. There is nothing like the smell of food cooking to ease complaints in those kinds of situations. I loved "being tactical" and making sure everyone complied with the division directives. I even published a little Headquarters Commandant Memorandum that discussed the tactical posture that was expected in the DIV MAIN CP.

Everyone complied except one of the Assistant Division Commanders, Brigadier General Morris Brady. I told the Chief of Staff about BG Brady's cot and he told me to make sure that the CG saw it. When the day arrived for the Exercise to start and the CG came forward to the field, one of the first places I showed him was that ADC's tent. I noticed that not long after that the cot was replaced with three cases of C rations with a blanket and air mattress on it. That little action just confirmed my assertion that you can win in any game as long as you know the rules and I was learning the rules of the game of power very well.

Not long after our field training exercise (FTX) at Fort Campbell we flew into Camp Mackal, North Carolina, for an 18th Airborne Corps CPX. Actually we flew into Pope Air Force Base and convoyed out to Camp Mackal. Of course we were the Air Assault Division and we had more helicopters than anyone else in the Army. We were, however, allocated a certain number of Air Force airframes to move the division and the reduction that I had to make with the CG's Mess was substantial. The former CG's Mess went to the field on two duce and a half (2½) ton trucks plus my jeep. They had things like real china, silver flatware, and crystal stemware. General Cushman would drive out to the field site, after it was set up, in a sedan dressed in a Class B (khaki) uniform.

With MG Berry it was entirely different. We didn't wear camouflage paint but we were otherwise completely tactical including a three meter interval between soldiers in line at the troop mess hall. When we got to Camp Mackal we were the "main show." I remember other divisions had stuff like wooden plank floors in the CG's Mess and a lot of the trappings that we had before General Berry arrived in the 101st Airborne Division. COL Basonez left it to me to determine our tactical posture and I played completely by the book. One night during that CPX I came upon someone answering the call to nature at the latrine area with their flashlight on. I said "Turn off that light." The person answered, "Do you know who I am? I am Colonel Holroyd." Actually he was a lieutenant colonel aviator. I answered, "I am the Headquarters Commandant and I don't give a damn who you are. Turn off that flashlight!" About that time a high pitched voice came out of the darkness and said "This is Colonel Honeycutt, turn off that flashlight Colonel." That incident jump started my career and from that point on I never looked back. When we returned to Fort Campbell the chief of staff called me in and told me to go down to the 3rd Brigade and see the Brigade Commander, Colonel Wendell "Tiger" Honeycutt. I went down to the 3rd Brigade and reported to Major Sonny Tucker, the Adjutant, and LTC Stanley Bonta, the Executive Officer. After a bit of small talk with those two, I was escorted in to see Colonel Honeycutt. His opening line was "I heard you like to fight. If you want to fight I'll give you a chance." I didn't quite know what to say but replied with a smile "Well, we can go outside if you want to and we'll get it on now." Honeycutt smiled and told me he had an opening in one his battalions for a battalion executive officer. He went on to say that if I wanted the job it was mine but I couldn't tell anyone for a while. I accepted! Honeycutt called the division chief of staff while I was standing there and told him that we would have to work out a reporting date but that the job was mine. I really liked the idea that he didn't want me to tell anyone, especially the lieutenant colonel that was my rater in ACofS, G1. In those days one had to be under the supervision of a senior officer for more than ninety days before that person could give them an evaluation. I didn't want that officer's name any where in my personnel file. COL Basonez and I worked out a reporting date and only we knew when I would be leaving to become the Executive Officer (XO) of the 3rd Battalion, 187th Infantry. Colonel Basonez also rated me with a “special evaluation” when I left the division headquarters.

The battalion commander of the 3rd battalion, 187th Infantry was a pleasant sort of guy who drank too much sometimes, but otherwise was a decent guy for whom to work. I saw him at a formal gathering the night before I was supposed to report to the battalion for duty and started to approach him. He nodded me over to the side and pointed to the guy that I was about to replace, another major. He then whispered to me that the other guy did not know that I was his replacement and that he was going to tell him that night. He asked me not say anything to anyone about it. I felt a little uncomfortable about it but I really didn’t care one way or another. I trusted Colonel Honeycutt and he had told me that it was my job. I had found out in the interim that Colonel Honeycutt had commanded the 3-187 Infantry when they went up Hamburger Hill in Vietnam. That outfit was near and dear to his heart and he was not about to see it fail in peace time. I did approach the major that I was replacing and listened to his drivel to a small gaggle of young officers. He opened the conversation, rather loudly, with “Well if it ain’t the headquarters comedian. Are you still sucking around the division flagpole? When are you going to come down to a battalion and get some real work?” I wanted to say “Listen you idiot, you are about to be relieved. You’ll be the real division joke by this time tomorrow.” However, I didn’t say a word. I just took his ridicule and moved on through the crowd of Rakkasan officers who were wearing dress white uniforms and impersonating officers and gentlemen.

The following morning, Saturday, on or about the 10th of February 1973, I went to the headquarters building of the 3rd battalion, 187th Infantry (Rakkasans) to report for work. I arrived at about 0745 and entered the building without fanfare. As I approached the adjutant’s desk the person that I was going to replace came through an interlocking door and asked why I was there so early in the morning. I said to him that I was reporting for work. I did not know at the time but the battalion was also getting a new operations officer that day. Major Stephen Yedinak was the officer taking that job. I asked the major that was asking me questions if the battalion commander had briefed him. He said 'no." I took him back into his office and said to him without sensitivity "I am your replacement." I wanted to add, you dumb jackass, but I thought better of it and didn't. He sat back in his chair and was as pale as a ghost. He got up and sheepishly, offered me his chair. I refused and left the room so he could regain a modicum of composure. About that time, voices rang out with "Attention!" Through the front door came the battalion commander with a blustering flair and jaunt that I would grow to dislike immensely. He answered the call to attention with a loud, boastful response "Carry on!" He spotted me and the look of "Oh my God!" came across his face as he realized that both the guy that I was replacing and I were both present. He immediately asked the other guy into his office with telling me something like "I'll talk to you later." I went into my new office and started to get settled. In about ten minutes the old executive officer came out and left immediately. That was the transition. He didn't even empty his desk. So I had one of the clerks to box up all of his belongings and we sent them to him at his new location when we found out where it was. Needless to say everyone in the Rakkasan Battalion was in a state of shock. Captain Rudy Simard was the S1/Adjutant and he was visibly shaken. He had an assistant that was a former Special Forces enlisted man who received a Vietnam era commission and he was speechless. LTC James B. Bramlett, the battalion commander, came out and asked me into his office. He told me that he had not planned for me to report that early and he was sorry for any inconvenience that may have occurred. I did not answer him. I decided that I would go to the brigade headquarters and let Colonel Honeycutt know that I was at work. I also relayed to Honeycutt the way that I had been "welcomed" to the Rakkasans. He acted like he was happy to see me. He told me that he wanted me to go down there and "clean that place up." I said words to the effect "I am not the commander I am only the executive officer." He answered, "If you don't clean it up in thirty days I am going to get rid of you." So while I was standing there he called the battalion commander saying, "Jim, this is Honeycutt. Steve Stephens is here in my office. I am putting you on leave for a while. Enjoy the time off." He turned to me and said, "Go down there and clean it up!" I left his office totally perplexed and surprised. However, I had my marching orders and heads were going to roll. I did not know anyone in the unit. I was brand new and I was going to clean up the mess...fast. I stopped by the Office of the Executive Officer at 1st Battalion, 503rd Infantry. I was told that this guy was the best battalion XO in the brigade. I wanted to size up the competition as soon as I could. He told me, in a bragging manner, to go and look at his motor pool. I did go by his motor pool on the way back to my office. All of these locations were within walking distance of each other so I was able to move from place to place rather rapidly. I looked at my watch and it was about 1130 hours, so I went to the mess hall or as we call them now, the dining facility.

Upon entering the mess hall I met probably the most able Mess Sergeant that I have known. He knew his business from A to Z. The Rakkasans had a good mess hall and that was the first positive thing that I had seen there so far. Of course by now the word had spread and everyone wanted to see the new XO. The battalion commander had taken Colonel Honeycutt at his word and left to go on leave, immediately. The only thing that he said to me was "I have been in command about a year and it has not been fun, I'd like you to help me enjoy the last six months." I was in charge! I left the mess hall and headed for the motor pool. The first thing that happened was I stubbed my toe on an old oil pan that was being used as a door stop and knocked the toe off of my spit-shined jump boots. The place was absolutely filthy. I was ticked off immediately and everyone in my sights was about to feel the wrath of the acting battalion commander. I was in charge and I took charge! The battalion motor officer was Lieutenant Robert Oncken. He was the son of William Oncken, the famous management analyst and consultant. I tore into Bob Oncken's butt like a hot knife through butter. I gave him instructions on how I wanted that place cleaned up and that I would be back before the day was concluded to check. It was about 1300 hours on Saturday. I found out later, that normally was about the time on Saturday that many of the officers went and bought a six pack of beer and brought it back to the battalion classroom for an officers' call with the battalion commander. Well I continued visiting different places in the battalion and talking to different people. We did not have officers' call that day. I met with Lieutenant Roy Helsing, the S4/Logistics Officer. He turned out to be one of the best officers in the battalion. He escorted me around his area and briefed me on what he was trying to do. I felt pretty good because I knew that doctrinally the XO was responsible for personnel and logistical matters in a battalion and it appeared that I had sane individuals with whom I could work in the S1 (Personnel) and S4 (Logistics) jobs. LT Helsing had a cut-throat lieutenant that was his Support Platoon Leader who was also a former enlisted Special Forces soldier that was commissioned during the Vietnam era. He was ruthless. I found out later that he could get things done and so I used him to lead interference on the hard stuff that I didn't have time to fool with. I met the Headquarters Company Commander, Captain Bill Poole. A Company was commanded by Captain James Isabel. The B Company Commander was Captain Tony Witter assisted by 1st Sergeant Jungles. C Company had an officer in command whose name was Captain Dan Lundsford, and Delta Company was commanded by a lawyer named Captain Tom Smith, assisted greatly by First Sergeant Adamski. The captains were just along for the ride for the most part. The first sergeants were really in charge. I had known a lot of the NCO's from my first tour at Fort Campbell. Initially, I was okay with that. All I had to do was make this bunch a team that believed in themselves.

The battalion Command Sergeant Major (CSM), Joe Dayoc, came into my office at about 1500 hours and expressed his satisfaction that I was there. It turned out that we knew each other when I was a lieutenant in the 1st Battalion, 327th Infantry, back in 1962. He was the First Sergeant of B Company, 1-327. He briefed me on all of the old noncommissioned officers that I should know from the old days. Half of the First Sergeants knew me from the old days and they knew that I was coming to the Rakkasans through the brigade Command Sergeant Major, Scully McCulloch. I thanked him for approaching me first and reacquainting himself with me. With that bunch of NCO's and their network, I knew then that I was going to be alright. It was about 1600 hours so I called LT Helsing and we went back to the motor pool. LT Oncken worked for him and he was ready to toss him under the bus immediately. The Motor Pool was still a cesspool but I decided that I would tackle it again the following week. I took LT Helsing and the Support Platoon Leader, LT Dave Orofino, and we headed for the Officers' Open Mess. We had a couple of drinks and I got home about 1830 that evening. I decided to enjoy the weekend with my family because something told me that I would not have many free evenings for a while.

On Monday morning I went in to work at what would become de facto my battalion. The first thing that I tackled was about 20 to 30 Articles 15 and Summary Courts Martial proceedings that were in varying stages of completion. I started giving three to four Articles 15 a day until I finished. Then I started on the Summary Courts Martial and cleaned them up in about two weeks. That made me a hit with Tiger Honeycutt and from that point on I was one of the "fair haired boys" of the division. Everyone knew that I was fair and unbiased and that I did outstanding work. I did not fool around when it came to work. Of course I learned that I could also play as hard as I worked, at the proper time. I had some great experiences in the Rakkasan Battalion. Colonel Bramlett told me again when he came back to work that he had worked extremely hard for the first year of his command and that he wanted to enjoy the remaining six months. I don't remember what I said to him exactly but it was words to the effect, "Stay out of my way and we'll make it happen." He didn't bother me and I tolerated him. Everyone knew who was in charge. I knew by then that you could not fool the troops. If you were not genuine they would see right through you. They knew that I was the "real deal." One day a black soldier sent word to me by LT Helsing, that if I did not come and meet with him immediately, he was going to jump from the roof of C Company. I sent word back to him that I was going to the officers' club for lunch and I wanted him to be in my office when I returned. Everyone was shocked that I did not hustle down to that building and try to keep the soldier from committing suicide. When I returned from lunch he was sitting outside of my office door. I brought him in, chewed his butt and dismissed him. Everyone knew that I was a stern disciplinarian and I treated everyone fairly and equally. Whatever I wanted to do was what we did in that battalion.

LTC Bramlett and I never had a conflict except one night after we had gone to a battalion hail and farewell affair in downtown Clarksville, TN. Upon leaving the affair he suggested that we stop by an insurance salesman's office on Highway 41A and meet up with the 3rd Brigade Command Sergeant Major and his wife. I was reluctant to do so but agreed to go. Upon arriving at this little party, I knew that I had made a mistake. The Command Sergeant Major was drunk and making a fool of himself and there were soldiers from our battalion present. After a very short period, I said politely that Olivia and I were leaving. LTC Bramlett shouted out so everyone could hear "Major if you leave this party I will put it in your efficiency report." I replied just as loudly, "Colonel, I don't care if you crap in my efficiency report, we're leaving." Olivia and I left! The next morning he came into the office and apologized. He did that a lot. He was prone to drink too much alcohol and often made a fool of himself. Another incident occurred one Friday evening when after a few too many at "Happy Hour" LTC Bramlett insisted that Major Yedinak the battalion S-3 and I, along with our spouses, go to his quarters around midnight for a nightcap after dinner. He did that often but never this late before. Well, on this occasion, we deliberately stayed at his house until sunrise the next morning. He never asked us over that late again. My guess is his wife was furious with him for doing that little stunt. Finally, on the night of his battalion farewell party, the officers put on a skit that depicted his penchant for calling our quarters after midnight. In his drunken stupor he was not always able to recognize that one of our spouses had answered the telephone and would immediately begin cursing and screaming about something that went on at work that day. He took the skit in good nature but I knew that he was embarrassed. Both of his parents were present. From that day forward I made sure that I knew the content of skits at officer's parties before they were performed.

LTC Bramlett was replaced after six months by LTC Tom Kehoe an entirely different personality. He was an Academy graduate, had a graduate degree, and had served in the greater Washington, DC area. He was savvy! I had also worked for him before as the RR/EO. We had a previous run-in when he sent our monthly RREO report to FORSCOM Headquarters back to us marked up in red pen. I snatched it from Mr. Barrington's hand and left for LTC Kehoe's office with Mr. Barrington pleading with me to "Take it easy Bro." I walked in and tossed it on Kehoe's desk and asked him what the problems were with the report. He answered that he had passed the action to MAJ John Gorley and he had sent it back to us. I knew Gorley from Panama. MAJ Gorley was not at his desk at the time. I was furious and let everyone know it. No one could tell me constructively what was wrong with the report. So I had the RREO secretary retype it verbatim and sent it directly to FORSCOM and copied Kehoe's office. We never had trouble with our reports again. Mr. Barrington was elated. He just shook his head and said "Bro, you are crazy."

I stayed with LTC Kehoe for less than a year at the Rakkasan Battalion. He rated me and cut me a couple of points. That ticked me off. I went to COL Honeycutt and let him know that I was interested in becoming the next brigade adjutant. Major

Sonny Tucker was moving on to become the executive officer in the 3rd Battalion, 503 Infantry under LTC Stanley Bonta. LTC Art Kinzel had become the brigade executive officer and accepted me as the S1/Adjutant. For about six months, Tiger Honeycutt, Art Kinzel and I were an unbeatable combination within the division for the lowest AWOL rate, the highest reenlistment rate and the doubles champs in racquetball. The 101st Airborne Division, at that time was the best assignment that a young warrior could get. MG Sid Berry left to become the Superintendent at the United States Military Academy (USMA) at West Point, New York and was replaced as the 101st Division Commander by MG John McEnery. Colonel Lou Menetrey left the position of Division G3 to become the Commander of the 2nd Brigade. His replacement in ACofS, G3 was LTC Fred K. Mahaffey. COL Mahaffey also followed COL Menetrey as Commander of the 2nd Brigade. Both of these men went on to wear the four stars of a full general. Even the Commander of the 101st Aviation Brigade, a colonel named Robert Roper, was promoted to brigadier general. He was replaced by Colonel Charles W. Bagnel who also became a lieutenant general. What I remember most about Roper was that Happy Hour could not officially start at the Open Mess without him. At that time the First Brigade commander was Colonel Charles W. Dyke. Dyke retired as a lieutenant general.

Colonel Tiger Honeycutt was selected for promotion to brigadier general and was replaced by another stern disciplinarian named Colonel Joseph T. Palastra. Palastra was also a West Point graduate, had a master's degree and had served in the greater Washington, DC, area, specifically in the Office of the Secretary of State. He was the beginning of a wave of outstanding leaders that would astound the Army for quite a while. MG McEnery took Tiger Honeycutt when he was selected for brigadier general as one of his assistant division commanders (ADC) the other ADC was BG Jack McMull. Mcmull went on to command the 18th Airborne Corps at Fort Bragg, NC. General McEnery finished his eighteen months and moved on to become the Commandant of the Inter American Defense College. He was replaced by MG John Wickham, a young general who came out of the Office of the Secretary of Defense in the Pentagon. That was one of the most memorable arrival ceremonies that happened during my thirty odd years in the Army. General Wickham was about five feet, six inches tall. The host for the ceremony was none other than the flamboyant, six feet, five inches tall LTG Henry "Gunslinger" Emerson, Commander of XVIII Airborne Corps. The Change of Command was conducted in the post stadium in the afternoon with the troops seated in the bleachers. Their leaders, Brigade and Battalion Commanders and their Command Sergeants Major, represented their division units on the parade field along with Company Commanders and their guidon bearers. This was done so the troops could view the change of command ceremony. They were marched into the stadium in unit formation and seated together in designated areas. Well, when the command group, MG Wickham on the left, and LTG Emerson on the right entered the stadium, the troops went wild with cheers and chants.

The command group mounted the reviewing stand and the ceremony began with Adjutant's call and the subsequent commands and ceremonial acts taking place. LTG Emerson leaned over to MG Wickham and said words to the effect: "This is a wonderful ceremony." About that time the troops from the 2-502nd Infantry, the battalion Emerson commanded in Vietnam started chanting, Gunslinger! Gunslinger! Gunslinger! Gunslinger Emerson leaned over to MG Wickham again and said: "I love them (expletive deleted)." The microphone was hot, and the 2-502 Infantry troops heard what he said and went wild again. I think Gunslinger Emerson knew the mike was hot and said the expletives deliberately. Toward the end of the ceremony, MG Wickham made remarks and stated how happy he was to become the commander of such a distinguished division. He got carried away and offered the troops the next day off. The troops in the bleachers went wild. Gunslinger was so taken aback that he stepped to the microphone, pushed Wickham aside and said: "You troops look so damn good today I am going authorize you to take off now and go home." It was late in the afternoon and the company first sergeants in some cases had not completed assigning unit details for the day. You guessed it! For their part, the troops left the stadium and "headed to the house." That would have been in February 1976. Those ceremonies in the post stadium were always a treat for soldiers. They looked forward to them.

By the way, young Mr. Donald Rumsfeld was the Secretary of Defense at that time. He flew in from Washington to attend the Change of Command. I was fortunate enough to meet the Secretary at MG Wickham's welcome reception at the Fort Campbell Officers Club. Someone gave MG Wickham a beer at the reception and he held it for about thirty minutes and never took a sip from it. I was amazed! All of the Brigade Equivalent Commanders were changing also. The 1st Brigade had COL Bill Dyke. We called him the "six million dollar man." Rumor had it that he ran physical training (PT) with all of his units every morning. At that time he had the distinction of being the youngest person to graduate from The United States Army Officer Candidate School (OCS). COL Fred K. Mahaffey a ROTC graduate from the University of Denver who had been a super star in DCSOPS in the pentagon commanded the 2nd Brigade. Finally, COL Joe Palastra who graduated from USMA, and commanded an aviation battalion and an Infantry battalion in Vietnam took the 3rd Brigade. Replacing COL Bob Roper at the helm of the 101st Aviation Brigade was an Academy graduate named COL Joel Bagnal. The new Division Artillery Commander was an Academy graduate named COL Sandy Samouse, and COL Harold I. Small assumed commanded the Division Support Command. The 2-17 Cavalry was commanded by LTC Gary Luck, the 326th Engineer Battalion was commanded LTC John Moellering and the 801st Maintenance battalion was commanded by LTC Jackson Rosier. These guys were all top notch. All of them, except Samouse, became general officers. I should also point out that during that time frame there were four black battalion commanders at the same time in the 101st Airborne Division. LTC Lewis Wright commanded an aviation battalion, LTC Jackson Rosier commanded the maintenance battalion, LTC Roger McLeod assumed command of the air defense battalion and of course LTC Willie Wright was placed into command of the 1st Battalion, 327th Infantry by MG Sidney Berry.

I spent about six months as COL Palastra's S1/Adjutant. LTC Art Kinzel was his XO, Major Jack McGuiness was the S2 (Intelligence), Major Rod Granneman was the S3 (Operations), and Major Jim Humphries was the S4 (Logistics). The Assistant S-3 was a Captain named Carl F. Ernst. That was the first time in my life that I served in a high performing unit. Each one of us thought that we were the best in the division at our jobs. Now if one were inclined to take that thought to its illogical conclusion, i.e., the 101st Airborne Division was the best division in the Army, and the 3rd Brigade was the best brigade in the division, then we had to be the best staff officers in the Army at what we did for a living. That was our story and we stuck to it. We won every conceivable award in the division including an intra-division track meet where I ran the anchor for the 3rd Brigade in the mile relay. We also won the combat football, combat volley ball, and combat basketball awards for the division. We also led the division in reenlistment, combined campaign fundraising and the fewest errors in the personnel accounting system. We were tough and everyone knew it. We were so good that the Sergeant Major in the S-3, Operations unit had a large sign made that read, "Lead, follow, or get the hell out of the way!" Even our spouses and our children strutted around with a winning swagger.

After about six months COL Palastra called me into his office and told me that he had agreed to let me go to be the Deputy Assistant Chief of Staff for Personnel, G1 at division headquarters. I had been in the Brigade, including my time at the 3-187 Infantry battalion, about two years. I had learned a lot. Colonel Tiger Honeycutt taught me how to be steadfast in tough situations. COL Joe Palastra taught me how to navigate the bureaucracy and how to get the important things done from an organizational point of view. Both of them had given me a chance to prove myself without regard for my ethnic background. I remember Tiger bursting into my office after I had been there about a month and emotionally blurting out, "You're not here because you're black. You are here because you're good." I was startled but surmised that someone had made a derogatory comment to him about hiring a black guy to run the front office. The subject never came up again with him. Although he was from Mississippi he never showed one scintilla of prejudice or discrimination toward me or my family…ever.

COL Palastra's first meeting with the 3rd Brigade staff was classic. The meeting was scheduled for 1300. Well, he was there and LTC Kehoe, LTC Bonta, Major Granneman and others were milling around like we did before Tiger's meetings. COL Palastra left the room and I followed him out. Once we were outside of the conference room he asked me, "What time is the 1300 meeting?" I was flabbergasted and answered "Right now sir." I reentered the conference room and announced, "Gentlemen the Brigade Commander." He walked in behind me and proceeded to talk about how happy he was to assume command of the brigade and how he admired COL Tiger Honeycutt. He even mentioned that they had worked together before in the Office of the Division Commander, MG William C. Westmoreland when Tiger was a captain and Palastra was a lieutenant. Then he said something that I have used numerous times when I assumed a leadership role in an organization. He said, "I know that all of you admired my predecessor and you were very loyal to him. If you feel that you will not be able to transfer that loyalty to me I will understand. If you truly feel that way you can leave this room in the next sixty seconds without retribution and there will be no hard feelings." He continued to speak in conversational tones for a few more minutes and suddenly looked at his watch and said, "Well about three minutes have passed since you had the opportunity to leave and no one left the room. I will assume that I have everyone's complete loyalty and cooperation." I thought that was a great way to open a transition meeting with a new command and I used it over and over.

I reported to the Office of the ACofS, G1 in the summer of 1975. I went to work for the first genuinely gentle man that I had ever worked for to that point. His name was Colonel Paul Gentry. He was from Texas, spoke with a southern drawl, and had a son attending Texas A&M University. He and his wife rank very highly among the best people that Olivia and I have known in the Army. They were just plain good, God fearing down to earth folks. Gentry and I only had one run in during the time I served as his deputy. The Chief of Staff for the division was a flamboyant aviator named Colonel Ted Crozier. We called him "Wild Turkey Crozier" because that's what he drank, Wild Turkey Bourbon. He had a tendency to fritter away the morning hours with mundane activities, take a long lunch break and handle paperwork in the early part of the afternoon. At about five o'clock he would call for the staff principals to come to his office for a meeting. Well they would be tied up with him until well past 1800. One evening I let everyone go home at about 6:30 PM and actually left myself. Well COL Gentry angrily called me at home and I went back into the office to talk to him. He wanted to know why I let the staff leave. I was cool. I just explained that most of us on his staff came in for PT around 0600 every morning. He normally was not in the office at that time. I further explained that even if we waited for him to return from the evening staff meeting he would then have to clean up his notes and we would usually not get briefed before about 1900 hours in the evening. I further explained that we had young families and we wanted to spend some time with our spouses and children. Well, after I explained that to him he was not angry any longer. In fact, he apologized and said that we could go over his notes in the morning and that he was glad that I had let people go home at a reasonable hour. As I said earlier he was a genuinely good man. My assistant in that job was Captain Richard

Wright. Rick's father was a general officer and had commanded the 101st Airborne Division in Vietnam. I really enjoyed working with Rick. We were a two man team that managed all of the officer assignments in the combat division and the garrison side of the fort. Our secretary was Specialist Fourth Class Diane Davies. She was a "stripes for skills" recruit that could type 135 words a minute without mistakes. She was great! I remember when Lieutenant David Grange came to the division from IOBC. LTC Stanley Bonta requested him, by name, for assignment to the 3rd Battalion, 503rd Infantry. I also remember Colonel Bill Dyke came to see me and brought his organization's officer personnel chart and tried to work out replacements six months in advance. Wow, I learned a lot from that. I also remember that shortly after Colonel Palastra was selected for promotion to general he came by my office and asked me to ensure that LTC (P) Colin Powell was taken care of with the assignment of good people. He also arranged for LTC Art Kinzel to become one of Powell's battalion commanders and he really had a compelling interest in seeing that Colin Powell would be successful in command. LTC (P) Colin Powell replaced COL Fred K. Mahaffey as Commander of the 2nd Brigade.

I thoroughly enjoyed that deputy job in the Office of the ACofS, G1. Almost on a daily basis I had to call the MILPERCEN on Stovall Street in Alexandria, Virginia. I communicated with the officer side of the house and Major Chris Wise, another officer in our Fort Campbell office talked to the folks on the enlisted side. I was constantly requesting personnel files for evaluation, of potential replacements for the field grade officer ranks for both the division and the garrison units. Personnel files usually arrived by facsimile in the Office of the Adjutant General. The lieutenant that usually notified me that the facsimiles had arrived was First Lieutenant Michael D. Rochelle. Because we thought of ourselves as the best fighting division in the Army, we thought that we deserved to receive only the best officers in the inventory for replacements. That was my story and I stuck to it. The desk officers at MILPERCEN hated to talk to me because they knew that I was a tenacious "pit-bull" that would not let go until I got what I wanted. In one instance General Wickham, the division commander, called me about 8:00 a.m. and told me that he had relieved the battalion commander of the 501st Signal Battalion. He also said that he wanted a replacement for him immediately. I called MILPERCEN and got the usual run-around, i.e., not having ample notice and etc. They mentioned that Major (P) Alonzo Short was designated for the command but he had not gone to his pre-command training. I worked with them for a short time that day and finally I called the 101st Airborne Division Support Command (DISCOM) and asked if a major that was assigned there could become an interim battalion commander for about ninety days. The DISCOM Commander, Colonel Harold I. Small, reluctantly said yes and I called General Wickham back and proposed the solution. He agreed and I proceeded to call MILPERCEN and tell them that Major (P) Alonzo Short could continue his pre-command training but we wanted him present for duty within three months. Everyone agreed. I thoroughly enjoyed days like that because it appeared that I could do things that no one else could get done. One reason was because I was a CGSC graduate and many of the people with whom I had to deal at MILPERCEN were classmates or knew one of my classmates. They all knew that a negative answer to me was grounds for escalating the matter to the next command level. Or said another way, saying no to me was an opportunity for me to excel. The deputy commander of MILPERCEN was Major General Edward Greer, a graduate of West Virginia State College. I never used him but I always felt that I had leverage to get things done, if I ever needed it. I did drop his name a few times.

During the course of my tour at Fort Campbell and the 101st Airborne Division the Army went through a downsizing drill. When the Vietnam War ended there was an apparent excess of officers in the company grades. Officers with whom I spoke in MILPERCEN always talked metaphorically about the U.S. Army officer inventory being three drawers. They spoke about the top drawer, the middle drawer and the bottom drawer. I insisted upon getting officers for the 101st Airborne Division from the top drawer. During the reductions in force (RIF) that followed the war many believed that the two bottom drawers were eliminated and there was only one drawer remaining that was divided into thirds. I did not care how they sliced it, the 101st Airborne Division deserved the best and I insisted that our replacements come from the best that the system had to offer. I developed a good telephonic relationship with the desk officers and their assistants and the 101st. Airborne Division fared well.

In early January, 1976 I made a liaison visit to MILPERCEN. Olivia and I had discussed the possibility of moving our family to the greater Washington, DC, area in order to enhance my career. I often said that "If you work at Sears, you need to, at some point, go to work at the home office. If you work for the Army, the home office is Washington, DC." Listening to COL Honeycutt and COL Palastra talk about how hard it was to live in DC I was reluctant to make the commitment. I remember Olivia's words on that account. She simply said, "How did they survive there? Did anyone in their family starve? If they made it we can make it. We will be okay!" That was all of the support I needed. So I took off for Washington, DC really on a reconnaissance mission to scout out the territory. I arrived late in the evening and went to the Holiday Inn hotel near MILPERCEN. I contacted Major Bill Edwards who was an assignment officer for Quartermaster Corps officers. Bill had been one of my classmates at CGSC. He and his wife, Merlyn and their children lived in the government subsidized housing area with us in Kansas City, KS. We were very close friends. Bill took me home for supper that evening and we discussed living in the National Capitol Region (NCR). The next day, I made a cursory stop by the personnel records section to review my official file. I went in to see the Chief of Staff at MILPERCEN and talked to a few assignment officers. That made my trip legitimate. Then I was off to visit Major Donald Tapscott who was my assignment officer and his assistant Ms. Cynthia Hansen. I had met Don at Fort Benning, GA, when I was a student in the Infantry Officer's Advance Course. I had also gone to visit him when he arrived in the class behind me at CGSC in Fort Leavenworth, KS. Don and I talked and he showed me my records folder. He announced loud enough for everyone within 20 feet to hear, "Oh you're wearing jump boots in your official photo." Little did he know that was the official uniform for airborne Soldiers. Then we went into one of the small interview rooms. He left the room after showing me a hand written derogatory note that had been entered into my file by LTC McLeod. The note was a result of an inquiry from the 101st Airborne Division asking if I could get an assignment to MILPERCEN. McLeod's hand written note was sent to the Chief of Infantry Branch, Colonel Elliott P. Sydnor and pointed out that I had received less than a maximum efficiency report as a company commander in combat from LTC Joe Wasiak. While Don Tapscott was out of the room I removed the note from my file and destroyed it. McLeod was the same officer that had given me a hard time at an earlier date when he sent me back to Vietnam for a second tour. I never figured out why this guy had negative feelings against me, but then I haven't lingered on it either. I think he retired as a colonel. When Major Tapscott returned I asked him the question about getting an assignment to the greater NCR. He was not immediately agreeable to it and muttered a negative answer to me. I asked if I could see MG Greer. He told me to go upstairs and ask the general's secretary if I could see him. I asked Ms. Hansen for directions and she volunteered to call ahead. I am not sure that MAJ Tapscott knew that I would pursue the course that I was taking to go and see a general? I went upstairs and MG Greer's secretary said that the general was having lunch. I told her that was okay I would just wait until he was finished. I sat down just outside of his office. She went back in to tell him that and he said for me to come on in to see him. Upon entering his office I explained that he probably would not remember me but I was the cadet that called the auditorium to attention when he spoke to the Corps of Cadets at West Virginia State College, 15 years earlier. I further explained that I was from McDowell County, West Virginia. He said with a big grin, "This beats the hell out of loading coal doesn't it?" I agreed with him and he offered me a cup of soup like he was eating. I refused and told him that I would not take a lot of his time but I needed his assistance to get an assignment to the NCR. He asked what I was doing now and what had I done in the past. I gave him a quick sketch of my career and he appeared to be satisfied and even impressed that I was doing the right things. He told his secretary to get Don Tapscott on the telephone. He simply asked him if he could get something for me in "the building." Don's answer was an immediate "Yes sir." He even started talking about the job. I was surprised because it appeared to me that he could have done that with me when I was downstairs. MG Ed Greer then turned to me and asked, "When do you want to come here." I said that somewhere around the 4th of July would be fine. He looked at his desk calendar and asked if the 7th of July was okay? I said yes. He still had Tapscott on the telephone and he said to him, words to the affect, that I would report on the 7th of July. I was a little miffed at Tapscott initially but soon learned that it was easier for him to tell Colonel Sydnor, the Branch Chief that MG Greer had assigned me to the building than it would have been for him to go in and try to get approval to assign me there. The procedure was known as "a brother-in-law action." I would find out that most of the good Army assignments in the National Capitol Region (NCR) were done that way. By assigning me to the building, I was now eligible to earn the very much sought after U.S. Army Staff Badge. I called Olivia and told her the good news and said that we could start packing.

I left MILPERCEN around noon and caught an afternoon flight back to Nashville, TN, where I had left my car and drove back to Fort Campbell grinning like the cat that swallowed the canary.

I started getting ready to leave immediately. However, I was careful not to talk about it in the office until I got my orders. When the orders arrived everyone was surprised that I was going directly to the pentagon and the Army General Staff. Fort Campbell, Kentucky had been good to me and Olivia this time. I had met a lot of general officers and quite a few other officers who would become general officers. I had performed very well in five different jobs. I understood how a division really functioned better than most and I knew all of these "super hot" leaders who were going places in the system. I had learned the protocol business and I was an extremely proficient field soldier. Thanks to COL Honeycutt and COL Palastra I had also become a pretty good golfer. In fact, there are general officers that I see today who identify me as the guy who used to play golf with the colonels. Most of all they taught me how to be firm and steadfast in the face of opposition. My parents had taught me to stand up for what I thought was right, but these two men raised that concept to the level of a principal worth dying for. I also had an opportunity to learn how to read official officer record briefs (ORB) and gauge the outstanding performers, average performers and the ne'er-do-wells. For a country boy from the coal fields of southern West Virginia, I was pretty savvy about the Army. Of course our family hated to leave our many friends and acquaintances in and around Fort Campbell and Clarksville, TN. We were particularly saddened to leave Perry and Ruby Barrington and their son Michael. As I reflect back to our assignment at Fort Campbell from April 1973 to June 1976, it is clear to me that I started to lose most of the prejudices and apprehensions that I had about working with white officers in the U.S. Army. MG Berry, COL Honeycutt, COL Palastra, COL Gentry and others convinced me that I was acceptable as a quality officer and could excel based on merit and that the color of my skin was not necessarily the major factor in my ability to succeed or fail. During my previous assignment in Vietnam I developed an attitude of distaste, disdain and distrust for the white hierarchy of the Army. Thank God the second tour at Fort Campbell turned me around and got me on the track of treating everyone with decency, respect, and compassion. It also renewed my trust in the basic goodness of mankind.

During the month of June 1976 we packed our household goods and loaded up the old station wagon that we bought back in the summer of 1971, on the way to Fort Leavenworth, and headed out to the NCR. Olivia and the children left a few days ahead of me to spend some time with her parents. I followed in my 1973 MGB with the hatchback. When I went to work at the 3rd Brigade Headquarters for COL Tiger Honeycutt we bragged about the number of sports cars in the front parking lot. Tiger had a 240 Z, I had a MGB, LT Giboney had a Porsche 914 and CPT Ernst also had a Porche 911. It was simply a 3rd Brigade status symbol to own a sports car.

MY FIRST TRIP TO THE BUILDING

When Olivia and I went to the NCR hunting for a house we did so on Easter weekend, 1976. We left the children with her parents in Bishop, VA, and proceeded to go to Bill and Merlyn Edward's home. They were so nice and cordial to us. In fact, they gave us their master bedroom and they moved into one of the spare bedrooms. We asked them not to do that but they insisted. That was the way Army families treated each other all over the world. We got started early in the morning with a realtor who was impressed that I would be assigned to the Office of the Deputy Chief of Staff for Personnel (DCSPER) in the pentagon. This guy was a retired major and he handled us like we were slabs of bacon. As it turned out all he did with us was fill out initial paperwork and determine our price range. The reason we went to this real estate office was because the broker was the wife of one of our classmates from CGSC and was a multimillion dollar seller in northern Virginia. She and her family lived in the government subsidized housing area in Kansas City, KS, with us. We thought that she was going to be our agent but she pushed us off to someone else. The person she gave to us started taking us to see houses in the upper level of our range right away. She showed us absolute junk the first day. She also offered to treat us to lunch, at McDonalds. When she offered to pay I would not let her. I was not about to let her think she was "treating us" at McDonalds. The next morning I was rather stern and emphatic with her. I told her to show us some decent housing or I was going to get another realtor. She called the person that we thought we were going to be working with in the first place and about an hour later we had them both showing us around. We were off to Lake Ridge, one of the suburbs of Woodbridge, VA, and we were shown some decent houses albeit, above of our price range. I didn't care. I knew that if I was going to buy a house it would not be a Major's house. It would be a full Colonel's house, because I thought that someday I would become, at least, a full Colonel. We finally settled on a house at 12211 Captains Court, in the Point Subdivision of Lake Ridge. Of all of the houses we saw and we looked at forty or fifty, Olivia's eyes lit up as soon as we walked in the front door. It was mid afternoon and the sun was shinning perfectly through the dining-living room patio doors and picture window and the hard wood floors were clean and gleaming. The eat-in kitchen, to the left as we entered, was perfect with all of the proper appliances. The stairs to the downstairs family room were to our immediate right. The place showed well. I instinctively knew that this was the place that Olivia wanted. I also knew that if there was any way possible I would get it for her. That place became our family's home and base of operations for more than twenty years.

I had learned from friends that too many officers had gone to the NCR without their spouses and bought a house. In fact one of our closest friend's said to us that her husband bought their house and she thoroughly disliked it, but did not have the nerve to tell him. I did not want that to happen to us. My theory was that Olivia would spend a helluva lot more time in those quarters than I would and she needed to be comfortable with them. I thought that I would be buried with work at the pentagon. So after a little private talk we decided that we wanted the house at 12211 Captains Court and we made a full price offer. That was probably a mistake but who cares now, that's what we wanted and that's what we bought. We left the realtor's office and went back and told Bill and Merlyn and took them to see it. It was only about five miles from their home. We were the first black family to move into "The Point" subdivision and fifteen years later there had only been one other. The homes were a combination of well constructed brick and siding, about 2500–3000 square feet of living space, with ample yards. Only a few houses had garages but all of them had off the street parking. In this particular house each of our children had their own bedroom and we also had a large family room and an eat-in country style kitchen. We also had a small patio out back. For a couple of skinny little kids from the coalfields of West Virginia we had scored again. We had a lot of good times in that house and our friends and our relatives seemed to enjoy it more than we did. It seemed like we always had house guests when we lived in Lake Ridge. As the years went by we added a two car garage to the house.

We arrived in the NCR on the 20th of June, 1976 and took lodging at the guest quarters at the Marine Corps Base at Quantico, Virginia. The biggest shock that I had was when we looked at the house closing documents and determined that we had not calculated the amount of escrow needed for insurances and taxes. Wow! What a mistake. The cost of living shot up drastically. We went from thinking that we would pay $515.00 a month to $607.00. That is a large increase when you are living on the margin. Our house was beautiful though, and we bought furniture for the kids for the first time. I very quickly became the typical NCR home fixer upper who lived for the weekend to start a new project. I was pretty handy around the house with the exception that I didn't mess with the plumbing. The one time that I did cost me an arm and a leg. The situation was that I had a broken spigot handle on my outside waterline. I decided, early on a Sunday morning that I would replace the broken handle. I went to Hechinger's, a local hardware vendor, and bought an entire spigot because they did not stock spigot handles. I went back home and got out my pipe wrench and adjusted it on the spigot and gave it a full turn. I broke it off inside of the wall. Oh, I forgot to mention that I did not turn the water outlet to this line off from the inside. So I had an immediate rush of water into our family room while I scrambled to get inside and shut the water off. I wrestled with that project all day that Sunday and at the behest of Olivia, paid a repairman to fix it the next day. As I remember that little home improvement error cost me about $120.00.

Inside of the pentagon, I went to work in the Leadership Division within the Directorate of Human Resources (DHRD), Office of the Deputy Chief of Staff for Personnel (ODC-SPER). The division chief was a black colonel named Clarence Miller. COL Miller was the first black senior officer for whom I worked. He and his wife, Margaret were perfect role models for me and Olivia. They lived on the Maryland side of the NCR. They entertained the entire division at their home regularly. They also attended the small parties that were given by the branch chiefs and action officers, both military and civilian in our homes. We had a great time working and socializing within the Leadership Division in the Pentagon.

The working environment and routine in the Pentagon was unlike anything that I had experienced in the military prior to that time. For example, in a regular tactical fighting division in the field one might see a general officer, up close, about once a month and probably speak with one once or twice a year. In the Pentagon you would see a general officer, up close, every day and brief one about once a week. The organization of the Pentagon was strange but functional. On the Army military side, there was the Office of the Chief of Staff. All military Army staff work eventually found its way to that office. The guys that controlled what went in and what came out the Chief's office were called "dwarfs" as in *Snow White and the Seven Dwarfs*. Snow White was a Colonel's position. These guys worked directly for the Office of the Director of the Army Staff. They were usually considered to be the best and brightest on the way up in the system. They had been recommended by a general officer through the assignment desks at MILPERCEN and were normally, usually, generally, and almost always the result of a "brother-in-law" action. They knew that they were in the cue to move up so they were usually arrogant. The truth is that they were no smarter than the rest of us around "the building" but they just happen to know someone who knew how to help them get ahead. Actually, the most powerful officers in the building were the guys with the title of executive officer or better known in the pentagon jargon as "the XO." In the old days we called them 'the gate keepers or the horse holders." They could get you in to see the boss or they could tell you the boss is "too busy" to see you and have you wait for up to three days or so. You did not want the XO angry with you or you'd be put on the docket late Friday afternoon or even early Saturday morning. Most of the general officers went into work on Saturday morning. However, no action officers wanted to get stuck working on Saturday because you could not get the honey do's done at home if you were at work at the pentagon.

Below the Chief of Staff's office and the Director of the Army Staff's office were the Deputates. Okay so it is not a word! It is pentagon jargon. The Deputates were headed up by three stars or Lieutenant Generals and they were normally referred to as the Deputy Chief of Staff for something. We worked for the Deputy Chief of Staff for Personnel (DCSPER). The DCSPER when I arrived in the Pentagon was LTG Hal Moore, the Vietnam hero battalion commander of the 1-7th CAV when they fought in the Idrang Valley. I had commanded a troop in the Gary Owen Battalion later in the war and I felt a deep sense of pride to work with a former commander of that battalion. Under the Deputates were the Directorates, headed up by two stars or Major Generals. The Director of Human Resource Development, at that time was MG Kenneth Dohleman. Dohleman was one of the hardest working men that I ever met. He had an expandable brief case that he carried home full of work every night. When he returned in the morning he would have read each paper and put his mark on it. That's what I learned from him and I still do it today. I do not hold papers in my possession more than twenty–four hours. He also wore the government issued (GI) uniform, including the shoes. The US Army Uniform Board was part of the Leadership Division. He felt that if he had to decide on the quality of the clothes being issued to the troops, he should wear them. I joined him and started wearing them too. In fact I became a model for the board in 1977. Some of you may have seen me in the Army

Times newspaper modeling the first black pullover sweater, the first black overcoat and the Army's first green shirt. The Leadership division was sort of a catch all for everything that required leader input. We wrote the first Army manual on ethics, the first alcohol and drug abuse regulation, the first organizational effectiveness concepts and we wrote major portions of the speeches for the Chief of Staff and the Secretary of the Army.

COL Miller, our division chief, was a great guy to work for with the exception that he smoked other people's (OP) cigarettes. I was a smoker at the time and he would ask for a cigarette at least once a day. He was trying to quit smoking…by not buying cigarettes. He was so bad at this habit that once on April Fools' Day he came in early and put a package of cigarettes on every smoker's desk. He led an office of odd, strange but very intelligent staff officers. Our lead secretary was named Sylvia. She was the typical "little ole lady in tennis shoes" that the pentagon is so infamous for having in an O6's office. As I explained before an O6 is a full bird colonel. They were generally outstanding colonels who for one reason or another were not selected to become a general officer. However, they came in early and stayed late almost everyday because they were committed to doing a good job. They were rarely awarded anything special; they lived in expensive neighborhoods in the suburbs; and they normally had separate office space with a door, a conference table, and a secretary. They checked the papers of the action officers to ensure that they were in the right format, made the right points, and were grammatically correct. When you took the paper into them for the final reading before you sent it forward, the first thing that they would do is reach for a pencil and start cutting the verbiage. During my years in the pentagon I learned a lot of lessons. One of the most valuable lessons was that a decision paper cannot be too short. One had to cover all of the points but you had to be brief. In fact General H. Norman Schwarzkopf had something called an executive summary (EXSUM), when he was the Deputy Chief of Staff for Operations (DCSOPS) that was a total of fifteen lines. Action officers were required to forward him all they knew and wanted to say about a subject in no more than 15 lines. That is another idea that I shamelessly adopted and used in my career.

My initial assignment in the Leadership Division was in the Alcohol and Drug Abuse Control Program (ADAPCP) Branch. The Branch Chief was COL Ervin Kattenbrink. When I was introduced to him by COL Miller, he simply said call me Erv. I was stunned. I had come from the most gung-ho division in the Army where Sergeants First Class and below braced against the wall when an officer walked down the hallway. Now I was at the so-called "corporate headquarters" for the entire defense industrial complex and this O6 tells me to call him Erv. It took me approximately three years before I could bring myself to do that. Other members of the team were Ms. Helen Gwinn, a Department of the Army Civilian (DAC) and a bevy of lieutenant colonels and majors. I did not have a problem calling the lieutenant colonels by their first name but not the colonels. I knew for certain that someday I would become a colonel but I did not have the complete vision – not just yet. For the first few hours that first day every time Erv would come near my desk I would stand up. Finally toward the end of the day he said to me, very casually, "If you are going to stand up every time I come near your desk you will be on your feet most of the day and not get any work done, because I will be coming to your desk often." I said yes sir but it still took me about a week to relax around him. They made me the Statistical Analyst for the entire Army ADAPCP. What a mouth full! I had difficulty saying it let alone doing the work. However, after about six to eight weeks I mastered that little bit of trivia like I had everything else in life to that point. That first day on the job went very well for me. LTC John Shannon, from the Office of the Secretary of the Army came by to see me and welcome me to the building. He was followed by LTC Bobby Moore from the Office of the Deputy Secretary of Defense for Minority Programs. Both of these officers were pentagon veterans who knew their way around the building. They were also African Americans. My sponsor was a major named Wilson Barnes. He was also a CGSC classmate. He didn't do very much for me. He did, however, tell me to call him if I needed him. I never did. It was Wednesday, July 7th, 1976.

My very first action/task in the pentagon was to work with the Office of The Judge Advocate General (OTJAG) on the quadrennial review of the Manual for Courts Martial. At that time the manual was revised every four years and the U.S. Army was the proponent for the revision. The OTJAG action officer brought me the portion that the DCSPER needed to approve and I had to get the endorsements to the changes from the other services. The staff process at the pentagon was very interesting. Staff actions were meted out from Snow White's office to the executive officers in the Deputates. The routing slips were color coded with tear off manifolds. Action officers (ACTO) got the "white tails" or white copy of the routing slip. The blue copy was kept by the division chief' secretary and put into a suspense file. Other color copies were kept at the Deputates and/or at the Office of the appropriate Assistant Secretary's of the Army (ASA) office. Generally the divisions were given 14 days to complete an action. That meant the ACTO had, at best eight days to complete the action because the division chief had to put his mark on it before it went forward to the Office of the Director of Human Resources Development (DHRD). The Directorate normally had a three to five day suspense buffer before an action cleared the Deputate's office en route to one of the ASA and other upper echelon offices on the "E Ring." I worked with the OTJAG officer and commenced getting the approvals and endorsements from the other services. This approval process was called getting everyone's "chop."

I went up on the hill from the pentagon to the Navy Annex and talked to some officers in the Marine Corps and they agreed with the paper I was carrying. Then I went to the fifth floor of the pentagon and talked with a U.S. Air Force female brigadier general. She agreed. From there I went to see the guys in the Navy area of the pentagon. During all of these visits I failed to get even one signature or initial. In fact no one told me that I needed to do so. When I turned in the action, the branch chief and the division chief signed off on it. They let it go to the Director's office before I was called in and told that I did not have a completed action. It was at that time that I learned that there were four staff positions available for an action and all staff actions had to have one of them on it before an action could be passed forward. The staff positions were: concurrence; non-concurrence with comment; noted; or has seen. In any case, the party to whom you spoke about the staff action had to give you their chop or said another way; you must get at least an initial from the person with whom you spoke. The DHRD, MG Dohleman, was very instructional with me and he sent me out to do the action all over again. He also taught me how to get an action extended. In order to extend the time on a staff action one had to go to the source of the action. In this case it was the Office of the General Counsel in the Department of Defense. Most sources of actions had programmed time for at least one screw up and could grant a three day extension. Once you obtained the extension you had to notify everyone in the chain so that they would not be looking for the action on the original due date. For Army personnel actions, that usually meant that you had to go by and see COL Bill Merrill in the Office of the Assistant Secretary of the Army for Manpower and Reserve Affairs (ASAM&RA). What a great guy he was. He was past his mandatory retirement date but he was also the person who approved the requests for extensions beyond the mandatory retirement date. He would simply approve his own request to extend every year. He wore civilian clothes every day and most people thought that he was a bonafide DAC. From his office you had to backtrack to the DCSPER executive office where the yellow tail of the routing slip was kept and they would alter the due date for the action. The pentagon had a complicated, bureaucratic system of tracking actions but they rarely got lost for any appreciable amount of time. The last stop was back at the director's office before stopping by the chief clerk's or secretary's office in the division. I redid the action and sent it forward. Once a staff action cleared ASAM&RA you did not hear about it again. You always kept your file copy of the action but the pentagon jargon said it best: "A passed action is a completed action." So if you could pass it either laterally or upward your job on that particular action was done.

My second action took me to see the Vice Chief of Staff of the Army (VCSA), General Walter T. "Dutch" Kerwin. I was given this action because I was fresh out of a combat division. The action involved moving a battalion from the Continental United States (CONUS) to an overseas area for an extended period of time. The staff action was to determine if we needed to give everyone a urinalysis test for drugs prior to movement. I took the action and without a great deal of coordination determined that urinalysis testing could be done. After all I had just left one of the best trained divisions in the Army and we did this kind of thing all of the time. You just had to line 'em up and have 'em urinate in a bottle and send it forward. It sounded simple enough for me. I took the action around to different staff sections and everyone concurred. I had chops from everybody. I sent it forward and everyone in the chain signed off. I got a white tail about two days later from the VCSA that simply read, "See me!" Of course when that happened, everyone and his brother got involved. First I had to back brief the branch chief and the division chief, together. The next morning we were on the DHRD calendar for a briefing. It was at this time that I learned something that has stood me in good stead for a long, long time. That is simply, if you are the principal staff action person on a project, you know more about that action than anyone else. It was an Army policy at that time, that an action officer would brief his action all the way to the top. So when I finished briefing the DHRD, my next step was to go into the private Office of the DCSPER and brief him, alone. I say again, the DCSPER was LTG Hal Moore. I was absolutely in awe of this guy. He was having back problems at that time and had to stand up the whole time that I briefed him. He appeared to be satisfied with my briefing and said that he would be going to the

Vice Chief's office with me. Well when I got back and debriefed Colonel Miller, he called the Director immediately and I was informed that there would be four people in the party to see the VCSA. They were to be LTG Moore, MG Dohleman, COL Miller, and me. Later I found out that this was a way for the senior officers to get face time with the "pachyderms." I made arrangements with the VCSA's secretary and got us on the calendar. Strangely enough everyone else was able to adjust their calendar to fit VCSA's available time.

As I remember, we were on for like 0830 and we met earlier to make sure that we had our act together. I was designated to do all of the talking and the others would only speak if necessary. I was pretty excited. After all I had not been in the building more that about three weeks and I was going to brief the number two man in the entire uniform hierarchy of the Army. Wow! Olivia had been right about going to Washington. I was about to see how the other half of the Army lived. We met briefly in General Moore's outer office and proceeded upstairs to the third floor, E Ring. We were taken in immediately to the VCSA's office a sure sign of the efficiency that one would expect at that level. The secretaries were well dressed, poised, and extremely courteous. Their office also smelled good with the fresh smell of flowers and perfume. Just seeing the efficiency with which things were being handled was enough to impress me. The VCSA was a small framed man. That surprised me. I had seen pictures and taken him to be much larger. He asked me to sit in the chair closest to his desk. They all knew each other including Colonel Miller who had a prior special relationship with VCSA. Instead of asking me to brief him the VCSA asked me, "How many battalions have you commanded Major?" I answered none sir but I have been a battalion executive officer. He replied, "How many battalions have you commanded?" I got the drift and said sheepishly, none sir. He then went on to explain to me how much was on the battalion commander's plate with the deployment to Europe and that guys like me were only adding things to it by putting a Department of the Army requirement on him to conduct an activity and report it back to the Department. He then wanted to know if I thought it made sense. I looked around that room for support from the crew of straphangers who had horned in on the meeting with me and I got nothing. We had all agreed before we left the DCSPER's office that I was right and all of those guys turned on me in a flash. I answered that it did not make a lot of sense to do the little drug drill and with that I got one of the best the pieces of advice that I ever got in the military. General Kerwin reminded me that the commanders in the field have enough to do without having some "staff weenie" in the pentagon, offer them additional requirements that did not always make sense. I left the VCSA office that morning with not only a high regard for the staff action process in the pentagon but also a profound degree of respect for General Kerwin. He had taken what was to many an insignificant action and given it his personal attention to protect a battalion commander in the field and to teach a new pentagon staff officer to consider all of the consequences before making a Department of the Army (DA) staff decision. When we arrived back down stairs LTG Hal Moore went to his office and MG Dohleman went to his office but Colonel Miller took the time to talk to me about pentagon decision making. He was very deliberate about how we should ensure that we consider everything before making decisions in what he called the "ivory tower" and about what should happen in the field. The analogy that he used to illustrate his point was: "You should picture yourself driving an aircraft carrier down the ocean and the word would come to the bridge that you were going one hundred and eighty degrees from the direction that you should be traveling. You would be given orders to turn the ship around and go the other way. At that point you would have some choices. You could start a right angle turn on the starboard side and come around to the 180 degree mark or you could possibly reverse you engines and slowly crab your way around on the port side to the 180 degree mark." The point he attempted to make was that no matter which choice you made you and the ship would have to continue traveling for a certain distance down the ocean in the original direction before the required change could take place. It was a long story to make a minute point but I clearly understood.

Eventually, I learned to love my job in the Leadership Division. After about six months on the job I became "the go to guy" for the division, the directorate and occasionally for the DCSPER's office. Part of my success is owed to then LTC Walter F. Johnson. Wally and I had gone to college together at WVSC. He retired from the Army as a Brigadier General, the first African American Chief of the Army Medical Service Corps. He was a year ahead of me in college. Our paths had crossed while I was a student at CGSC while he was in graduate school at the University of Kansas. After graduate school he was assigned to the pentagon and remained there forever. He knew his way around the building and he taught me how to navigate through the bureaucracy associated with the Department of Defense (DOD). He showed me where the support service centers were located, where the audio visual support center was located and he briefed me on how to go in on Sunday and find useful furniture in the hallway. The truth of the matter is that if you needed to prepare for a presentation you could not depend on the secretaries to get the basics done for you. They simply were not trained to do briefings. They did their jobs extremely well but briefing generals was the domain of the actions officers and the good ones made their own slides. This was well before the days of power point presentations and required a little hands-on approach. However, if you knew how to use the copy machines, use the paper cutters and, and use the equipment in the audio visual center on the first floor of Corridor 10 you could do your own work. You could also teach your secretary how to do it. Our branch secretary was Lois Stevens. She was great! I remember interviewing her for the job and going into the boss and asking him to hire her. Lois was married to a Navy commander who was assigned to the Navy Annex just up the hill from the pentagon. His name was Jack. She had a daughter in high school and a younger son. She was just what our office needed. Her work ethic was perfect. She and her husband had just returned from attaché duty in Iran. She had worked for the military over there. She was an eager learner, she did not skip out early, and she would even come in early if she had prior notice. Because our last names were pronounced the same we would introduce ourselves to people as brother and sister. Over time she and I became very close and I actually did think of her at times as the sister that I never had. In order to get an action past MG Dohleman, you would have to redo the paper three, four, maybe even five times. Often, by the time you got to the fifth version back it looked a helluva lot like the first version. Lois would suffer through that and when she saw Dohleman in the hallway and he would ask "How's it going Ms Stevens?" She would tell him about it.

There is nothing worse than going down the E Ring at about four forty-five o'clock in the evening proof reading the final version of a staff paper that is due that day, and suddenly find a mistake on page five of a seven page document. Lois never put me in that position. If she gave you a document, it was typed exactly the way you had given her the draft. In addition, all of the words were spelled correctly and the punctuation was perfect. Lois replaced a young branch secretary who was not that dependable. In fact, there were times when one of our prior secretaries would show up in the clothes that she wore the day before because she had spent the night out, all night, and had not gone home. That particular young lady would come to me sometimes on Tuesday and say, "If you have an action that is due on Friday you need to get it to me by tomorrow because I will be out sick on Thursday and Friday. Lois Stevens was a welcome breath of fresh air to the ADAPCP branch. She was always neat, always attended additional training and she and her husband always attended the division's social events. Over time she went on to become a directorate secretary and I understand that she was in the DCSPER'S office complex on the morning of the 9-11-2001 terrorist strike at the pentagon. Together, she and I would take on any staff action, for any time frame, from any office. We were good at completing actions and we knew it!

I need to point out that this was well before the advent of personal computers on everyone's desk. This was during the days of the International Business Machines (IBM) magnetic tape and later the magnetic card typewriters.

After about two years in the ADAPCP Branch I was selected for promotion to lieutenant colonel. We went through a couple of branch chiefs after Colonel Ervin Kattenbrink left us that did not work out too well. The last one was a former battalion commander who showed up for work every day with a fresh *Washington Post* newspaper and read every word of it by noon. He was a great guy but he did not care for the job he had in the pentagon. In fact, he hated working in the pentagon. At about 1100 each day he opened his second package of cigarettes and started planning for lunch. He didn't even try to learn the office routine or the manner in which we did staff actions. He just signed off when we brought him the staff actions. My guess is he did not even proof read them. Shortly after he arrived he was selected to attend the U.S. Army War College at Carlisle Barracks, Pennsylvania. So he was just biding his time to get the Army Staff Badge and move on to greater things. It took a year on station in the building to receive the Army Staff Badge. Normally there was an award ceremony with the certificate being presented in the office and the division chief would buy donuts. You were not given the badge along with the certificate. You had to purchase the badge separately yourself. I remember that my children took their allowance money and bought my Army Staff Badge. I still wear that badge today whenever I wear my uniform. The ADAPCP branch chief was just waiting on his badge. In the meantime we were very busy in the office. I remember one afternoon we were called to the DHRD office to make a presentation about the progress of our program. The action officer's briefing kit consisted of an easel, a pad of butcher paper (chart paper) and a box of colored magic markers. As I began to set up my kit for the briefing, MG Dohleman asked the branch chief why I was doing the set up. The chief answered, "Oh sir, he will be doing the briefing." Dohleman said, "I want you to brief me Colonel." The branch chief confessed that he was not prepared, at that time to brief. The Director said, "I want you to brief me tomorrow morning at 0830." We left the office immediately and needless to say, I would have a long night trying to get the branch chief ready to make the presentation. Down deep I knew that we did not have enough time. So the next morning I was in early and we again attempted to get him up to speed. At about 0815 we packed him up with the briefing kit and he went around the corner to the Director's office on the 7th corridor just after passing the General Officer Management Office (GOMO) and just short of the E Ring. He was back in about 15 minutes with a sad look on his face. He said, "I have been relieved of my duties as branch chief and I will be reassigned out of the building." I felt sorry for him briefly, but I saw this as my chance to become the ADAPCP branch chief. I was a "promotable major" and I thought I was the best qualified officer on board for the job.

NEVER ACCEPT SECOND BEST

Besides Lois and me the action officers in the ADAPCP branch consisted of two Medical Service Corps officers, a Chaplain, and a female civilian (GS 12 or 13). I was the only grunt in the bunch. I had served in the field, i.e., a combat division and I served in Vietnam on the ground. I knew soldiering and they were essentially staff weenies. I went to Colonel Miller, the division chief, and made my case to become the branch chief. He told me that he had decided to make the female civilian the branch chief because "It would be a good political and strategic move" for the Army. I was disappointed. Actually, I was ticked off. I felt like I was carrying the branch and I felt that I deserved the position and I was positive that Lois and many others felt the same way. I was so angry that I had to take a walk down the corridor. I ended up in the office of a college friend, LTC John Radcliff Robinson. Rad, as we called him, was the personnel officer for the Joint Chiefs of Staff (JCS). I asked him if they had any openings in the Joint Staff. He said that he was trying to fill a military secretary officer position in the Office of the Director of Operations (J-3). I asked him if he would float my ORB to the XO in J-3. He called me about two days later and told me that I had a scheduled interview with the XO. On the day of the interview I put on a pressed uniform including my blouse, went and got my shoes shined on the pentagon concourse and got a fresh haircut. I was interviewed by Colonel Tom Eddins, a West Point graduate, who had relatives in Welch, WV. He was an Armor branch officer and very neat. I was at my best for the interview. By this time I was absolutely confident that I could perform any duty in the pentagon. I knew that if I got the chance to interview, I'd get the job. I got the job! I did not say anything to anyone until I cleared it through

MILPERCEN. J.J. Johnson, my old friend that I served with at Fort Benning was now my assignment officer in MILPERCEN and I knew that I could get his okay. As soon as I got the orders cut, I walked in and told COL Miller. He was surprised and probably angry but he knew that he had not done well by me with the branch chief position and so he did not fight it. I hated to leave Colonel Miller. For the most part he had been good to me. He had nominated me for membership in the ROCKS, Inc. and he had supported me in becoming his replacement as chairman of the ways and means committee of that organization. I considered him a friend. However, my move to JCS was not personal or anything against him. It was just business!

I went to work for COL Tom Eddins and never looked back at DCSPER. The Director of Operations (J-3) for the joint staff was LTG C.J. LeVAN. That was the way he spelled it and that's the way he always wanted to see it. He was different. He sat back in his office about fifteen feet from the entrance. When you took something for him to sign you had to cross the empty space and wait until he acknowledged your presence. When he finally looked up at you, it was time to speak. All of the action officers were intimidated by him. I refused to let him intimidate me. I played the waiting to be recognized game but otherwise I ignored the office idiosyncrasies that everyone followed. I did not like the guy so for the most part I avoided him and worked around him through COL Eddins. My desk mate was an Air Force officer named MAJ Margolis. At first I was in charge of the military secretary's office. The Army promotion system was so slow at that time that Margolis was selected for promotion to lieutenant colonel after I was selected and was subsequently promoted before I was. That was my very first drill in being in charge when you are outranked. However, he and I got along well. I was also selected for battalion command that year and everyone knew that I would be leaving as soon as I got enough time to get my JCS Badge. Like the Army Staff Badge you had to have a year on station to get it. When my promotion day came, I asked Brigadier General (BG) Joseph T. Palastra, my old brigade commander and friend to come down to J-3 and promote me. BG Palastra was at that time the executive officer to the Deputy Secretary of Defense. In the process of all of my office duties in J-3 one of my most important duties was the retirement of LTG LeVAN. Because of my protocol background in the 101st Airborne Division it was a piece of cake. He wanted to retire in the U.S. Navy Yard so his colors would fly from the flag staff. He wanted a company of troops to review and I made the mistake of saying, as a joke "What about him riding in on white stallion?" That was a mistake that took several hours for me to overcome as COL Eddins casually mentioned it to him and you guessed it. He wanted to ride a horse to review the troops. He was replaced by LTG Philip D. Shutler, a three star Marine. General Shutler was the best flag officer for whom I have worked, bar none.

I learned a great deal from General Shutler. The first thing that he did was move his desk to the front wall of his office. When action officers entered the door he was sitting right there a few inches within the door. He was accessible! He was also friendly and helpful. Unlike LeVAN he talked with everyone, and he discussed actions with the action officers. Staff actions in the JCS staff were a lot like staff actions in the Army except that you now had to get consensus from all of the services before you could send a paper forward. It was referred to as "going purple" meaning that it wasn't blue for Air Force, green for Army, or navy blue for Navy and etc. it was purple and had everyone's initial chop. Of course I didn't have to worry about any of the leg work, I ran the processing office. I also had the privilege of starting up and running the first word processing center in the joint staff. We operated with computers made by the Vydek Corporation. They were "tempest cleared" or said another way they were so quiet they could not be detected by Russian electronic monitoring devices. There were three ladies in that group who worked on flexible time schedules. We were open from about six o'clock in the morning until about eight o'clock at night. Officers could drop off their drafts and expect to get them back within an eight to ten hour period. If there were rush jobs they were brought directly to the executive suite and one of us would establish the priority for work completion. Everyone learned very quickly to get their papers to me early. Their procrastination did not constitute an emergency for me. I did not care if the ACTO looked bad because his or her paper was not done on time. It did not take long for folks to realize that I was not a push over in the front office.

Going to work in the J-3 staff changed my work schedule completely. Now instead of riding the bus to work, I had to drive my car. My hours for starting work were somewhat predictable however, going home was different. We normally stayed in the office until the J-3 left and then we would clean up the place and set up for the next day. Sometimes that would not occur until around seven o'clock in the evening. The executive office staff had to be there before the J-3 arrived and we stayed until he left for home. That usually meant that finding a parking space in the pentagon parking lot was not a problem. When you arrived early and stayed late there was always parking available. We worked for the executive officer. We also worked on what we called a half day schedule on Saturday. Actually we did not start on Saturdays until about eight o'clock and we stopped when all of the signal lights turned red. There was a set of signal lights in the suite that were supposed to indicate the location of the president, Jimmy Carter, the vice president, Fritz Mondale, and the secretary of defense, Dr. Harold Brown. The lights were red, amber and green in color. They were suppose to signal green when the principals were in their offices, amber if they were in transition to or from the office but still available, and red when they were completely out of the office. Saturdays were the days that we caught up on backlogs of correspondence, staff actions and other activities such as speech writing. General Shutler sat at a location in the office so he could observe the signal lights. Late in the evenings and particularly on Saturdays he would look up at the lights and say, after they had all turned red, "Well, let's call it quits for today, we've been here long enough." Normally the Deputy J-3, Air Force MG Jerry O'Malley played tennis on Saturday mornings and came in around 10 or 11 o'clock. MG O'Malley was a really good general officer and very easy to work with. He was promoted to full general and died in an airplane crash. LTG Shutler always bought lunch for us on Saturday from the Chairman's Mess. He had an account there and we charged our lunch to his bill. The Chairman's Mess prepared the best hamburgers that I have ever eaten besides the ones prepared at our home by Olivia.

There were a number of crises that occurred during my tenure in the J-Staff. Probably the most significant was the Iran hostage crisis. We activated the Crisis Action Center (CAC) and ran it around the clock for about six weeks. Brigadier General Andrew Chambers was brought in to chair the CAC. I was responsible for the logistical support to the CAC. That meant that I had to have typing support available, 24 hours a day, for the entire period. That was the first time that I realized that the pentagon could not survive a crisis period with the hired help. After about three weeks, the clerical support started to crumble. The ladies that did the typing were, for the most part, married and had to go home to their families. There was one young lady that was not married. I do not remember her full name but we called her Mo. Mo was a crisis saver for us. Sometimes she would stay on duty for twenty-four hours at a time, catching "cat naps" during the time. The best part of working on the CAC was the quality time that I spent with BG Andrew Chambers. He talked to me and advised me daily. It was at that time that I started to have serious thoughts about becoming a general officer. General Chambers went on to retire as a Lieutenant General. He was always one of my favorite role models.

As the Military Secretary to the J-3, I was involved in everything that the joint staff did. I knew about the aerial surveillance program with the SR 71. I knew how the Moscow-Washington telephone program called MOLINK worked. I also knew where the president, the vice president and the secretary of defense were located most of the time. It was a great job. It was before the days that everyone had cell phones and sometimes I wonder how we survived with only reliable landline service. By the way I also knew what the AT&T telephone bill for JCS was each month.

While in this job I was selected for battalion command. It could not have happened at a better time. I was winding up about three years in the pentagon and I would leave with two, not one but two, skill badges for my blouse. I was selected to command a battalion at Fort Lewis Washington. That's where General Chambers was serving as an Assistant Division Commander. I talked to him about serving in the great northwest and he told me how good it was going to be. I was literally leaving a job where my rater was a three star general to go to work for a colonel. I had developed a technique where I could chew action officers up and spit 'em out and they would never know what hit 'em. I had no fear of going to this new job. General Shutler rated me and said in my performance rating: "Stephens is signally head and shoulders above his contemporaries." At first I thought that he had made a typing mistake and meant to say "singularly" head and shoulders…It was not until I read it several times that I realized that he was waving semaphore flags for me. I should point out that this was the first performance evaluation that I had received, that I did not write a draft for, since Tom Kehoe marked me down at my executive officer position in the 3rd Battalion, 187th Infantry around 1974. From that time on I was in on the writing of every report. Most of the time, the raters submitted them exactly as I wrote the draft. I have found that some people actually mark themselves down on draft evaluations. Not me! You want to know how I felt about my performance. It was outstanding! Anyway LTG Shutler said some nice things about me and it probably helped for my next promotion. So I got my JCS badge and left for the west coast after attending pre-command courses at Fort Benning, GA, and Fort Leavenworth, KS.

Before going into command, all prospective commanders were required to attend pre-command courses. One phase of the training was done at one's basic branch schoolhouse and the other phase was conducted at the U.S. Army and General Command and Staff College. The first phase was conducted with your peers from your branch of service. On the evening before I was supposed to leave for my pre-command courses, Stephanie, our oldest daughter, came home crying. She had been mistreated by two women who coached the Woodbridge High School Women's Track Team. Apparently, the team members were told to run several laps. At the end of the designated number of laps Stephanie was told to run another lap. She asked why and one of the coaches said words to the effect, "Because you are black. Everyone knows that you will be asked to do more because you are black." Stephanie refused and was suspended from the track team. I was furious. I got in my car and went to the school and went and found one of those women. I leaned over on her desk and said: My daughter is at home crying and you'd better tell me why." Her eyes welled up and she started explaining that the other woman was the culprit and she had not said anything. Of course the other woman was gone home. The next morning I went to the school bright and early. All of the parking places in the teacher's lot were taken except the principal's. I took it! I went into his office and sat to wait on him until he arrived. He came into his office angry that someone was in his parking space and started to speak to his secretary about it. I interrupted and told him that I was in his space and I wanted to speak with him. I was about 185 pounds and I was ripped. If he had made the wrong move that morning I was going to kick his butt. He was cool. I explained Stephanie's side of the story and he was apologetic. Stephanie's version of how the kids on the bus from Lake Ridge reacted when they saw my car in the principal's space made that little diversion worth while. As I think back I am surprised that I did not grab the coach that evening and give her a good shaking. However, she was a little person and I knew she was scared. My children always knew that I would protect them.

I left the principal's office after about thirty minutes and headed for Fort Benning, GA, to become "re-blued." Among other grunts that were with me was Lieutenant Colonel Fred Peters. Fred and I were friends from a previous assignment at Fort Benning. What a great guy to have around to ensure that all situations were thoroughly analyzed in the school house. With Fred Peters around single issue analysis on any subject was not possible. He would nail an instructor with a question that would take thirty minutes or more to settle. In our pre-command course at CGSC we were placed in a larger group that included all branches of the Army and it also included the officers selected for Brigade command. Colonel Gary Luck stands out in my mind from that class. What a classy leader he was. We all knew that he was going places in the military business. He retired as a four star general. I went to Fort Benning alone with all of my personal effects in a 1973 hatchback MG. Olivia joined me on the last day of classes at Fort Leavenworth and we drove across country together to Fort Lewis, WA. Stephanie was reinstated on the Woodbridge High School track team.

During one of the pre-command sessions at CGSC, the Chief of Staff of the Army, General Bernard Rogers made a presentation. One of the officers fell asleep from jet lag during the presentation. I have never seen a senior officer humiliate a junior officer the way Rogers did this guy. It was brutal! He yelled at him, called him lazy and threatened to keep him from going into command. The guy was an air defense artillery officer whose name I cannot remember now. However, no one else fell asleep after that. I consider General Rogers' behavior that day totally unacceptable for a person in his position.

TAKING COMMAND

Olivia and I left Fort Leavenworth during the afternoon of May 25th, 1979 and headed west. Our first stop was a motel in Hayes, KS. The next morning we left early and traveled to Laramie, WO. From Laramie we went to Boise, Idaho, and developed car trouble, i.e., we broke a belt. We got the car fixed and headed west again following some guy we met at a service station driving a Jaguar. He explained that he was driving the car for a company that employed drivers to drive cars across country for people who for one reason or another could not drive themselves. He gave us a business card for the company. We arrived on Monday evening, the 28th of May at the Fort Lewis Guest House and started unloading the car when my prospective brigade commander showed up with a bottle of wine and a bouquet of flowers. He offered his welcome to us and asked if I could come to a meeting the following morning at 10 o'clock with the division commander. The prospective commander, Colonel Richard Jarrett turned out to be a good guy. I was extremely irritated with him that evening though. In those situations I always wanted to ask, what if I had said no. I just arrived after three days of hard driving and, oh by the way, I am not unpacked yet. I knew what to expect though. I had a starched uniform with the patches already sewn on and my spit shined boots were packed away in old socks and ready for display. I went to bed and slept like a baby. The next morning I got up and pressed my uniform again and got dressed to go to the 1st Brigade Headquarters and meet Major General Richard E. Cavazos. Cavazos' first words to me were "Hello Stephens, you pentagon weenie. What are you doing here?" I think he was showing off for the group. He had a tendency to do that. Until now every flag officer that I had met was poised, and comfortably aloof. Most of them were so glitzy that you could put a picture frame around them and hang them on a wall. MG Cavazos was none of the above. He was one of the troops. He was truly a soldiers' soldier. General Andy Chambers had briefed me about him so I knew what to expect. General Cavazos was also announcing to that group of officers that they were getting a pentagon savvy officer. I warmed to him in a matter of seconds. I do not think until this day that he knew I would be present at that meeting.

That morning I also met the officer that I would be replacing, LTC James Burns. He was cordial but not overly friendly. For example, he did not invite me to visit the 2-39 Infantry battalion area. That was okay with me but I made a promise to myself to never do that to an officer who was replacing me. My model had been Joe Palastra replacing Tiger Honeycutt. Tiger shared everything with Joe and the transition was almost seamless. LTC Burns set a time for us to meet and talk. It was exactly one hour before the change of command ceremony commenced. I am certain that General Cavazos thought that the guy was giving me briefings and tours of the outfit. Nothing was further from the truth. COL Jarrett knew he was not showing me around but did not comment. You see LTC Burns was one of Cavazos' right hand men. In fact, he was not leaving the division but was going to become the 9th Division's Assistant Chief of Staff for Operations, G-3. He was replacing the longtime, well respected LTC Bobby Jolley who was retiring. People spoke of these guys as if they were icons in the system. They were in fact, only demagogues at Fort Lewis. I respected them as I did everyone else but I had served on the general staff of the famed Screaming Eagles of the 101st Airborne Division and I had two, not one but two, pentagon skill badges from the Army General Staff and the Joint Chiefs of Staff. These guys were not insignificant to me, but I had no fear of doing well in that outfit and I think everyone sensed it.

I assumed command of the 2nd Battalion, 39th Infantry (Falcons) at 0900, Friday, the 1st of June, 1979. That was a big day in our lives. We had for all practical purposes reached every goal that we had set in the near term. Olivia was there dressed in a nice blue suit, including a hat and gloves and looking like a battalion commander's wife. We were off to the challenge of commanding in the 9th Infantry Division, a straight leg division. After the change of command, we went to the Officer's club for a reception. I do not know until today if the reception was for Jim Burns' leaving or my welcome. In any case it cost me a pretty penny. I did not mind I just figured it came with the turf. At about noon I left and went back to the battalion headquarters. Olivia went back to the guest cottage that we had rented. That morning Jim Burns had given me a run down on his assessment of the leaders in the battalion. He started with the Command Sergeant Major. All he would say about him was: "I consider him a friend." I thought okay that means I will have to fire him. Then he talked about the operations officer, S-3, CPT Michael Tesdahl. I got the feeling that he put this guy in the position to ensure my failure. I determined from jump-street that neither, CPT Mike Tesdahl nor I was going to fail. I knew for sure that I was going to succeed. In order for me to succeed, CPT Mike Tesdahl had to be outstanding. Next, LTC Burns talked about the company commanders. A Company was commanded by LT Nolan Bivens, B Company by CPT James Amondson, C Company by CPT Lyle Brooks, D Company by CPT Donald Tieg, and Headquarters and Headquarters Company by CPT Alex Angel He had good things to say about all of them except the African American lieutenant named LT. Nolan Bivens. Apparently LT Bivens' company had shot a mortar round outside of the safety fan at the artillery range and LTC Burns never forgave him for it. Rumor had it that Burns wanted to relieve LT Bivens for that incident but the brigade commander saved him. The one guy that he omitted talking about was the battalion executive officer, MAJ Art Ballin. What a Godsend he turned out to be! What a fine gentleman he turned out to be! He, his wife Sally, and their children took to me and Olivia as if we were kin folks. The entire personnel briefing from Burns took about fifteen minutes and so I thought he would talk about some of the unit's standing operating procedures (SOP). He did not and I did not push him. After all, I had literally commanded the Rakkasan Battalion under LTC Bramlett. I knew what had to be done and I knew what I was going to do. I was going to be in charge and I would take charge. During my brief change of command remarks I gave the regular troops the rest of the day off after the parade. I scheduled a meeting with all of the officers at 1300 that afternoon.

I opened the meeting like COL Joe Palastra. I praised Jim Burns and said that I knew that they were loyal to him and that it might be difficult for them to switch their loyalties to me quickly. I went on to say that anyone who thought that they may have severe difficulty switching their loyalty to me could leave the room within the next sixty seconds without retribution. I continued to talk for about another two minutes and said casually that the sixty seconds had passed and from now on, I would expect complete loyalty from everyone in the room. Everybody was absolutely stunned. I had their undivided attention. Colonel Joe Palastra had taught me well. I went on to outline my goals for the battalion in the near term. We were going to the field on Monday to evaluate another battalion's Army Readiness Training Evaluation Program (ARTEP). I knew how to train troops. In fact, I thought I knew how to train troops better than anyone, at my level in the Army. I was almost wrong. I knew the 101st Airborne Division way to train. I did not know the 9th Division way. General Cavazos had a policy that a new commander had to go to the field within the first thirty days of assuming command and lead his battalion through an ARTEP within the first six months of command. A command tour was only eighteen months so training leaders took some planning. MG Dick Cavazos was the best that I have ever seen at training battalion commanders. The officers call meeting lasted about an hour. I released everyone for the day except the battalion XO and the SI. It was approximately 1400 hours. I met briefly with the Adjutant/S1 and asked to see the battalion officers' benevolent fund books. He said that he did not keep books but he had the fund in the glove compartment of his car. I immediately accused him of stealing money from the officers' fund. This guy was a West Point graduate and I had insulted his integrity and he let me know it, as well as a lieutenant could let a lieutenant colonel know it. I told him to go and get the money. He went out to his Triumph, TR3 and brought back a paper bag with the money in it. I made him count it and told him that I expected him to deposit it in the bank on Monday morning and that we would have a meeting and elect officers and select another person to counter sign the checks. I also told him to chill-out. I knew that he had not taken any money from the fund but if he were officially accused he would not have a leg to stand on. I did not tell him that I had administered an officers' fund at least twice in my career. After that episode I let him go home. He left in a huff. Then I turned to the XO and asked where my damn welcome packet and information materials were. With tears in his eyes he produced a folder with all of the welcome materials that he had assembled for me. He said that he wanted to send it to me before I arrived and had been told not to do so. I listened to him snivel and absorbed a host of the complaints about LTC Burns and decided that I would close up the office and go home. I had broken the water pump on my MG upon arriving at the post and needed to replace it. Olivia and I had moved from the guest house to one of the post VIP guest cottages. I replaced the water pump in the front yard of the guest cottage where we were staying. Olivia and I spent the rest of the afternoon driving around the post and getting to know Fort Lewis. The next morning, Lucius "Peanuts" Reeves, a guy we knew from college who now lived in the Seattle area took Olivia and me to the Seattle Airport. Olivia flew off and I went back to the battalion. Because I did not have any family distractions for about a month the staff didn't know it but they were about to be exorcised or said another way, I was going to work them to death.

On Monday morning I had an 0700 appointment to see the division commander. I arrived fifteen minutes early and he was already at work. He again welcomed me and expressed his delight in my being in the division and alluded to the fact that he was glad that I would be bringing some pentagon skill and diversity to the command. He did not only mean racial diversity, I was bringing a new way of thinking with me. The 9th Infantry Division was unique in that it was about as far away from the pentagon as you could get without leaving the lower forty-eight states. It had developed a culture of its own. In my opinion, Fort Lewis is the most beautiful of all of the U.S. Army military installations in the continental United States. Because of the climate it almost never snows and it does not become unbearably hot in the summer. During the month of June, Mount Rainer can be seen from the post. General Cavazos talked about all of the beauty of the post and what his vision of the future of the installation was at that time. He concluded by telling me a story of a previous battalion commander who had conducted a Dining In for his unit at the secluded officer's Little Club over on the lake. It appears that the battalion officers were in formal dress uniforms and prepared for the party of their lives. Someone invited a strip tease dancer from one of the strip clubs downtown and she put on a show for them. Afterwards, apparently some of the bachelors decided to have sex with the woman in plain view of the others. After a while several of the married officers decided to partake of the offerings and a line formed. The two African American noncommissioned officers who were bartending that evening decided that they wanted a piece of the action and also got in line. This upset some of the white officers and they began to utter racial slurs at the bartenders and degrade them. The black bartenders became angry and walked away. Unknown to the battalion officers, they called the military police (MP). When the MP's arrived they found several officers with their pants off, the woman completely naked, and the battalion commander passed out drunk. According to MG Cavazos, the incident was reported to him at about 0600 in the morning and he officially relieved the lieutenant colonel from command at 0615. His final words to me were: "While you are in command here you will not conduct a Dining In. Is that clear?" I said "yes sir." It was my turn to speak and I expressed my gratitude and told him how glad I was to be there and thanked him for his candor. I left his office in awe! It was about 0730 on the morning of 04 June, 1979. It was time to go to work.

What General Cavazos did not tell me was that there was a Fort Lewis clique. It consisted of a closed group of officers and noncommissioned officers who had been around the Fort Lewis area for three or more years. They were very protective of each other and they were also reluctant to take in new members. As I looked around the First Brigade I made a quick assessment and some fast judgments. My immediate competition was LTC Bill Powell who commanded the 1st Battalion, 39th Infantry (Bar None). LTC Powell was a typical hard-charging officer who had a solution for every problem, a comment for every situation, and an aloof strut most of the time. At the time I met him he was a "short-timer" in the brigade, already selected to command the 2nd Ranger Battalion up the street from 2-39 Infantry. The Ranger Battalion was being commanded at that time by Lieutenant Colonel Wayne Downing. Ranger Battalion commanders were normally in their second battalion command having proved themselves worthy in their first command. Unfortunately, Powell was killed during a training exercise while commanding the Rangers. He was a nice guy and cordial but he offered me little help. His replacement in the Bar None Battalion was Lieutenant Colonel Ward Lutz. Ward was one the nicest and straightest gentlemen I ever met. He, like me was brand new to the division, therefore considered an outsider. The other battalion commander in the brigade was Lieutenant Colonel George Kirschenbauer. George commanded the 2nd Battalion, 1st Infantry. He was a quiet and reserved West Point graduate who had been around Fort Lewis for a long time and was part of the clique. He was a nice guy and cordial but offered no help. About my third day in command Lieutenant Colonel Donald Scott, a Lincoln University, Missouri graduate came by my command and offered help.

LTC Scott was also a member of the clique at Fort Lewis. He had been there for a while and was a consciously close friend of BG Andy Chambers. BG Chambers was close to MG

Cavazos and therefore everyone assumed that LTC Scott was close to MG Cavazos. He may have been but he never expressed it to me. Don showed me his training charts and briefed me on how he kept track of the post/installation cycles of training and support. There were three installation cycles at Fort Lewis. They were: post support, post training support and post training. They were approximately three months long and technically you were in the different cycles four times a year. When your battalion was in the support cycle you received all of the normal post details such as, post police, funeral details, parades, and off-post support trips. A typical mission during the training support cycle was aggressor detail for a unit that was undergoing an ARTEP. I always used that cycle to augment my training plans. When a unit was in the training cycle they were untouchable for any of the support or training support missions. You simply did training. If you managed those cycles well as a commander, you would ultimately command a good unit. Don Scott showed me how he did it. Of course I took examples back to my guys and CPT Mike Tesdahl and I sat down and made it fit our unit. From that point on we were tough to beat for training. I will be forever grateful to Don Scott for his friendship during my early days at Fort Lewis. Don went on to become a general officer. I used to tell him all of the time, “Boy, you’re gonna be one!”

Prior to my arrival, the 2-39 Infantry weekly training meeting was conducted at 1300 in the commander’s conference room every Friday. I saw no reason to change the time or the location. In this meeting each subordinate commander would brief me on what they had accomplished during the current week—a sort of after action review. Next they would go over their plans and activities for the coming week. I would ask how I could assist them, if appropriate. Finally, they briefed their plans for the next six weeks. The real value of this meeting was that every leader in the battalion had a chance to see what each other was doing. The first week that I was in command, LTC Jim Burns, the new Division G-3 and former Falcon Battalion commander, showed up for the meeting. Because he was a guest from the Division

Headquarters I was cordial and allowed him to interrupt and clarify some of the things that the company commanders were telling me. The second week in command, at about five minutes before meeting time he drove up for the meeting again. I met him about half way up the 2-39 Infantry Headquarters walkway and asked him if I could help him. He told me he was down again to attend my training meeting. My answer, paraphrased here, was very crisp. "Please feel free to visit the battalion anytime that you have time. However, the training meeting is mine and if I feel the need for you to attend I'll send you an invitation." He turned and left and he never came back to the battalion the entire time while I was in command. Jim came to visit me later in my career in Bangkok, Thailand. Upon his return to duty in Korea, he sent me a very nice wall plaque with the Falcon Battalion brand and logo that is hanging in my home today.

As I alluded to earlier we (my battalion staff and company commanders) were on tap to conduct an evaluation of an ARTEP for one of the second brigade's battalion commanders during my first week of command. The evaluated commander had been in command for approximately six months and this would be his opportunity to test the results of his training since he assumed command. During an 18 month command tour there were a finite number of things that a commander was expected to do well. One of them was to have a successful ARTEP. I had extensive experience with the evaluations while I was an executive officer in the 3-187 Infantry back in the 101st Airborne Division. During that time the scores were: satisfactory, fail, or sometimes a marginal satisfactory. A rating that was instituted in the 101st Airborne Division, by the Assistant Division Commander for Operations, BG John Brandenburg. If the unit failed the ARTEP they had to be reevaluated within six months. However, failure was simply not an option. The rules were essentially the same at the 9th Infantry Division with the exception of how the marginal satisfactory results were awarded. What I did not know was that there was a collegial relationship among the Fort Lewis Infantry battalion commanders that unofficially required the evaluator to grant a pass for almost every major event and pick one minor event to report as a failure or a marginal satisfactory. No one told me about this arrangement! I went about this task as I had tackled every task since Dr. Lorna Kemp failed me on my college comprehensive examination at West Virginia State College in 1962. I did it to the best of my ability and by the book. The evaluated battalion commander failed two events and I awarded him a failing score on both. He was a West Point graduate, a gentleman, and he never disputed my decision. When the ARTEP was over our team was given the opportunity to compile our notes and make a formal presentation to the entire evaluated battalion in the post theater about a week after the evaluation. My preliminary evaluation to the Office of the ACofS, G3 (LTC Burns) indicated that the battalion had failed two events. The major events of the ARTEP were rather standard. The ARTEP normally began with a movement to contact that included a forced road march and an attack on some intermediate objectives. Upon securing one of the intermediate objectives, the unit was required to go into a defensive posture. Normally a unit was allotted twenty-four hours to set up the defense. The time period usually ended at Before Morning Nautical Twilight (BMNT) with a morning or early afternoon visit by the Division Commander. General Cavazos was the best general that I have ever seen at this kind of visit. He climbed into bunkers, get down and checked fields of fire and talked to soldiers about how they set up their position. After the defense, the evaluated unit started an approach march to attack a coordinated objective during daylight hours followed by a night attack in the early evening, just after End of Evening Nautical Twilight (EENT). Upon hearing that I had failed the unit on two events, I received visits from other commanders including Don Scott and they were all very careful not to ask me to change my evaluation but they were also very vociferous about the collegial atmosphere that existed in the "Old Reliables." I listened to them and I stuck to my decision. I was not about to have my staff think that I would bow to pressure after we had worked so hard as a team. Because like it or not, from my point of view, that was a teambuilding exercise for me and my staff more than it was an evaluation for that battalion commander. They had their agenda and I had mine. Captain Mike Tesdahl, Major Art Ballin, and all of the other 239 Infantry staff members were evaluating me and I was evaluating them.

When we arrived at the post theatre for the final critique and description of the evaluation, the Division Commander, MG Cavazos, met me outside and said, "Steve, I am going to support your evaluation of that battalion." That let me know that someone had discussed it with him. However, his comments were heartwarming for me because he let me know that he respected my judgment. MG Cavazos opened the evaluation with one of the most stirring speeches that I had ever heard from a general officer. He made the troops laugh and he laughed with them. He told war stories about soldiering that held them spellbound. He made them cry and he cried with them. I was mesmerized. That speech went into my mental notebook for further refinement and use. I did not realize until that day but the ARTEP was really about rallying the troops. To hell with the battalion commander's ego! To hell with the battalion commander's evaluation! To hell with the unit's pass or fail! The officers and NCO's went about that three day field exercise without going to sleep as if it were exam week at some university. I left that theatre saying to myself, "It is not about me. It is about them...the troops!" I believe that was the day that I decided that I was not necessarily in competition with Lieutenant Colonels Lutz and Kirschenbauer. I was in competition with myself. From that point on I was determined to do what was right for the soldiers of the Falcon Battalion. From that episode in the theatre I went back to my battalion headquarters and designed a "transition model" week for my officers to get to know me better. For this event I arranged for us to meet at the officers' club at McChord Air Force Base. We rented meeting space for three days. We met there at 0730 in the morning, and left at 1600 in the afternoon. I left the battalion in the able hands of the noncommissioned officers. The officers and I discussed operations and training, logistics, personnel matters, and every other thing that needed to be discussed. When we left there after three days that unit's officer cadre was well on its way to becoming cohesive. Next, I asked the CSM to arrange a meeting for me with the noncommissioned officers. He arranged the meeting at the Fort Lewis Rod and Gun Club. I arrived at 1300 hours to find that they had been there since about 1100 and had drunk beer for their lunch. There were at least two who were well on their way to becoming totally inebriated and there were at least two others who were either retired or on leave from another battalion who wanted to get in my face. I was cool. They had a table and chair in the front of the room at which they wanted me to sit. They also had a bottle of beer on the table. The CSM briefly introduced me and I sat down. I spoke about leadership and responsibility for about ten minutes and asked if they had questions. There were none. During the presentation I was all business. I cracked no jokes, made no slurs and did not discuss my family. I ended the remarks with giving them my marital status, telling them I had three children, and giving them my shirt size. My final words were; "That's all you need to know about me." They were stunned. I didn't touch the beer and I got up and left. By the way, when he returned to the battalion, I asked the Command Sergeant Major to think about retiring. He put in his papers the next week. I found out later from First Sergeant Cowan, the battalion's noncommissioned officers were in total shock. They came away from that meeting knowing that they were going to have to perform or find a new place to work. Their primary duty at that stage of the Army was to keep a *Job Book* on each soldier. The job book concept was one to the most controversial things that we ever did in the Army. In my opinion, there were some good points to the concept but for the most part it was a mistake.

When the Command Sergeant Major departed I was told that I would not get a replacement immediately. That did not bother me because I had already figured out who was the ranking First Sergeant in the battalion. I called him to my headquarters and appointed him a Sergeant Major (SM) I could not call him a command sergeant major but he was mine and my troops' sergeant major. He was First Sergeant Cowan. He did an outstanding job and retired from the Army years later as a command sergeant major. On one occasion in the field he was with me at supper time and I had the normal bevy of staff officers around and we were eating the evening meal. I always removed my helmet when I ate meals no matter if I was inside or outside. Sergeant Major Cowan walked up and said' Sir are we tactical here in the field?" I answered: "Yes we are sergeant major." His reply was: Well you officers need to get tactical and put your helmets on like the rest of the troops." I immediately put on my helmet and so did the other officers. I finished my meal and said to him; "Let's take a walk." Everyone knew by the tone of my voice that I was ticked off. I told Cowan, words to the affect, "If you won't embarrass me in public I'll never embarrass you. What you did was embarrassing. If you ever pull another stunt like that I will chew your ass out in public." He never embarrassed me again. He was outstanding as an advocate for the troops, an administrator, and a gentleman. I can say unequivocally, he was one of the best troop sergeants major I have ever known. Eventually, I was sent a CSM by the Brigade headquarters. The new guy had his heart in the right place but his head was in the wrong place. I kept him for a few months and tried to make something of our relationship but it didn't work out. He was evidently an affirmative action pick to meet a quota. I let him go. Then I was sent a system designated command sergeant major that was branch Military Police Corps. I knew what the Army was trying to do so I took him and commenced teaching him how to become an Infantryman. He worked out fine.

Commanding a battalion was the best job that I had at that point in my career. I was in charge and I took charge! I was in charge of approximately 627 soldiers, responsible for the well being of the families of the married guys, and often judge, jury and executioner for those who broke the rules. In that regard, one of the most effective tools that I used was my ability to memorize the opening statement of the non-judicial punishment proceedings. I would show the soldier to whom I was administering justice a copy of the opening statement and ask him to follow along as I looked them in the eye and recited it, verbatim. I also memorized the oath of reenlistment. While I was in command, the battalion only received first place for post reenlistment a couple of times, but we were second within the division fourteen months in a row. I would call undecided soldiers in and ask them if I could call their parents. While they sat in my office I would call their parents and ask if they objected to their son reenlisting. That was a very effective tool that I had learned from Colonel Tiger Honeycutt. Often times I would have to sweeten the pot while a parent was on the telephone with something like "Your son wants to go to dental assistant school. I do not have any seats for that military specialty at the moment but I can offer him dental technician school instead if he will commit for an additional two years. I am going to leave the room and let you two talk this out and visit." I would leave and wait until the soldier opened the door. Most of the time, it worked. I want to point out that I only did that for exceptional soldiers. I would not repeat, would not, reenlist anyone with a record of unauthorized absences and/ or frequent violations of the rules and regulations, a history of debt, or one who told me up front that he was reenlisting for the bonus money. If I had reenlisted everyone in that group we probably could have been number one several months. Colonel Joe Palastra had taught me not to reenlist poor performers. I think I was a good administrator, a fair disciplinarian, and a friend to good soldiers and their families. During my meeting with the battalion members, every month, in the theater across the street from my headquarters I encouraged them to bring their spouses and children.

After six months in command we took our battalion ARTEP and we were evaluated by LTC Hugh Shelton. Shelton went on to become Chairman of the Joint Chiefs of Staff. He failed me in two events during the ARTEP. I accepted his evaluation without question although I did not necessarily agree with it. For me it was the quid pro quo that I had begun when I evaluated one of his fellow battalion commanders in his brigade. Just before my evaluation, both General Cavazos and Colonel Jarrett left the Division. When Colonel Jarrett and his wife Karen left the brigade and they were replaced by Colonel Joe Quinn and his wife Marilyn. I had no memorable bad times with either of the brigade commanders or their spouses. They were good and faithful military families and the Army was a great place for me to work at that time. I do remember that Karen Jarrett was the first person to ask us to attend an Episcopal Church service. Both COL Jarrett and the Assistant Division Commander, BG Edward Trobaugh, provided lukewarm comments for my performance rating. However, MG Cavazos intervened with a separate endorsement that I am sure helped push me over the top for early promotion to full Colonel. He did not have to do that and I will be forever grateful that he thought that much of me. I saw COL Jarrett in the pentagon after I was promoted to Brigadier General and en route to Thailand. I was cordial to him and he reciprocated.

General Cavazos was replaced by MG Howard Stone. Howie and Helen, his spouse, became friends with me and Olivia. He was completely supportive of me while I was in command and extended me, along with Hugh Shelton to twenty-four months in command. I do not know if we were the first commanders in the Army to be extended but we were the first at Fort Lewis. Colonel Joseph Quinn was a breath of fresh air for the First Brigade. He was low key, mild mannered and friendly with everyone. Jarrett had been flamboyant, somewhat arrogant, and he displayed what he called "élan" whenever possible. I welcomed the opportunity to work with COL Joe Quinn. Of course by the time he arrived I was a seasoned battalion commander that, for the most part, was capable of calling my own shots. I normally led the brigade in all of the rated categories and my guys and I certainly knew how to capture the spotlight for any minor accomplishment. On the down side, I lost my executive officer, MAJ Art Ballin to an Army reduction in force action. Art was my right arm and I knew that he would be difficult to replace. However, the Army sent me another very capable executive officer in Major Bruce Braun. That's when I realized that if you take the time you can train an officer replacement to be as good as or even better than the person that they replaced. Also during the first year Mike Tesdahl was promoted to Major and changed permanent stations. He was replaced by Major David Hammond.

The highlight of my command tour came when instead of being sent to the National Training Center at Fort Erwin, California, for training, I was allowed to take the 2-39 Infantry to the U.S. Marine Corp Amphibious Warfare Center at Coronado Beach, CA. As a group we were elated. We deployed as if we were going to war on a complete load-out by aircraft, landed in Miramar Naval Air Station, California, and mounted buses to Naval Amphibious Base (NAB) Coronado, San Diego CA. We dismounted the buses at NAB Coronado at about 1700 hours on a Friday evening and we immediately required everyone to get settled. I addressed the troops at about 2000 hours and laid down the ground rules for the entire trip. The bottom line was I did not want anyone getting hurt and I wanted to return to Fort Lewis with everyone with whom I left. Early the next morning, around 0630 we started our morning run with a Jodie cadence. I had learned this technique while I was in the 101st Airborne Division. When you go to a strange post get up early and wake up everybody for miles around! Let 'em know that the "best damn outfit in the world" has arrived. When we returned from the run, I had an expected message to see the Marine Corps Colonel who commanded the Amphibious Training Center. He initially attempted to chew me out for the noise we were making but ended up smiling, saying that it made him "feel good" to see such a spirited outfit down to visit them. I smiled and thanked him and told him that they would only have to endure us for about fourteen days. He told me that my next appointment was with a Navy Commander who was the local base commander and that he may not be as friendly. I asked the

Colonel to tell me what the guys rank was again, he laughed out loud and said "Commander." We both knew that I was not about to back down from a Navy person of the same rank. The Navy guy was cordial and asked that I keep my troops in tow. I assured him that I would. Little did I know that there had already been trouble in the chow line that morning, while I was in to see the Marine Corp Colonel. We spent the rest of the day getting settled in and preparing for the beginning of the amphibious warfare course to start the next day. We had a lot of fun doing that training. The officers were separated from the enlisted men and so it turned out to be another team building exercise. One of the noncommissioned officers had a relative, his wife's brother, to come and get him over the weekend that we had off down there. On Monday morning, he was reported absent without leave (AWOL). I was not upset or worried but called his wife back at Fort Lewis and asked her if she had heard from him. About an hour later he showed up. He was scared to death that I was going "bust" him. Instead, I told him to call home his wife was worried about him. He was still telling that story ten years later when I saw him at a conference at Fort Benning, GA. The fact that he had to call home and explain his actions to his wife was a helluva lot worse than any butt chewing or non-judicial punishment I could have given him. Part of our trip involved three days at USMC Camp Pendleton Training Center, California, where we had a beach assault that began on a Navy ship 1400 meters out in the ocean and culminated with a live-fire exercise at the reservation. We returned to Fort Lewis with everyone except one guy who was sent to the hospital. That was a great exercise for us and from that point everything was really downhill until I relinquished command. Except during my last week of command, some of my troops went swimming on a Sunday afternoon in one of the lakes at Fort Lewis and one of them drowned. That was by far my worst day at Fort Lewis Washington during that tour.

During the battalion command tour at Fort Lewis, the Chief of Staff of the Army took a real interest in training troops to perform well at battalion level. In fact, the Army called on Retired Lieutenant General Arthur Collins to visit selected Infantry battalions and evaluate their training. He came to visit my battalion and stayed with me for almost a whole day. I never saw any results but I knew that he was impressed. The Falcon Battalion was a top notch training outfit and I knew it. If we could not "dazzle them with brilliance we would baffle them with bullshit." I had learned in the 101st Airborne Division that impressing visitors was more art than science and I knew how to be artful.

We met some really nice people during that assignment. One of the life long friendships that we established was LTC (Ret) John and Glenda Malloy. Both of them are deceased at this writing but they will remain always as two of our closest and dearest friends. They felt it was their duty to take care of the African American leaders that were assigned to Fort Lewis at that time. I should point out that selecting black officers to command Battalions and Brigades was not a routine matter in those days. However, during the time that I commanded the 2-39 Infantry there were six other black lieutenant colonels in command positions at Fort Lewis. They were LTC Donald Scott who commanded an Infantry battalion; LTC Jerry Fields who commanded the Division's Medical battalion; LTC Johnnie Wilson who commanded the Division's Ordnance Battalion and toward the end of my tour LTC David Foye took command of one of the Infantry battalions in the brigade in which I was serving. LTC James Monroe commanded the Division Maintenance Management Center (DMMC) which was a battalion equivalent command appointment. There was another black lieutenant colonel in charge of patient administration at Madigan Army Hospital, a position that was equivalent to battalion command. Just before I left Fort Lewis, Brigadier General (Doctor) Guthrie Turner, an African American assumed command of Madigan Army Hospital. We occasionally met as a group and swapped lies, ate barbeque and drank Scotch Whiskey and Dram Buie (Rusty Nail) at John Malloy's house.

John was fond of saying "What goes on here stays here. You can always feel safe to relax in our home." He meant every word of it and all of us took advantage of his and Glenda's hospitality.

At the end of my tour, I wanted to stay at Fort Lewis. I asked the Division Chief of Staff, Colonel Joe Felter if he would appoint me as the ACof S, G1. He tagged me along for weeks and finally said no. I then called Brigadier General Colin Powell and asked him if he would bring me back to the pentagon. He told me to send him a civilian type resume and he would see what he could do. I sent it to him but did not hear anything. I called LTC John Mackey whom I had sponsored to DCSPER earlier and who now worked in the DCSPER's front office as one of the executive officers, and asked him to get me back in the building. Although he was four years younger, John and I were childhood friends. We attended the same church in War, WV. In fact, his mother and my mother were as close as sisters. His father was my high school football coach and John was my brother's roommate during his first year of college. John brought me back to the building as a bona fide Branch Chief in DCSPER. I went to work back in the Leadership Division. This time I worked for Colonel Robert Carroll, a 1962 year group contemporary who had gotten an early promotion to Colonel. During this assignment, I was a real rarity in the building at that time. I was an ex-battalion commander with Army General Staff and Joint Chiefs of Staff experience.

My son, Bob, graduated from Lakes High School about a week before we left Fort Lewis. He received an appointment to the United States Army Military Academy Prep School. Stephanie, my oldest daughter was a rising senior and would have to move for her senior year. That was one reason why I had groveled and asked the Division Chief of Staff if I could stay at Fort Lewis. Stephanie also owned a couple of Washington state track records for the women's low hurdles. She could fly on the track! I knew that she would get scholarships from all over the western part of the United States for track. Little did I know that she wanted the family to move back to Lake Ridge, VA, so she could attend Woodbridge High School her senior year. She told me that one afternoon just before I called John Mackey and pleaded with him to get me back to the pentagon. We still owned our house in Lake Ridge and only had to serve notice to the folks who were renting from us at the time. I did not think that moving was a wise decision but I did not want to disappoint my daughter. Plus it meant that I could tell COL Joe Felter to kiss off. It would also put us closer to Bob who would be attending the West Point Prep School at Fort Monmouth, NJ. We moved back to Northern Virginia in June 1981.

I must tell one last Fort Lewis story. The Army Chief of Staff scheduled a visit to the 9th Infantry Division to assess small unit readiness. The idea was to have an Infantry platoon complete a force march, assemble in an attack position, and vigorously assault a platoon size objective shooting on a live fire range. Almost invariably these visits took place on Monday morning which meant that the ammunition had to be drawn on Friday afternoon and it had to be stored and secured over the weekend. This was because the civilians that ran the ammunition distribution point were too lazy to come to work early on Monday morning. During a previous VIP visit one of the units did not secure the ammunition on Friday and the soldiers assaulted the targets saying “Pow, Pow, Pow.” Well BG Lincoln Jones, the ADC for Operations, told me that he wanted a real show for the Army Chief of Staff and most of all he wanted the division’s soldiers to look good. I selected LT Nolan Bivens’ company and gave them instructions. March a rifle platoon in the force march into the attack position. Have another platoon ready in the attack position with the proper camouflage, protective masks and live ammunition to come up out of the attack position screaming, shouting and firing like madmen. I also supplemented the sounds with an excessive number gas operated machine gun simulation apparatuses and trip flare operated smoke grenades. It was fabulous! I had learned how to put on a show in the 101st Airborne Division. Needless to say all of the generals were elated at the soldiers’ performance.

THE RETURN TO WASHINGTON, DC

We drove across the United States in two cars. Olivia, Bob and Christa were in the Oldsmobile station wagon and Stephanie and I were in the Datsun 280Z. We had CB radios in both cars and communicated with each other at all times. That was a great trip for us as a family. Our first stop was at Mountain Home Air Force Base in Idaho. There was not much to Mountain Home Air Base so we went to bed and left early the next morning. We headed for the Great Salt Lake City area and visited the Mormon tabernacle. We spent that night at Dugway Proving Grounds. That was a real adventure because Dugway appeared on the map to be eighty miles from everything else in the world. We decided that it was probably not at the end of the world but you could see the end from Dugway. Our kids had a ball there that night. The fitness center was open all night and Bob and Stephanie were out very late. Because Christa was about six years younger than Stephanie she had to turn in earlier. We left after a late breakfast at the community club and headed for Denver, CO. The trip over the Rockies was unforgettable. The old station wagon almost conked out at the 14,000 feet mark. The old wagon was kicking and coughing, with Bob driving, and Olivia on the CB radio. Stephanie was reading The Book of Mormon. After we cleared the top of the Rockies and started down the other side, the old Datsun 280Z started acting up. We nursed both cars into Lowry Air Force Base at about six o'clock in the evening. We rented a guest cottage and decided that we had to get the 280Z fixed before we could travel further. The trouble was in one of the levers on the steering column. It not only controlled the turn signals but also the headlights. We had to wait a day for parts to be brought in so we took off for the U.S. Air Force Academy in Colorado Springs. Stephanie was impressed and expressed an interest in attending there. Bob had already received an appointment to the USMA Prep School. We had a great day there and they provided us with a guided tour. What a lovely campus. After Denver we headed into Kansas and stopped at the VIP Guest House at Fort Riley, KS. After a good night's rest in the VIP quarters, we let Olivia sleep in and the kids and I went to breakfast in the executive dining room of the VIP guest house. That was a great experience for Christa. The sergeant who ran the place kept referring to her as Ma'am and it always cracked her up. She was 10 years old. We brought some breakfast back to the room for Olivia and we left for Kansas City, KS, at mid-morning. We made a detour to Fort Leavenworth, KS, to visit with George and Karen Kirschenbauer, our former neighbors at Fort Lewis, and continued east until we reached Scott Air Force Base, Illinois. We spent an uneventful night there and headed for southern West Virginia the next day where we would spend some time with Olivia's parents in Bishop, VA.

We left Bishop and moved back into our home in Lake Ridge. Nothing had changed except we had some new neighbors. The Fetzer's, our next door neighbors were reassigned to Hawaii and had rented their house to a young couple. We very quickly got back into a routine that had been sort of standard for us, i.e., I worked at the pentagon, Olivia taught at one of the elementary schools and the children attended the local public schools. Bob was off to the West Point Prep School in July and Stephanie decided that she would not run track for those women who had mistreated her on the track team, before we left for Fort Lewis. I went back to the old office in the Leadership Division where Lois Stevens was now serving as the Division Chief's Clerk. She was in charge. I was proud of her.

The Leadership Division had changed a lot in the three years that I was away. I had spent a year in JCS and two years at Fort Lewis before returning. However, there were still reports and papers in the files that had my signature on them. This time though I was the Branch Chief for the Leadership Branch. I had a gaggle of guys working for me who for the most part were very smart officers but they had not spent much time in the trenches. On the day I arrived, the three star DCSPER billet also changed, and LTG Maxwell Thurman became the DCSPER. Max, as he was called, was a person that some people called the smartest general in the Army. I will grant that he was smart but I would rather call him the hardest working general that I ever saw. He was in at about eight o'clock in the morning and he left with a brief case full of work at about seven o'clock at night. When he traveled he carried two brief cases of work. He also worked a normal eight hour day on Saturday. However, he would not start work on Sunday before 1300 hours because he wanted to allow people the opportunity to go to church. A favorite ploy of his was to tell an ACTO late Friday afternoon to "Brief me again tomorrow at 0900." If you waited until nine o'clock to show up you would not get in before noon because he would have told at least four or five other ACTOs the same thing and you had to get in the cue in the order that you arrived. In an earlier assignment he had been in charge of the planning and budgeting process for the entire Army. He was a "numbers guy" and he really wanted everyone else to be numbers guys. Late one evening while I was briefing him he stopped me abruptly and said: "Are you a numbers guy?" I did not answer him directly. I said to him, "I am a leader, sir." I kept on briefing him and he never questioned me about that again.

What I remember most about that year was all of the false starts that we had as a group on leadership items that Max Thurman rejected. We thrashed around like a bunch of rookies trying to find the proper words for him to say in a speech or write in a paper. Aside from Lois Stevens my best friend at work was LTC Bill Bollen. He was also an ex-battalion commander, branch artillery. He was pretty good on the computer and had a pleasant personality. One afternoon LTG Thurman said that he thought that the Army Alcohol and Drug Abuse Regulation,

AR600-85 was too long. Bill Bolen and I went up stairs and got a copy of the Air Force's regulation on alcohol and drug abuse and came in early on a Saturday morning, worked all day and rewrote the Army's Regulation in one sitting. We cut it from about 200 pages to less than 20 pages. We sent it forward and Max paid us a visit with the draft in hand and praised us in front of everyone. We passed it to the ADAPCP staff and they stalled it with technicalities. Another time I was on a briefing team that was preparing a briefing for Max to deliver to a joint meeting of the Secretary of the Army and the Chief of Staff of the Army to be delivered in the Secretary of the Army Conference Room. After what appeared to be weeks of preparation, we started the final process at about six in the evening in the DCSPER's Conference Room on the C Ring. LTG Thurman came in and announced: "We're all naked here, so state your piece freely." He really meant it. He appeared to listen to everyone no matter what their rank. That was a valuable lesson for me. Remember this was well before briefings were regularly given in power point. In those days illustrating your point in caricature was very popular at the pentagon. It was so popular that I found a soldier who could sketch what I was saying as I spoke. I kept him in our office to illustrate our thoughts as we articulated them. He was so good that I got him reassigned from Fort Myer to the pentagon, secured quarters for his family at Fort Belvoir, VA, and had him literally on call twenty-four, seven (24/7) to come to the pentagon any time we needed him. Max would start talking and I would think of how to illustrate what he was saying and the soldier could draw it. COL Robert Carroll, the leadership division chief, and others, COL Don Phillips, LTC Robert Burns, and a civilian named Tom Johnson, fancied themselves as the thinkers and they would come up with concepts that they thought Max would like. As a group we called ourselves "the skunk works." On the day before a briefing we would get a speaking piece to a certain point and it would be time to rehearse. We would go to the DCSPER conference room and invite so called subject matter experts from all over the Army to vet the results. At about seven o'clock in the evening we would really get serious and work until around midnight and go home shower and change clothes and head back to the pentagon because Max would want to rehearse again at about six in the morning. Rehearsals even included how LTG Thurman was going to make the gestures during his presentation. We would determine if he was going to point up in the air or down at the floor to make his point. If the briefing was scheduled for 0800 we would still be changing slides at 0755. Again, this was of course before the days of power point presentations and so you had to make the slides at the audio visual support area on the first floor of the 10th corridor. That meant that one would leave the briefing area in corridor six and a half, run downstairs and across the inner court and into corridor ten make a new slide and get it back to the briefing room and slip it in so that the briefing sequence was not interrupted. I was good at getting this done and Max appreciated it. Now with computers and power point all of that seems ridiculous but it took skill and tenacity to get this done back in the day.

During the course of working at the pentagon that year, the War College Selection List was posted and the Colonel Promotion List was also posted. All lists for promotion and schooling were posted in the seventh corridor on the DCSPER Bulletin Board. Everyone knew about a day in advance when the lists would be posted. I was not really concerned because I was confident that I would be selected for the war college. I was selected. What I did not sense was that I would be selected for Colonel, early. Promotion lists are categorized as zones. The zones correspond to dates on a calendar. The primary zone is where the bulk of promotions for any grade will come. A few people will be selected from above the primary zone which usually means they were selected during or after a second look by the selection board. The real prize is to be selected for promotion below the primary zone which means that you are selected early and on your way to higher success in the military business. To my great surprise I was on the Colonel promotion list also.

From that point on I was in the fast lane. In fact, that year was over before it started. There are five senior service colleges within the military education system for senior officers. They are the Army War College in Carlyle, Barracks, PA, the Air War College at Maxwell Air Force Base, AL, the Naval War College at Newport, RI, the Industrial College of the Armed Forces and the National War College both co-located as part of the National Defense University at Fort McNair, Washington DC. I requested to be sent to the National War College (NWC) instead of the Army War College. I submitted the request, in writing, to the DCSPER and LTG Thurman approved it. The reasons for my request were simple enough. First, I was living already in the National Capitol Region so the Army would not have to pay for a family move. Second and more important, the National War College had a twenty percent production rate to flag rank. Finally, although not discussed openly, the word on the grape vine was the twenty percent general production rate climbed to forty percent for minority officers at NWC.

SENIOR SERVICE COLLEGE

The National War College is located on the Potomac River at Fort McNair, DC. Fort McNair is also the headquarters for the Military District of Washington. The edifice that actually houses the National War College was designated as the most beautiful building in America in 1902. I was invited over to tour the NWC by LTC Fred Leigh who was a student at the time. I had helped Fred when he arrived in the 101st Airborne Division back in the mid-seventies and I think he was attempting to return the favor. I went over and made the tour and had lunch with Fred and I left saying to myself how proud I was of my choice to attend senior service school in Washington, DC. There was even a little nine-hole executive golf course available on Fort McNair. This was going to be fun.

I arrived early for the first day of classes at the National War College and found that the pace was going to be very slow. There were a few us who were there early but most of the class would report at the appointed time. One of the early arrivals that I met that morning was LTC Daniel W. Christman. We were placed in class sections, issued our initial materials and told to report back the next day for orientations. At the orientation it was clear that a large portion of the class work would be done in groups. It was also very clear that the nightly readings would be awesome and that you were expected to be able to participate in the discussion groups every day. For the most part we conducted class discussions on Monday, Tuesday and Thursday, had a high powered lecturer on Wednesday and did organized athletics and visits to places like Capitol Hill on Friday. All of this was completed by three o'clock in the afternoon most days and we were on our way home by 4:00 PM. This was great for me and everyone else because we had not had such good working hours since attending Command and General Staff College. The student population was made up of one quarter U.S. Army officers, one quarter U.S. Air Force officers, one quarter U.S. Navy officers including a contingent from the U.S. Marine Corps, and one quarter federal civilians including members of the U.S. Coast Guard.

I was placed in a homeroom section with LTC Wesley Clark who went on to become a four star general and Commander of the North Atlantic Treaty Organization (NATO) and LTC Butch Neal who became a four star general and went on to become the Assistant Commandant of the Marine Corp. Butch Neal was a long distance runner and worked very closely with all members of the class who wanted to train for the next Marine Corp Marathon which was held every fall in Washington, DC. I trained with them and in the final week of training decided that I could not run the race because I was a "smoker." Now I never smoked more than one pack of cigarettes a day but I had smoked for approximately twenty-five years. After all of that work I "chickened out" because I could not kick a very bad habit. I did continue to run with the guys and became very close to a civilian student named Barton House. He was a little short guy like me and we had similar strides. Bart would stay with me and talk until we reentered the main gate at Fort McNair and he would kick in a faster pace and beat me back to the War College. I knew I was in better physical condition than he was but I did not have the ability to finish as fast as he could. One day I decided that the only way to teach this guy a lesson was to leave him downtown. We normally ran from the National War College at Fort McNair down the Washington Mall to the Lincoln Memorial turned and ran back up the Mall to the National War College. After I left him at the Washington Memorial a couple of times he started to finish with me instead of showing off for the bystanders.

I played on the softball, soccer and golf teams for the National War College. We had an annual Field Day (Jim

Thorpe Day) at Carlyle Barracks in the spring where all of the students from all of the senior service schools would congregate with their families for a weekend of sports play and festivities. It was a great weekend. One could easily tell that a large number of the egotistical "Type A" personalities from the U.S. military industrial complex were harnessed in one location. This group included some pretty self-centered civilians too. It was during that weekend that I met Brigadier General Dallas Brown. He was also a graduate of West Virginia State College and a member of Alpha Phi Alpha Fraternity, Inc. I made a point of introducing myself to him and he was very cordial. I explained that I was just traveling from West Virginia State College that weekend after being inducted into the West Virginia State College Military Hall of Fame the preceding day. I'll never forget his response. He said "Are they now taking babies into the Military Hall of Fame?" At first I was upset but decided maybe I was a little young for that kind of honor. I think that even today I am still the youngest person that was ever inducted into the West Virginia State College Military Hall of Fame.

The highlight of my year at the National War College was the annual field trip abroad. There were approximately twelve trips available. Everyone wanted to go to China. I wanted to go to South America because I spoke Spanish and I felt that I would have an opportunity to help with the trip. As it turned out I was called on a great deal to assist because I could speak Spanish. We visited Brazil, Argentina, and Chile, in that order. At each location we were expected to present a gift to our host. Most of the time, the requirement to present the gift was given to me, because of my facility with the language. We had a great time for about fourteen days and bonded as a group. When we returned it was time to write our final papers and move on to greener pastures.

I teamed with a group and we wrote a paper about the Congressional Military Reform Caucus. It was a conscientious group. I remember taking one member, LTC Hugh Shelton, to some congressional offices on Capitol Hill. In particular we visited the offices of Senator Slade Gordon of Washington. These trips to the capitol were all in preparation for writing our paper. We had an Air Force Judge Advocate General officer, LTC Nolan Sklute, in our group and he took control and wrote most of the text. We actually turned in a nice piece of work. Of course it never went anywhere. In fact, I would be hard pressed to find a copy of the paper among the myriad of stuff that I have not unpacked since I retired from the Army more than fifteen years ago. In that work group, we had six officers. At least four of us made general officer including Hugh Shelton who went on to become Chairman of the Joint Chiefs of Staff, the aforementioned Air Force lawyer who became the Judge Advocate General of the Air Force, and a rather glib and articulate Marine Corp officer named Jeffrey Oster and of course, me. Four out of six ain't bad!

While at NWC I worked hard on my personal physical fitness. It seemed that everyone did. The National War College had an affiliation with Dr. Kenneth Cooper and the Cooper Clinic in Dallas, TX, and so all of us worked out almost every day. We always had a lunch break of at least an hour and a half and so one could run five or six miles easily and get back for whatever activity that was scheduled for the afternoon. Most of my running was done with the group that was training for the Marine Corps Marathon. There was a Navy Seal, Captain Ronald Bell, who trained with us that was also a smoker. He ran the marathon. I did not. The race was run on a Sunday morning. I went to the race and as I watched my classmates finish, I became so angry with myself that I almost cried. I watched all of the guys that I had ritualistically trained with every single day go by me and finish a race that I could have also run if I just had the guts to try. Toward the end of the race I stood at the bottom of the hill leading to the Iwo Jima Memorial and watched my former classmates start up the hill to the finish line. I almost became physically ill. The lesson in fortitude, determination, and stamina for me came when a black disabled veteran, double amputee was coming along in a wheel chair. He started up the hill toward the Iwo Jima Memorial and he couldn't make it. He started a second time and he didn't make it. At this point a bunch of us were going out to push and help him up the hill. He waved us off! He turned the wheelchair around and reached down low on the front of the wheels and pulled himself up the hill...backwards. By the time he got to the top of that hill we were all cheering madly and tears were streaming down my face. I resolved right then that I would run the marathon the next year "come hell or high water." Even if I was a smoker I could, at least, have as much self discipline, confidence and courage as a guy with no legs to complete a marathon.

In the realm of road races, a marathon is not to be taken lightly. Webster's II New College Dictionary defines a marathon as "a cross-country footrace of 26 miles, 385 yards or approximately 42 kilometers." That doesn't sound like much in the short term but it is not something that you just go out and do.

I was really embarrassed at school the next day because the runners with whom I had trained were strutting around like bantam roosters and I had failed not only them but I had also failed myself. I continued to train with them though and to their credit they never said a word about me not running the marathon. I knew however, that would never happen to me again. In my lifetime I had failed to go to Ranger School when I had the chance. I had failed to allow my troops to recommend me for a Silver Star instead of a Bronze Star with "V" when I was wounded in Vietnam, and I had failed to run a marathon when I had the chance. The first two I could not fix but the latter I could. I resolved to quit smoking and work at running the marathon the next year. Of course I told Olivia about my disappointment and she went out and bought me a book that had a fourteen week training plan in it. Olivia, my best friend, always believed in doing it by the book. Thank God for her! The timing was about right because the marathon would be run in November the following year and she bought the book as we were coming up on the June Graduation from the War College. In the meantime, I was looking hard for a job in the NCR. I went to see Colonel John Stanford who was one of the

Executive Assistants to the Secretary of Defense (SECDEF). John had been a classmate of mine at CGSC in Leavenworth, Kansas. I thought that he would help me find a job in the pentagon. At this point in my life I wonder if I did not expect too much from others in those days. I always helped friends and classmates when they asked and I guess I just expected everyone to be the same way with me. That was not always the case. Since the SECDEF was out of town that day John Stanford ushered me into the SECDEF's private office and spent the thirty minutes that he had allotted me sitting on nice furniture talking about buying a car for his son. At about the 30 minute mark he glanced at his watch and told me he had to leave for an appointment. I thanked him for seeing me but knew full well that I would not get a recommendation for a job at the Department of Defense (DOD) from him. I also stopped in, one afternoon, to see the Executive Assistant to the Under Secretary of the Army, LTC "Doc" Sawyer. I also thought he would help me. Again, he postured with the importance of his position and I received no words of encouragement. Since I was not able to turn up much in the building I widened the search. I went to see MG Art Holmes who made a phone call and directed me to the Office of the DCSPER for U.S. Material Command, MG Hank Doctor an African American general officer. I got the run around from his executive assistant. In fact, I could not even get in to see him for an interview. Finally, I went by to see Colonel Carle Alton, the African American Garrison Commander at Fort McNair. Colonel Alton, who we called Joe, was friendly and cordial. He was everything that one expected in a full Colonel. He was staid, formal and extremely capable. Joe told me that the Commanding General of the Military District of Washington (MDW) was looking for an Inspector General (IG). He went on to say that he would "carry the water" on this matter and ask the commander if he would interview me for the job. I left him fully confident that I would get an interview with the CG of MDW. I also felt that if I got the interview, the job would be mine.

The Commanding General of the Military District of Washington is de facto the Ceremonial Chief of the National Capitol Region (NCR). He has under his command, among other entities, the 3rd United States Infantry (The Old Guard), and the U.S. Army Band (Pershing's Own). The MDW commander at this particular time was Major General Jerry Curry, an African American. Throughout my career in the military I never worked for a finer gentleman than MG Jerry Curry. He interviewed me and told me during the course of the interview that the job was mine. He was a fair man and he didn't cut any corners in the ethics arena. He was a straight arrow. I met with him once a week and gave him an update on the audits, inspections, and investigations I was doing and he acted decisively in every case. He was a completely no-nonsense leader who read poetry, conducted minor maintenance on his own car, and fancied himself as a historian. He was a great role model for me because I never saw him lose his temper or deliberately mistreat anyone. He was a gentle man!

General Curry promoted me to full colonel on the morning of September 12, 1984. The ceremony was conducted in his office with Olivia and our daughter Christa present. I kept my lieutenant colonel silver oak leaf insignia and passed them to my daughter Stephanie, who was now a cadet at the U.S. Military Academy at West Point, NY. It was a quiet, discrete ceremony with only the immediate staff in attendance. General Curry brought Olivia, Christa and me into his inner office about thirty minutes early and told me, in their presence, how to become a flag officer. We listened and nodded when he asked if we were up to the challenge. He said "If you do what I tell you, three years from now you will be a general." I listened and I came out on the selection list for general rank three years later. Of course I did not pin on the rank insignia for another year or so after that.

According to Ms Helen Camuguay, the secretary to the MDW Inspector General, I was the twenty-eighth officer she would train to do that job. She also announced on the day that I arrived that she would be retiring at the end of that year, so I had a short window of time to learn. It was the middle of June, 1984. Her assistant was an attractive, African American woman named Anne King. These two women gave me a crash course in how to perform the duties of an Inspector General. I learned quickly and we were off to building one of the best outfits in which I have ever been a part. The staff consisted of two lieutenant colonels, a major, three sergeants major and a couple of sergeants first class. Everyone was a seasoned veteran and knew their stuff. Aside from Helen and Anne I had a lot of contact with LTC Ted Bridges, the branch chief for the Complaints Division. The other division was the Inspections and Compliance Division. Sergeant Major "Val" Valentine became a very close friend and associate and he helped me quite a bit with learning about logistics. The IG job was probably the best learning experience that I had in the Army because there was so much with which I had to be proficient. In addition, the application of people skills was never more important any place than in that job. In that regard, I remember a situation where I had received an anonymous tip that a Colonel in the NCR had spent approximately $12,000 on furniture for his office. LTC Bridges went to check it out and came back saying "Boss, you will not believe what this is going to uncover." As it turned out the colonel spent more than $12,000 on office furniture for his entire office suite. He had purchased a desk, a credenza, a conference table with twelve matching chairs and all of the coffee tables and end tables to round out the display all done in some famous trademark motif. He also outfitted his secretary's office with the same designer furniture.

The office suite was absolutely beautiful. When I went to see it the next day, the Colonel announced his retirement and decided to tell me that the real culprit was the Air Force Lieutenant General upstairs. I called the general and asked if I could come and visit and he became defensive and refused to talk to me, initially. The next morning he called and wanted to know if I had time to come and see him. I had the purchase orders on all of the items and I carried them with me. The misappropriation and abuse was atrocious. For example, the drapes in this guy's office suite cost more than $10,000, the carpet was about $3,000 and the leather chairs in front of his desk were also very expensive. That was not the bad news. The real find was the amount the general allegedly spent on "his executive dining room." Since the organization was only a tenant on the MDW property we turned the action over to the IG at the Joint Chiefs of Staff for further investigation.

I continued to train and work on getting ready for the Marine Corps Marathon. When the day came, I was ready. As an office we made a pact to quit smoking as part of my training. About a third of the people on the IG Team smoked. Since I was the person in charge, I took charge and set the example. First I changed some of my habits. I stopped drinking coffee in the morning. I was normally the first person to enter the office every morning and I turned the coffee pot on. It would have been charged with coffee in the filtering unit the night before by one of the staff. I routinely turned on the coffee, opened the Washington Post, stood by the coffee pot until it finished brewing and lit a cigarette. So the first thing I did was to stop drinking coffee. I also stopped smoking in my car and Olivia and my children would not allow me to smoke in the house. At about the same time the DOD made it a violation of regulations to smoke in DOD buildings or vehicles. So, I said to hell with it, I quit! I did very well until we had a visit from an old friend from my company grade years, David Tate and his wife, Arlene. They came in from North Carolina for a weekend visit when we were having our Christmas party for the IG staff at our home. I made it through the whole evening without smoking. Dave was a lawyer and worked in the Office of the General Council at R.J. Reynolds in Winston Salem, NC. He smoked two packs of cigarettes at the same time. He alternated between a regular cigarette and menthol flavored one every time he lit up. He was almost never without a lighted cigarette in his hand. As soon as the guests left I went to Dave and asked for a cigarette. He was more than eager to give me one. I lit it and drew in the smoke so hard it made me dizzy. By the time I had drawn in three drags the end of the cigarette was glowing red for about a half of an inch. I looked at that and became angry immediately at myself. I put it out. I have been cigarette free since then. That was at approximately 2300 hours, on December 4, 1984. All in all my time as an IG was a good two years except when I went to a party at a former high school and college friend's house on 30 December, 1984. I drank too much and wrecked my car on the way home. Thank God I was alone and there were no other vehicles involved. I spent New Year's Eve, 1984 in a hospital room in Fairfax County, Virginia, by myself, which gave me a lot of time to think. I still have the scars that were caused by that accident. The worst ones are the ones in my heart and mind that cannot be seen. I really made a fool of myself that night and I'll never be able to repay Olivia and the children for their support and understanding of that incident.

While I was at MDW we moved the IG office from Fort McNair to Fort Myer so the old office could be renovated and restored. The Military District of Washington is quite a historic place. A quick look at the Fort McNair website revealed the following.

"Fort Lesley J. McNair, on the point of land where the Washington Channel and Anacostia River join in Washington, DC, has been an Army post for more than 200 years, third only to West Point and Carlisle Barracks, Pennsylvania, in length of service. The military reservation was established in 1791 on about 28 acres of what then was called Greenleaf Point. Maj. Pierre C. L'Enfant included it in his plans for "Washington, the Federal City," as a major site for the defense of the capital. An arsenal first occupied the site and defenses were built in 1791.

The fortifications did not halt the invading British in 1814. With the British coming overland toward Bladensburg, MD, Soldiers at the arsenal evacuated north with as much gunpowder as they could carry, hiding the rest in a well as the Redcoats approached from two directions. About 45 British soldiers were killed and wounded from an accidental explosion.

Someone threw a match into the well and "a tremendous explosion ensued," a doctor at the scene reported, "whereby the officers and about 30 of the men were killed and the rest most shockingly mangled." The remaining Soldiers destroyed the arsenal buildings, but the facilities were rebuilt after the war.

Land was purchased north of the arsenal in 1826 for the first federal penitentiary. The conspirators accused of assassinating President Abraham Lincoln was imprisoned there in 1865, and after a trial found them guilty, they were executed there by hanging.

Among them was Mary Surratt, the first woman to be executed under federal orders.

A hospital was built next to the penitentiary in 1857, and Civil War wounded was treated at what then was called the Washington Arsenal. President Lincoln was a frequent visitor to the arsenal, coming to observe ordnance tests on new weaponry. He also attended the funeral for 21 women who on June 17, 1864, were killed by the explosion of a bin of gunpowder in the room in which they were assembling cartridge cases by hand. A spark ignited some fireworks drying outside the building causing the explosion, one of the worst catastrophes to occur in the city of Washington.

The arsenal was closed in 1881, and the post transferred to the Quartermaster Corps. It was known by the name Washington Barracks. A general hospital was located at the post from 1898 until 1909. Maj. Walter Reed worked there and found the area's marshlands an excellent site for his research on malaria. The major died of peritonitis after an appendectomy at the post in 1902. The post dispensary and the visiting officers' quarters now occupy the buildings where Reed worked and died.

About 90 percent of the present buildings on the post's 100 acres were built, reconstructed or remodeled by 1908. With the birth of the Army War College in 1901, Fort McNair became the Army's center for the education and training of senior officers to lead and direct large numbers of troops. Its first classes were held in 1904. The institution was reorganized as the Army-Navy Staff College in 1943 and became the National War College in 1946. The Army Industrial College was founded at Fort McNair in 1924 to prepare officers for high-level posts in Army supply organizations and to study industrial mobilization. It evolved into the Industrial College of the Armed Forces. ICAF and NWC became the National Defense University in 1976.

The post was renamed in 1948 to honor Lt. Gen. Lesley J. McNair, commander of Army Ground Forces during World War II. McNair was headquartered at the post and was killed in Normandy, France, July 25, 1944. Fort McNair has been the headquarters of the U.S. Army Military District of Washington since 1966. Also assigned to the post is Company A, 3rd U.S. Infantry (The Old Guard). This ceremonial company is known as the Commander-in-Chief's Guard. The Soldiers wear colonial uniforms and drill under orders published during the Revolutionary War in Baron Frederick Von Steuben's *Blue Book*."

Moving the IG Office to Fort Myer brought new challenges for the IG Team. However, it did bring the office's services closer to a larger number of soldiers and civilians that were employed by MDW. General Curry relinquished command and was replaced by MG John Ballantyne. General Curry was the second black officer that I reported to directly in my career and so far I was batting a thousand. He was absolutely great as a leader, a mentor and a friend. MG John Ballantyne was a classical cavalry officer. He had attended the U.S. Military Academy and graduated in 1954. He arrived to assume command of MDW in June 1984. He was tall, thin and in superb condition. He had been a gymnast at the Academy and he kept himself in great shape. He was the class leader when we attended the Air Assault course at Fort Belvoir in the summer of 1985. He was a very wise man and I valued his counsel. There were some really sticky situations that happened on his watch and he never lost his cool and guided me to the proper solution in every case.

One of the centers gravity in my life at that time was training for the Marine Corp Marathon. The fourteen week training program that Olivia had purchased for me was perfect. It was a gradual lengthening of the amount of miles one ran a week. Initially one only had to do about three or four miles a day. I was already past that distance just training with the guys at NWC. I did most of the long distance running on Sunday morning before we went to church. I would usually do ten to twelve miles and arrive back home just in time to get dressed and go to church with the family. I would normally fall dead asleep during the service only to feel Olivia's sharp elbow piercing my side. After about three weeks, I increased the number of miles to about fifteen on the weekends. Building endurance is not easy. I found that the best way to do it was not to count miles but rather, count time, i.e., how long could one run without stopping. I decided that I would add a half-hour each week until I got to five hours. I knew that the official counters stopped at six hours but quite frankly, I felt that I could walk the twenty-six miles at that rate. When the time came to run the race I had worked my way up to 20 miles. The training material talked about "hitting the wall at eighteen miles." I wanted to experience going through the wall at least twice before the actual race. I did not at anytime complete twenty-six miles during training. I always stopped short of achieving the actual distance. The other point that should be made here is that running for three or four hours is hard on your feet, your bladder and your head. Just finding a place to take a "leak" becomes problematic while you are running in residential developments. I also changed my eating habits and learned how to "carbo load." What I learned most was that you can push your body far beyond where you think it can go. Finally I ran the actual race in 4 Hours and 32 minutes. That's an average of nine minutes per mile but who was counting. I was 44 years old. I completed the race, showered, changed clothes and went directly to Christa's soccer match that afternoon in Woodbridge, VA. After the soccer game, I went home and slept for about ten hours. Oh, I almost forgot. I lost all of my toe nails the following week. Now, I strutted around MDW like a bantam rooster. It was November 1984.

During the spring of 1985, I received a call from Colonels Division at MILPERCEN. The Chief of Colonels Division, Colonel George Wilkins, III had been a classmate of mine at NWC. When the Army brigade command selection list was published in 1984 seven of us were called into the Commandant's Office at NWC. LTC Hugh Shelton was called in separately and told that he was a primary selectee. The other six of us including LTC Wesley Clark, were called in as a group and told that we were selected as alternates on the U.S. Army Brigade Command Selection List. Normally that meant that if someone serving as a brigade commander committed a serious crime or died you may get a call. I received a call from COL George Wilkins and was told that the Commanding General of U.S. Army South (USARSO), the Army component of the United States Southern Command (USSOUTHCOM) would be giving me a call. George Wilkins and Hugh Shelton were also a part of the special project on the Congressional Military Caucus that I worked on in NWC. About a week later I received the call from MG Fred Werner, Commander of USARSO and the 193d Infantry Brigade (Separate). He informed me that the 193rd Brigade command position was being downgraded to a Colonel /06 Command and that I would be designated as its first Colonel Commander. He also told me that I needed to report for a change of command on or about 01 May 1985. Needless to say I was elated. However, I was about to make my family jump through hoops again. Olivia was teaching in Woodbridge and Christa was a student in middle school. Olivia could break her contract, reluctantly but we would have to take Christa out of school with a month to go before the end of the year. I asked MG Werner if I could report to the command thirty days later. He answered with words to the effect, "If you want this command you'll come in April." The implication was that if I did not come then that they might give it to someone else. I got the hint loud and clear and so we made plans to move. I really hated to pull Christa away from school. She was the only child that we had at home at that time. However, our other children would also be affected Bob was attending West Virginia State College in Institute, WV, and Stephanie was a "Cow" at the United States Military Academy at West Point, NY. We made the decision to go and I started going to the pre-command courses and Olivia started packing. We shipped the car and the household goods and took off for USARSO in the Republic of Panama in late April 1985.

RETURN TO PANAMA

Upon arrival at Tocumen International Airport, the commercial airport in Panama City, we were met by Lieutenant Colonel Larry Gregg, the Task Force Bayonet Executive Officer. My arrival in Panama this time was in sharp contrast to my first assignment back in 1965. At that time I landed at Howard Air Force Base on the Pacific side of the canal and was met by a sergeant from the 8th Special Forces Group. Since it was late in the afternoon we were taken to a barracks on Howard, AFB and given a bunk bed for the night. The next morning we were taken to the Balboa Train Station and put on a train. We rode the train to the Colon Train Station on the Atlantic side of the Isthmus. We were loaded onto and transported by a pickup truck to Fort Gulick, Canal Zone, home of the 8th Special Action Force (SAF). This time, twenty years later, Olivia, Christa and I were met at Tocumen International, and put in a chauffeur driven military staff car. Our bags were loaded onto a pickup truck that followed us to the Guest House at Fort Amador, Republic of Panama (RP). LTC Gregg and his wife, Sharon, attempted to make us as comfortable as we could possibly get living in a military guest house. We stayed there approximately three days and subsequently moved into our command designated quarters. Our household goods were already in Panama when we arrived and all we had to do was unpack. We moved into Quarters Number 37 that faced Hole number 3, on the golf course in front of the house and out of the back door was the tee box for Hole number 15. The Pacific Ocean was about 100 yards away and visible from the front of the house. The quarters were approximately five thousand square feet and were also equipped with live-in quarters for a maid. The previous occupants were Colonel and Ms. "Rock" Hudson, the officer I was replacing. What I was not told before I arrived in Panama by MG Werner was the 193rd Infantry Brigade had not changed over to a bona fide Colonel command and that the Commanding General was the currently designated commander of the 193rd Brigade and I would command an Infantry unit within the brigade that was designated Task Force Bayonet. I immediately abandoned that designation and called it simply "The Task Force."

"Rock" Hudson as he was called was a full colonel with a background in the Rangers and a reputation of being a "Hard Charger." He was barely 5 feet six inches tall and spoke with a deep bass voice. He appeared to be in his late forties or older. We were invited to COL Hudson's home for an initial visit on our second day in Panama. While we were there they showed us around. He sold me the window air conditioner units and they provided some light hors d'oeuvres while we had a nice chat. The next day, Thursday, I met with Colonel Hudson in his headquarters and the meeting was quite reminiscent of my initial meeting with LTC Burns when I assumed command of the 2-39 Infantry battalion at Fort Lewis, Washington in 1979. After the initial meetings with the officers in Task Force Bayonet I felt pretty good about taking the command. The CG was away on a trip and so I met initially with Colonel Joseph Rafferty, the Chief of Staff at the 193rd Infantry Brigade Headquarters. I had known Rafferty briefly when he was at MILPERCEN in Alexandria, VA. He was a nice guy.

MG Werner returned from his trip just in time for the change of command. The ceremony took place on Friday, May 3rd, 1985 at 0900 on the Fort Clayton Parade Field. As usual, the troops looked magnificent in their jungle battle dress uniforms. After MG Werner thanked COL Hudson and his spouse, Delores, for their service to the command and praised the troops for their fine appearance, he stepped away from the microphone. COL Hudson then made the usual round of thank you comments to his family, the command, and particularly to the troops. It was now my turn to say how pleased I was to assume command and give the troops the rest of the day off. In this case it was very different. COL Hudson had convinced everyone that because I was coming out of Washington, DC, that I needed to go directly to the field. He was another officer that had avoided a Department of the Army assignment in the pentagon. I do not know why there was a small group of senior officers, at that time, who felt as if they beat the system if they avoided an assignment in the National Capitol Region. Hudson had planned a field exercise for me to commence on the afternoon following the mid-morning change of command. I was really upset about that to say the least. My family was not completely unpacked and I was headed to the field for a week. As I started to state my remarks to the troops, Hudson looked at his wife who was sitting in the seat of honor in the first row and she got up and they left. He simply said "Let's go Dee!" I was startled! MG Werner reached over and touched my shoulder and said to me, "Stand fast!" Hudson and his wife left the parade area without saying a word to anyone and never observed the troops as they passed in review. It stands, even today, as one of the most bizarre, rude, and uncouth acts I observed in a leader in more than 30 years of service. It was, for sure, the most bizarre thing that I had ever seen at a Change of Command Ceremony. They had loaded all of their gear in the staff car and headed directly for the airport. However, I did know this time that the change–of–command reception was being held for me.

That afternoon the troops of the brigade headed for the field. I changed uniforms and decided to go and make an early round of visits. My first stop was at the airborne battalion at Fort Kobe. The commander was LTC George Utter. At this point he was the most seasoned battalion commander in Task Force Bayonet. The Task Force consisted of an airborne Infantry battalion, a straight leg Infantry battalion, and a 105mm Artillery Battery. When we went to the field we received the ordinary complement of support and service support troops to round out the troop list. LTC Utter had set up his command post (CP) in the yard of his garrison headquarters and had proclaimed that day as "wives in charge day." According to him the spouses in the battalion were running the show. This was another bizarre revelation. By the way, the battalion headquarters was not able to communicate with any of the other Task Force Bayonet elements including his subordinate companies. I left LTC Utter's CP and went to the field location of the Task Force Headquarters. It was a disaster! Everyone was sitting around in camouflage paint and odd looking uniform attire and nothing was happening. They were set up in an old coastal artillery battery ruin area and they were not able to communicate with anyone. The only thing that I thought was how pathetic they were thinking that I needed field training. In all my years in the military, to that point I had never seen anything look that bad in a field exercise. From there I went to visit LTC Tom Sewell, the commander of the straight leg Infantry battalion. They were on a hillside on the east side of the canal camouflaged in elephant grass. They were not able to communicate either. Everyone with whom I spoke in Task Force Bayonet was embarrassed. COL Hudson's field exercise for me was a joke! At that point it was about 1600 hours and I canceled the exercise. I had everyone brought back into garrison, cleaned up their gear, and sent them home. It was my Task Force and dammit, I was going to train it my way. I was in charge and I took charge! Later, Sergeant Major Lupe Martinez, The Task Force operations sergeant major said to me, "Sir, I was never more embarrassed in my entire military career than when you came up to me and asked me what was going on in the field that first day." I really made the troops and their families happy by giving them an unexpected weekend at home.

The next work day, Monday, I set about observing and assessing the real readiness status of the brigade. We were the only American responders in Latin America for any crisis. Geographically, Latin America is an area that starts at the northern border of Mexico and goes southward to Antarctica. Technically, on any given day The Task Force could have troops deployed in every country throughout that area except Cuba.

We had a tactical mission in Honduras and Salvador and I had temporary support missions going to many of the other counties. In addition, The Task Force had a training affiliation with the Florida National Guard and the Puerto Rico National Guard. We were very busy and unit training was very difficult to schedule. I found in my initial observations that the battalions were very good at responding to spur of the moment requirements, particularly small unit activities. However, anything above platoon size operations was a mess. An example that comes to mind was an airborne operation that took the 2-187 Infantry across the Isthmus for a parachute jump onto Gatun Drop Zone followed by a forced march south back to Fort Kobe. I flew over by helicopter to observe the jump, the unit assembly, and the establishment of the airhead. These airborne soldiers did not know that I had jumped more than twenty times on that drop zone when I was a lieutenant and a captain. It was unlike anything that I had ever seen. Major Gary Khun was the battalion executive officer in the 2-187 Infantry and he was acting as the Drop Zone Safety Officer (DZSO) a duty that I had pulled on that DZ as a Captain. Major Khun had served with me as a Captain in the 3rd Brigade, 101st Airborne Division back in 1975. He knew that I knew how to conduct airborne operations and he was totally embarrassed for his unit that day. As it turned out, LTC Utter really wanted to take his battalion to the Atlantic Side of Panama and force-march them back along the Panama Railroad, a route that his father had taken several years earlier when he had commanded a battalion in Panama. My question to The Task Force staff was a simple one. "What does that have to do with the unit's Mission Essential Training List (METL)?" No one could give me a satisfactory answer. It appeared that my predecessor enjoyed doing those kinds of high visibility junkets and he would play them up as training advancements. In my estimation they were show-off activities that contributed marginally to the mission of The Task Force and at best marginally enhanced unit camaraderie. There were other snafus that were equally as bad. Part of the problem was the 193rd Infantry Brigade Staff's involvement with Task Force Bayonet's training.

The officer in charge of the Brigade G-3 (Operations) staff section was a person that I had known for many years prior to going to Panama. He was Colonel Gorham Black, a Howard University graduate, who had commanded a Training Battalion at Fort Dix, NJ. In that regard, his tactical unit planning experience and tactical unit training knowledge was limited. Colonel Black's staff always sent 193rd Infantry Brigade's support tasks to The Task Force…late. By receiving the support requirements late we would have to jump through hoops and change our plans almost on a daily basis.

I decided to institute the training rigor that I had learned and perfected in the 9th Infantry Division into The Task Force. First, we would have a training meeting every Friday at 1300 hours with all of the Task Force battalion commanders, brigade and battalion command sergeants major, and all of my staff present. Woe, be unto the person who was late for that meeting. I would embarrass them severely in public. The purpose of the meeting was simply to review the previous week's training and discuss the good, the bad and the ugly; talk about plans for the upcoming week and what problems remained unsolved; and finally discuss plans for the period that was six weeks away. This process was painful for the Task Force battalion commanders at first but after about six weeks it caught on and started to make sense to them. However, in order for the process to work I needed the cooperation of the 193rd Infantry Brigade staff. At first I tried to work with Colonel Black's operations staff but found that his staff was inept as tactical unit trainers and therefore, they were not able to comprehend what we were trying to convey to them. COL Black and I got along well together initially. However, over time our relationship deteriorated. He was later relieved of his duties by the Commanding General and eventually returned to the United States. During the interim I divided the training cycles between the Battalions and the Battery. I established a training cycle, a training support cycle, and a support cycle. That way the battalions could plan their training and conduct it in an uninterrupted manner during the training cycle. Generals Cavazos and Stone would have been proud of me. They had taught me how to train well. Then I assigned specific duties to the battalions for training the affiliation units. The Florida National guard would be the sole responsibility of the 2-187 Infantry Battalion, and the Puerto Rico National Guard would be the sole responsibility of the 1-4 Infantry Battalion. The Artillery Battery would support both.

Just prior to making all of the training changes, LTC Gregg, the Task Force Bayonet Executive Officer, announced to me that he had received orders to go to Honduras and command Task Force Bravo. I was a little upset because I was only about a month into command and apparently this had been known by everyone in the 193rd Infantry Brigade except me, from the day that I arrived in country. I was the FNG so I did not complain. I didn't think that he was my kind of guy anyway. I was kind of glad to get rid of him. He had been trained by Hudson and literally did not know very much about integrated unit training. I was sent LTC Arthur Holmes as a replacement for LTC Gregg. If one did not believe in providence and Divine intervention, the assignment of Art Holmes would change your mind. He was marvelous! Aside from being able to carry out my directives he was personable and everyone on the Isthmus respected him. He had been COL Black's deputy operations officer in the 193rd Infantry Brigade G-3 (Operations). He knew all of the knuckleheads up there in G-3 and that was a plus for The Task Force. I also decided by that time, I would not personally deal with the 193rd Infantry Brigade staff unless it was an absolute necessity. That would be LTC Holmes' job. For the most part The Task Force was autonomous from the brigade and I enjoyed that separation. That would all change with the arrival of MG James R. Taylor, the replacement for MG Fred Werner.

My first encounter with Werner led me to believe that he was in over his head from a field soldiers' point of view. He was, however, a good diplomat and representative of the United States of America to the countries and Missions throughout Latin America. He was a fluent Spanish speaker, his wife,

Jeannie, was from Cochabamba, Bolivia, and he was rather athletic. For the first meeting with him, he made me wait for about twenty minutes in his outer office and when he finally called me in, he was standing with his back to me looking out of the window with his right hand stuck in his battle dress uniform (BDU) jacket like Napoleon. Any one who knows me will tell you that I get really upset when I have to wait for an appointment, no matter who it is. I personally think that it is rude and inconsiderate to make people wait for you. It is really rare for anyone to have to wait for me. When he turned around, I greeted him with a hearty "good afternoon sir" or words to that effect. He replied, "Is that the way you report to your superior officer?" I became really ticked off, but immediately snapped to attention, saluted and said, "Sir, Colonel Stephens reports." He lazily returned the salute and commenced telling me that he was in charge. He made it clear that I would not get the 193rd Infantry Brigade Standard (flag) until he was given a flag for the USARSO Command. I did not answer him. He went on to tell me that he expected me to instruct my troops to salute him and treat him with respect. He also stated that he normally ran about thirty minutes late for appointments and everyone needed to take that into consideration. Finally he reiterated that the 193rd Infantry Brigade was his command and that I was not to assume any prerogatives that normally conveyed to an Office of Personnel Management System (OPMS) Brigade Commander. I was really, really angry with this man. I decided to let it show. He insulted my intelligence for the first part. I was not an idiot. I knew that a Major General outranked a Colonel and I also knew that he was in charge. I also knew that very few officers at my rank, saluted and reported to their superior officer in the confines of his office. I thought I detected a little superior to subordinate effort there to put me in my place. I did not, however, make an issue of any of this unpleasantness. It sure as hell was different from anything that I had experienced from general officers in the past. Not once during the entire meeting did he welcome me to the command or ask if my family was settled. Finally, he asked me if I had anything to say and I simply said that I was glad to be there and that it was my understanding that I was an OPMS Brigade Command designee and I expected to be treated as such. I ended by saying that, if there was a misunderstanding, maybe we should call MILPERCEN to clarify my status. He avoided an answer but instead invited me and my family to his quarters for dinner that evening. As I started to leave his office he told me that I should deal with COL Joe Rafferty, the Chief of Staff on matters pertaining to the Task Force. He iterated that COL Rafferty was to be considered the "first among equals" of the 06's assigned. I smiled to myself and said under my breath "When pig's fly! I have no equal here." I left his office and called Olivia and told her we were invited to dinner at the CG's quarters—that very night. He only lived about five houses down the street but we thought that it was unusual for him to ask us on the spur of the moment like that. We had been in the quarters more than two weeks. I think I got his attention with the offer to call MILPERCEN. The visit to his quarters turned out to be cordial and his wife was a gracious hostess. From that point on I got along with him. He came to the field only one time, in a year, to visit my troops. He was so full of himself, in his starched BDU's and spit shined boots that he did not relate well at all to soldiers. He went on to be selected and promoted to three and four stars billets and the title of Commanding General, United States Southern Command (SOUTHCOM).

Major General James R. Taylor, Werner's replacement in USARSO was entirely different. He was a tactician, a trainer, and a personable leader. He had worked for LTG Walter Ulmer one of the great executive management experts in the Army. After LTG Ulmer retired he became president and chief executive officer of the Center for Creative Leadership (CCL) one of the premier management training institution in the world. He had trained MG Taylor well at 5th Army headquarters at Fort Hood, TX. Taylor had also worked for General Joe Palastra, my mentor, earlier in his career. That meant that he and I would not have conflicting military philosophies on very much. Taylor was a real breath of fresh air for USARSO. He was a graduate of Texas A&M University. He was ninety-nine percent supportive of everything I did with The Task Force. He treated me with all the respect, dignity, honors and privileges appertaining to an OPMS Brigade Commander. I was normally in his foursome at the golf course on Saturday morning and our families socialized together regularly. It was an absolute joy to finally work for a gentleman who knew his job and did it well. One of the first things he did was to give me responsibility for the Aviation Battalion assigned to Panama. That meant that in addition to supervising two Infantry battalions and an Artillery Battery I would now take on the 227th Aviation Battalion under the command of LTC Michael Abbott. I learned more than I ever wanted to know about aviation maintenance and operations. The Aviation Battalion consisted of a great group of officers and families with whom to work and I am far richer for the experience. However, they were a little short on discipline at times.

General Taylor and his wife Lynn brought a ray of sunshine to our street. They opened up the CG's quarters and visited everyone in the neighborhood. Lynn was a smoker and I had quit smoking just before the 1984 Marine Corps Marathon. One night she lit up at a Task Force officers' party in our quarters that we were having and I asked her to please smoke outside if she wanted to smoke. Well if you have ever stood outside in the evening during the rainy season in Panama you would know why she became angry. She said to Taylor, "Jimmy, this colonel has just asked me to step outside to smoke." The room got quiet and everyone was waiting for his reply when he said, "well step outside if you want to smoke." Wow! He was a great person for whom to work.

During MG Taylor's tenure we conducted Operation Blast Furnace in the Republic of Bolivia. General Taylor and I went to Washington, DC, in late June 1986, to brief the Chairman of the Joint Chiefs of Staff, Admiral William J. Crowe, Jr. regarding the operation. Before we arrived in Washington we stopped in Atlanta, Georgia, at Forces Command (FORSCOM)

Headquarters to brief the Commanding General who at that time was none other than General Joseph T. Palastra. We went in and briefed General Palastra and he invited us over, to his temporary quarters where he was staying while the CG's house was being renovated, for dinner with him and his wife Anne. Both MG Taylor and I had worked for him previously and he wanted to get caught up on news about our families. Anne prepared a light meal and we caught a later flight to Washington, DC, in preparation for an early meeting the next day at the pentagon. Upon arriving at the Chairman's Office we were met by Mo a young lady that had worked for me in J-3 several years before. I was happy to see her and find out that she had progressed to be an executive assistant to the Chairman of the Joint Chiefs of Staff, Admiral Crowe. She had been a lifesaver for me in the CAC in the old days. MG Taylor and I made the appointment to see the Chairman. In those days the Joint Chiefs only met on certain days and they required a read ahead packet before they would debate an issue and put it on the agenda in the Gold Room. The Gold Room was normally referred to as "The Tank." We had about a two day wait so we decided to brief everyone that would listen in the (ARSTAF) and solicit help in preparing our information packet. I still had friends in the building and above all I knew my way around like a professional. I got the support we needed lined up and made sure that we got to briefing venues on time. I think that Taylor was happy to have me along. Of course, I knew that one had to be a general or flag officer to brief in The Tank so MG Taylor conducted the briefing in The Tank. At one point in the briefing Admiral Crowe asked who would be the commander on the ground. General Taylor told him that I would be in command. I stood up and he asked me one question. "What will you do if you have an American down on the ground during this operation?" I answered, "Sir I will not leave any downed Americans on the ground." There were no other questions asked of me. It was Friday afternoon. The Joint Chiefs approved the concept and we were on our way back to the Republic of Panama that evening. It was Thursday, 26 June 1986. The next week I was the

Commander of Troops (COT) in the U.S. Southern Command 4th of July Parade. I had been the COT of that parade as a Captain, in Colon, Canal Zone on the Atlantic side of the Ithmus in 1966, twenty years earlier. On Sunday afternoon 05 July 1986, we started preliminary planning for the deployment of troops to the Chapare Area of Bolivia in order to eradicate the laboratory production of cocaine. General Taylor and I along with an advance party departed Panama the following weekend and the troops followed shortly thereafter. 106 troops and six Blackhawk helicopters from The Task Force along with a small contingent of civilians from the Drug Enforcement Agency (DEA) landed in Santa Cruz, Bolivia on or about 14 July, 1986. MG Taylor and I flew down in his airplane, a King Air C-12. Actually the C-12 aircraft was assigned to The Task Force Aviation Battalion. The troops and helicopters were deployed to Bolivia by two U.S. Air Force C5A aircraft. The Blackhawk Helicopters were disassembled prior to deployment packed into the C5As and reassembled upon arrival. We spent one night in Santa Cruz and immediately redeployed north by helicopter to Trinidad Airfield to conduct anti-drug operations. This American Task Force along with 30 UMAPAR Bolivian national police officers and selected U.S. Drug Enforcement Agency officers set up a base to commence hunting and destroying coca-processing laboratories in the Chapare, Beni, and Santa Cruz areas of The Republic of Bolivia. One of my most vivid memories of Operation Blast Furnace, which included aviation support, counterinsurgency training, as well as helicopter logistical support, is standing alone on the airfield at Trinidad, Bolivia, and watching the Under Secretary of the Army, Mr. James Ambrose, and MG Taylor take off from the Trinidad Airfield in the Under Secretary's aircraft. I was left in charge and the weight of responsibility was very heavy. However, I was the responsible person so I took charge. Operation Blast Furnace focused on law enforcement raids against traffickers in local villages, which was de facto seen as an attack on Bolivian peasants. The four-month operation temporarily depressed coca prices, but its effects were short-lived.

Upon my return to Panama from Bolivia I was summons into the Criminal Investigations Command (CID) headquarters for questioning. It appeared that I had been living in government quarters for approximately eighteen months and illegally receiving my government quarters allowance. I was questioned at length by the CID agents in the CID office. They were rude, disrespectful, and above all unduly accusatory. They wanted me to take a polygraph examination and they also wanted to question Olivia. I refused both. I knew that I had not done anything wrong and I sure as hell was not going to let that bunch of quasi hoodlums browbeat Olivia. As it turned out, I was not the only senior officer that had happened to at that time. I was told the Commanding General of SOUTHCOM and the SOUTHCOM Chaplain among others had similar situations. We finally got it resolved and I was required to repay the government in equal payments over a three month period. I still burn when I think of how I was treated in that situation. I have often wondered if the other folks had to pay their debts within three months. The commanding officer of the CID Command in Atlanta made a special trip to Panama to apologize for the unprofessional and rude behavior of his agents. I listened to him but I never acknowledged forgiveness. One agent, a Mr. Waterman actually told me, during an interrogation session that he was upset with me because I had not taken him to Bolivia with me on Operation Blast Furnace. I thought, what a narrow minded jackass he was; but I kept my cool and I stood my ground. I knew that these guys wanted to embarrass me and I was not about to give them the chance.

Somewhere in the flurry of events under MG Taylor's watch I did receive the 193rd Infantry Brigade colors and was designated the Commander of the 193rd Infantry Brigade (Separate). I was so upset when I left that first meeting with MG Werner that I designed and had a flag made for The Task Force. I paid for it out of my own pocket and we marched with it in every parade. I never asked permission I just did it. He never questioned how I got it and I never told him. We had a retirement ceremony for The Task Force colors that I purchased upon acceptance of the brigade standard. The Task Force colors are in my home today. I figured I bought them, they are mine. At about this time the OPMS battalion command selection process sent me two outstanding replacement Infantry battalion commanders. They were LTC Robert Wagner and LTC Monty T.S. Hess. They were outstanding leaders and just what those Panama battalions needed to get a fresh start.

On Saturday mornings I held what was called Saturday Court. It was a simple meeting of every soldier and/or Task Force family member that received a military police moving violation or was involved in a family dispute during a specified period. I normally held these meetings once a month. If a soldier or his spouse or one of his children received a violation they were required to report to me at a specified time to explain how they were going to ensure that the incident would not be repeated. Normally, I started at 0900, and required the involved soldier to have his battalion commander, battalion command sergeant major, company commander, company first sergeant, platoon leader, platoon sergeant, squad leader, and fire team leader present at the meeting. My goal was to inconvenience as many people in the soldier's chain of command, as possible. I scheduled everyone at 0900.

By starting at 0900 I would ensure that their weekend was ruined. It normally only took about two of these sessions to make the troops start policing themselves. This was not true in the 227th Aviation Battalion. They always had people present for Saturday Court. Sometimes, I would get rather earthy in those meetings and use very strong language. I was called in by a promotable colonel who was assigned to the USARSO headquarters and he attempted to verbally reprimand me for using profanity with the Saturday Court bunch. I simply said that over time I had reduced the incidence of violations in my unit to one or two a month. I went on to say, "If you'd like sir, I'll discontinue Saturday Court and you can start seeing the violators." He quickly declined and allowed me to leave his office. I also saw everyone in the Task Force involved in a domestic disturbance. I had the normal cast of characters present but added all children over six years old. You'd be amazed at how embarrassed a senior noncommissioned officer can become trying to explain why he struck his spouse in the presence of his chain of command and his children. These were techniques that I had learned from Tiger Honeycutt. My guess is they will still work today, however one would probably not be able to conduct Saturday Court in today's military environment.

The USARSO deputy commanding general was a promotable colonel who for the most part was a good guy. Aside from the run in about how I treated the troops at Saturday court we got along well. One time he came by for a briefing from me and my operations officer, Major Greer, and he decided to tell an ethnic joke. I did not laugh and neither did Major Greer. We did not disrespect people in The Task Force no matter who they were and that meant we did not tell ethnic jokes about any ethnicity. He got the message and never did that again. He never knew it but the fact that I did not participate in ethnic joke telling was always part of my opening speech to new troops. Since an incident in a race relations conference in the 101st Airborne Division back in 1971, I neither told nor tolerated ethnic jokes again.

My two years in Panama ended too quickly and I was reassigned to the pentagon. It appears in hind sight that command of The Task Force was the best unit in which I served. After about sixty days on station, we did almost everything right. We had great camaraderie among the officers and their spouses. Most of all, we enjoyed respect from the rest of the Army. We stopped drugs in Bolivia for a while; we had a little shooting war going on in Honduras and El Salvador; and finally, we had every leader in the Army, in a high position of responsibility, who could figure out how to do it, coming to the 193rd Infantry Brigade (Separate), for a visit. Somehow I knew that I would be selected for general on the next meeting of a selection board.

Relinquishing command in the 193rd Brigade was a tough experience for me. For the first time in my career I was sad about leaving my troops. The new USARSO Commanding General, MG Bernard F. Loeffke, the person who replaced MG Taylor, had Olivia and I over for lunch after the change of command ceremony. Loeffke had just returned from Washington, DC, and apparently knew that I was on the general officer selection list. He did not tell me so but he gave me a cap with a star on it. Although it was a Chinese Army hat, it was enough of a signal for me to call Colonel's branch and ask to speak with Colonel Joe Ballard, the branch chief. I had served with Joe Ballard in the 101st. Airborne Division when he was the executive officer in the 326 Engineer Battalion. He told me "Sorry sir, I can no longer speak with you, your records are no longer in Colonel's division." That confirmed my suspicions and I felt really good about leaving Panama. I still did not tell anyone or celebrate because my mother had taught me many years before never to trust that you will be credited with an accomplishment until you see it in writing. Incidentally, Joe Ballard retired at the three stars level.

Upon arriving back in the United States, I was assigned to the NCR to wait on orders. I decided to go to West Virginia to visit family. I was at my mother-in law's house when a telephone call came in from LTG Robert Riscassi, the Deputy Chief of Staff for Operations (DCSOPS) or as we used to say the G3 for the whole Army. He told me that I was going to be assigned to the Office of the DCSOPS. He indicated that I would be working in the Training Division. I knew that the Training Division only had one general officer position and that meant that I would be a Director in DCSOPS. Hey, that was really big stuff! I even went by and talked to the incumbent director and started making plans to go to work upon his departure. As it turned out, I went to work expecting to be the Director of Training to find out that the Chief of Staff, Army (CSA) General Carl Vouono had brought one of his cronies in ahead of me and I was assigned to the Operations Directorate as a "surplus general officer, additional deputy director for operations." That meant among other things that I would not be frocked right away and that I would be referred to as a "promotable colonel" instead of a brigadier general. It also meant that it was possible that I would not have meaningful work. My new boss was MG J.D. Smith. What a wonderful guy he turned out to be. He treated me like I was already wearing stars and he conveyed that attitude to everyone else. He gave me meaningful tasks and assignments. He never over supervised me. He simply treated me with the decency and respect that I was due. I worked hard not to let him down. He put me in charge of the 0600 morning briefing to the DCSOPS and the monthly readiness briefing to the CSA. It was some of the best training that I could have asked for before I went to the field as an Infantry Division Assistant Division Commander.

SECTION III

FLAG RANK

Presenting Olivia with roses at my retirement ceremony at Fort Myer, VA—May 1993.

Olivia and I saluting during the playing of the National Anthem at my retirement parade ceremony—28 May 1993.

COL George Hudgens, Steve, Olivia, and BG J.J. Johnson immediately after my retirement ceremony.

Reviewing the troops at my retirement parade with MG Fred Gordon, Commander, Military District of Washington.

Meeting with Mr. Ron Brown at the Headquarters of the Armed Forces Inaugural Committee (AFIC).

MG Billy Streeter, Ron Brown, and Susan Livingston, Assistant Secretary of the Army for Installations, Logistics and Environment (ASA, IL&E) at Armed Forces Inaugural Committee (AFIC) Headquarters.

After receiving the Distinguished Service Medal during my retirement parade at Fort Myer, Virginia.

White House Reviewing Stand for the Inaugural Parade for President Bill Clinton.

Joint planning meeting with BG Stephens, Colonel Victor Tambone, Chief of Staff of AFIC, LTC (P) Jim Eicher, Operations Officer of AFIC, Mr. Harry Thomason, Presidential Inaugural Committee Choreographer, and Mr. Rahm Emmanuel, Presidential Inauguration Committee Operations Officer at the Inaugural Committee Headquarters.

Meeting with Ron Brown and Mrs. Tipper Gore, wife of Vice President Al Gore.

Having a light moment with the AFIC staff.

Meeting with Colonel Victor Tambone and Mrs. Hillary Clinton, wife of the President.

Escorting Assistant Secretary of the Army for Installations and Logistics and Environment (ASA, IL&E) through the Armed Forces Inaugural Committee Headquarters.

With Ambassador and Ms. Daniel O'Donohue in Bangkok, Thailand.

Promoting my daughter, Stephanie, to Captain in my office at JUSMAGTHAI, in Bangkok, Thailand.

A Stephens family photo at JUSMAGTHAI in Bangkok.

Working with Thai airborne soldiers.

Attending the King Bhumibol Adulyadej birthday celebration in Thailand—1991.

Having fun in the office at Inaugural Committee headquarters.

Discussing inaugural planning, personnel, and logistics with Sergeant Major Neely.

Right guide in the Presidential Inaugural Parade.

Stephens speaking at Military Hall of Fame night in WV—May 2000.

Stephens Family Photo in Charleston, WV—Christmas 1993.

FLAG RANK

Officers who typically command units or formations that are expected to operate independently for extended periods of time (brigades and larger, or flotillas or squadrons of ships), are referred to variously as General Officers (Army, Marines, and some Air Forces), Flag Officers (Navy). General Officer ranks typically include (from the top down) General, Lieutenant General, Major General, and Brigadier General. Flag Officer ranks, named after the traditional practice of showing the presence of such an officer with a flag on a ship and often on land, typically include (from the top down) Admiral, Vice Admiral, Rear Admiral and Commodore. In various countries, particularly the United States, these may be referred to as "star ranks" for the number of stars worn on some rank insignia: typically one star for Brigadier General or equivalent with the addition of a star for each subsequent rank. In the United States five stars has been the maximum used in all services (excluding the Marines and Coast Guard which have only used four).

Everyone knows that general and flag rank officers are considered to be the military's senior leaders.

The first general officer insignia was established by general order on July 14, 1775 which stated: "To prevent mistakes, the general officers and their aides-de-camp will be distinguished in the following manner: The Commander-in-Chief by a light blue rib band, worn across his breast, between his coat and waistcoat; the Majors and Brigadier Generals by a pink rib band worn in like manner;..."

Stars were first used as insignia to identify general officers on June 18, 1780 when it was prescribed that Major Generals would wear two stars and Brigadier Generals one star on each epaulette. Three stars were established in 1798 for the rank of Lieutenant General and were worn by the Commander-in-Chief, General Washington. Four stars were authorized for the rank of General when the rank was established by Act of Congress on July 25, 1866. Grant was the first officer of the Army to hold the rank of General and to wear the insignia of four silver stars.

The title of General of the Armies was established after World War I. No special insignia was developed and General Pershing wore four stars. He was the only person appointed as General of the Armies.

General of the Army was established by Congress on December 14, 1944, and provided that no more than four officers could be appointed. President Roosevelt appointed Generals George Marshall, Douglas MacArthur, Dwight D. Eisenhower and Henry H. Arnold. An Act of Congress, approved on September 15, 1950, authorized the President to appoint General Omar N. Bradley to the grade of General of the Army. The insignia of grade for General of the Army is prescribed as five silver stars set in a circle with the coat of arms of the United States, in gold, above the circle of stars.

I was promoted to Brigadier General on 01 July 1989. My frocking ceremony took place much earlier in September 1988. Actually MG J.D. Smith frocked me in a conference room in the pentagon. Olivia prepared a great reception following the ceremony and invited a large number of our NCR friends. My brother and his wife, Gloria attended the ceremony along with many close friends. I invited Lois Stevens and she attended. We left the ceremony and my daughter Stephanie who at the time was a First Lieutenant accompanied me to say goodbye to my friends in the pentagon like the lady who changed the light bulbs, the supply technician in the Joint Chiefs of Staff, and the many support persons with whom I had worked. Later that day Olivia, Christa and I headed west to Fort Lewis, Washington for a second tour in the great northwestern United States. Bob went back to work at the Airline Transport Association and Stephanie headed to Fort McClellan to finish her assignment there.

I thoroughly enjoyed my time as a general officer but found a lot of the transactions and activities to be stuffy, bloated, and too accommodating. Instead of being at a level where candor, selflessness and even rancor were acceptable I found that, for the most part, the higher ranks were looking for an acquiescent team player and in most cases, did not want to hear the unvarnished truth. In that regard, I think I was one of the best colonels to ever wear eagles in the Army but, in my opinion, not a great brigadier general.

INTO THE PENTAGON FOR THE THIRD TIME

The Operations Directorate (OD) of DCSOPS is located in the basement of the Pentagon. The basement of the Pentagon is unlike any other portion of the building. The room numbering system was entirely different and one could get lost down there very easily. The Operations Directorate was a twenty-four hour, seven days a week operation where the real action went on for the entire Army. We kept our hands on the pulse of everything that happened in the Army. The authorized deputy director for operations was Brigadier General Ronald Griffin, a CGSC classmate. Ron was also a great guy. Both J.D. and Ron had served as the Executive Assistant to the DCSOPS when they were colonels. They knew DCSOPS inside and out and they taught me a lot about the policies, procedures and practices of working within that Deputate. In order to stay ahead of the game I needed to be in the office no later than 0530 each morning for a pre-briefing on what happened overnight. MG JD Smith would arrive at about 0545 and the DCSOPS came down on selected days at 0600. The night shift guys in the Army Operations Center (AOC) were all top notch performers and had the routine down to a science. There was a balcony that overlooked the AOC floor where the action officers worked. For the morning briefing (0600) the night shift guys always stayed around until the briefing period concluded at about 0700. One of my first projects was to upgrade the information technology (IT) equipment in the AOC. In a short period of time I learned more about computers and associated equipment than I ever wanted to know. However, it did two things for me. First, I learned who the leading companies in the IT industry were at that time, and second, I realized that if I wanted to advance in the Army I'd better become personally, more familiar with information technology. I commenced learning everything that I could about computers immediately.

I interviewed for follow on flag officer jobs while I was working in the AOC. I was advised by two black general officers, LTG Henry Doctor and MG James Hall, to go for an Assistant Division Commander (ADC) position in one of the fighting divisions. One of the first interviews that I had was for a Department of Defense Security Assistance position for South and Central America. I was interviewed by a civilian. One of the first things that he said was that he was on loan to DOD from the State Department. He also let me know right away that he knew LTG Colin Powell who was serving at the time as the Deputy Assistant to the President for National Security Affairs. I figured out right away that I didn't want to work for this name dropping guy but it would be okay for the short run. We continued to talk and he asked me how I felt about General Manuel Noriega. I told him that Noriega was my friend and that I liked him. Little did I know, but that would be the kiss of death for that interview. I honestly did not know at that time, that General Noriega was an enemy of the United States. I had just left Panama where we were instructed to treat him as a head of state. I also counted the Panamanian Infantry battalion that General Noriega's brother-in-law commanded as part of my defense force for the Panama Canal. So we had trained together and socialized together, often. In fact, during one of the major maneuver exercises in the Republic of Panama (Operation Candella '87) I was asked by General John Galvin, the SOUTHCOM Commander, to spend a day with General Noriega showing him how his forces would be integrated into the United States defense plan for the Panama Canal. I knew General Noriega was a graduate of the Chorrios Military Academy in Peru with a degree in engineering. Upon graduation and returning to Panama, he became a sublieutenant in the National Guard. He was also a graduate of the Colombia

Lancero School. He was in my mind a well qualified soldier. He had treated me with decency and respect and I liked him. Anyway, that civilian must have thought that I was crazy because within six months after the interview, Noriega had been captured and imprisoned by the United States of America, and scheduled for a tribunal. Needless to say I did not get that job.

A good portion of the first year as a general officer designee is spent going to different schools and classes. There is the U.S. Army General Officer Orientation Course held in the NCR. That was conducted in Alexandria, Virginia, commencing on a Sunday afternoon and lasted for five days. Our spouses were also invited to attend. It was a very nice welcome and orientation to the general ranks where the CSA was the opening speaker, followed by the Vice Chief of Staff. The CSA's opening remarks reminded us that "for everyone sitting here, there are ten just like you that didn't get selected." The VCSA also spoke and told us to do something that I still do today. He said "Do not go home until you have answered all telephone calls." Today I take that a step further and answer as many emails as possible also. We were then treated to a seminar by Mr. Lou Tice, the Guru of the Pacific Institute whose success concepts had won him the reputation of being a world leader in performance excellence. I had heard Lou Tice speak before when I worked in DCSPER for General Maxwell Thurman. Lou was part of the small group of subject matter experts that included Dr. Charles Moskos from Northwestern University and COL Dandridge Malone among others who LTG Thurman kept on a string for advice to the Office of the DCSPER. Lou's presentation to us was great. We also spent a whole day in media training. Our spouses also received media training. We had a day with the current active duty three and four star leadership general officers where we could ask questions. My former commander from Panama, LTG Fred Werner was one of the presenters. He was cordial toward me and Olivia. The orientation and training culminated with a nice dinner party at the Fort Myer Officers' Club with most of the members of the ARSTAF present. Olivia and I had a great time with everyone there. Our good friends J.J. and Diane Johnson were members of that class as well as Johnnie Wilson and his wife Helen and Clara Adams-Ender and her husband, Larz. During that course Johnnie Wilson made it clear that he did not want to be seen associating with us too much from fear of the white members of the group becoming uneasy. As usual, Olivia was fashionably dressed, correct in demeanor, and she knew when to speak and when it was best to listen. She was as poised, elegant and intelligent as always. Later, I attended the Program, Planning and Budgeting training for general officers at the Xerox Training Center in Leesburg, VA, and several other day training sessions in the NCR. There was also the DOD General Officer Orientation Course at the Institute of Higher Studies located at the National Defense University. Part of that orientation course was a visit to most of the major DOD headquarters throughout the world. Finally, I was attending the Center for Creative Leadership (CCL) in Colorado Springs, CO when I received a telephone call from LTG H. Norman Schwarzkopf, the DCSOPS of the Army.

Shortly after I arrived at DCSOPS, LTG Riscassi was reassigned and replaced by LTG Schwarzkopf. By reputation Schwarzkopf was a legend in his own time. The legend had it that he was big, very intelligent and most of all a bully. He was big. I figured him at six feet four inches tall and weighing about three hundred pounds. He was so smart that he scared the hell out of most folks. He was a completely no-nonsense person. That's probably why he was called a bully. He just did not tolerate crap from briefers. You had to have your facts and figures together when you talked to him or he would tune you out. Upon hearing of his assignment to DSCOPS, MG J.D. Smith called me and Ron Griffin into his office and told us that we were never to allow a colonel to go in and brief LTG Schwarzkopf alone. He wanted a general officer present at every briefing.

I had two memorable encounters with LTG Schwarzkopf. The first was during a mid–east crisis in the Suez Canal when bong hammers were pulling up along side of our battle ships and tossing grenades. We wanted to shoot them out of the water with helicopters. Schwarzkopf could not buy the idea that the helicopter pilots were using a cross made by a grease pencil in the windshield of a helicopter to aim at the bong-hammers (Boston Whalers). It was my job to convince him that it was proper. As luck would have it, I knew that General Palastra had used this method as a young pilot in Vietnam. I simply had our guys to check with some of the stateside aviation commands in U.S. Forces Command and they confirmed the method. The second encounter was over my session with the General Officer Management Office GOMO) assignment officer. The assignment officer was one of the world's premier jackasses. He did not like to be questioned about the assignment that he determined that you should get. In an earlier life I had served as an assignment officer and I knew that the only aim of an assignment officer was "to force the square pegs into round holes." No matter what assignment people try to tell you about what's good for you they are merely trying to fill a personnel requisition. He offered me a job at MILPERCEN. Going on what the two black generals had told me previously, I refused the position and requested to see the CSA. That action not only ticked off the assignment officer, it blew his mind that I would have the audacity to go and talk to the CSA about it. He evidently called Schwarzkopf in desperation. Schwarzkopf called me in and started to chew me out but decided to ask me some questions first. The gist of the conversation was he told me he wanted me to work for him a year and he would get me an ADC job. I agreed. He then asked how long I had been in DCSOPS and I told him ten months and two weeks. We both smiled and he said okay. So his telephone call to me in Colorado Springs a month later was very significant. He kept his word! I have always admired how he handled that situation even though I only had about two weeks to pack, get frocked and go to the new assignment. He was true to his word and I will always be grateful to him for his forthrightness.

FROCKED AND READY TO GO

Because of the change in time zones General Schwarzkopf's call to me in Colorado Springs was very early in the morning. He told me that he had secured an ADC job for me with the 9th Infantry Division (Motorized) at Fort Lewis Washington, under MG John Shalikashvili. Shalikashvili asked everyone to call him Shali. Schwarzkopf concluded the conversation with "you need to tell your wife." I called home immediately. I told her about the "good news" that we were moving and her only words were: "You'll have to go alone." As luck would have it, she had just signed a contract to teach first grade in one of the local elementary schools for the coming year. We had discussed the matter all summer and finally figured that we would be in the NCR for another year. Almost every day when I came home she would ask if I had orders yet and I would answer, no. To add insult to injury, my youngest daughter, Christa, was leaving the house as I called, to have her senior class photos made.

Bob had moved in his junior year, Stephanie had moved in her senior year and now I was asking Christa to move in her senior year. I hung up the telephone and for a while could not be happy about the assignment. I wanted Olivia to go and experience the triumph and joy of serving as a "general's wife" on a post that had a fighting division. I had a couple of days to go before finishing the CCL course. I went ahead and finished my work at CCL without having my heart in it. All I could think about was I would be moving to a new assignment without my family. By the time I got back home things had changed.

It seems that as soon as Olivia hung up the telephone from talking to me, she told Christa about the news. She also told her that she had told me that I would have to go alone. That summer Christa had spent six weeks in the Governor's Language Academy at Averett College, in Danville, VA, where she was required to be totally submersed in the Spanish language. She had spent that time without us visiting her and for the most part was on her own in student housing like a college student. She had grown up over night. She was no longer Dad's little girl. She was a very mature young lady who happened to be a high school senior. As Olivia tells the story, Christa simply said in a calm voice "It is my senior year, my last year at home, and I think we should spend it as a family." After having said that, Olivia started calling the movers and packing. She also called her school principal and voided her contract. By the time I got home she had a time schedule worked out and we were in the throes of moving out of Northern Virginia to the Great Northwest. Someone knew a family that was moving from Fort Lewis to the NCR and we contacted them to find out that it was Colonel George Fisher the same guy who had assumed command of my company, B Troop, 1-7 Cavalry when I got shot in Vietnam. He and his wife rented our house in Lakeridge sight unseen. I arranged to have a frocking ceremony in the pentagon and Olivia called the secretaries in our office and they worked out a reception after the promotion ceremony. One of the things that I had done early was have my uniforms tailor made at the Army Quartermaster Depot in Philadelphia, Pennsylvania. I had them hanging in a closet with all of the accoutrements in place, ready to go. During the Bennett-Ramsey Triennial Family Reunion that summer in Charlotte, NC, we bought a new car. So all we needed to do was get our household goods on the road headed to Fort Lewis, Washington, move into the guest house at Fort Myer, Virginia, and wait for the big day to pin on the rank. We invited a lot of people even though it was on short notice. This was a very special day for the Stephens family! It was in many ways a culmination of a helluva lot of hard work, sweat and tears. It was also a new beginning for us. One perhaps we were not as prepared for as we should have been.

Just before I went to CCL I received a call from a friend who told me that Brigadier General Evelyn P. Foote, a CGSC classmate, was looking for an Aid de Camp and that my daughter, Stephanie was a finalist in the search. I called BG Sherian G. Cadoria and asked her to put in a good word for Stephanie. Both of the female generals were former military police (MP) officers and Stephanie was assigned as a military police officer at the time. The short and long of it was Stephanie got the job. She was in town on the day of my promotion interviewing with Pat Foote. Bob had a job with the Airline Transport Association and he arranged to be in town that day also. My brother Booker and his wife, Gloria, drove up from West Virginia. I had my whole family there and it was a great feeling. After the promotion ceremony and reception we took Stephanie to the Metro Station so she could fly back to Fort McClellan, AL, and pack for her move to the NCR. Olivia, Christa and I headed west. It was about 1300 hours on Wednesday the 7th of September 1988.

There were three drivers in the car. I had bought Christa a 280Z while she was a junior in high school. She could drive as well as either I or Olivia. We set out to do about a thousand miles a day. We spent the first night in Indianapolis, Indiana, at Fort Benjamin Harrison. The second night we pulled into Francis Marion Air Force Base in Cheyenne, Wyoming. This was really our first taste of being treated like a general officer's family. We pulled into Marion AFB without a reservation. I went to the front desk at the lodging office and the person at the counter assigned us guest quarters and started a conversation with me that delayed us for a short period. Then we were given directions to the VIP Quarters where we would be staying. By the time we arrived at the quarters by a designated roundabout route that the desk person gave me, my name was on a sign in the front yard, "BG STEPHENS." We were impressed! The VIP quarters was a four bedroom house with a formal dinning room, a formal library and a complete kitchen with the cupboards completely stocked with food. There was also a washer and dryer in the basement. We put our Cadillac Seville in the garage and went in to spend the night. I was a Major when Christa was born so she never underwent any of the hardships that Bob and Stephanie endured during the early years of my career. She was always the princess. So we put her in a bedroom suite alone. Among other furnishings, the suite had a chaise lounge that she curled up on as if she was really a princess. The next morning she liked the suite so well that she asked if we could spend one more day but the answer was no, we had to press on. The third night we stayed at Mountain Home, AFB, Idaho. As luxurious as the quarters were at Marion AFB was as austere as the accommodations were at Mountain Home AFB. We had a room with a space heater and blankets. Christa was next door in equally austere conditions. The next day we pulled into Fort Lewis, WA by about six o'clock in the evening. The command group was away doing something and we were met by Sally Taylor, the spouse of Brigadier General J.B. Taylor the other ADC in the division. We had already signed into the post guest house and decided that we would not move to one of the VIP guest cottages for that evening. Our household goods were already on post and would be delivered the next morning to our quarters.

The household goods moving van was waiting for us when we arrived at the quarters early (0730) the next morning. I supervised the move in while Olivia got Christa registered for school. We knew our way around Fort Lewis and our friends John and Glenda Malloy were there to assist us with everything. Thus began a great tour with MG Shali as the boss and BG J.B. Taylor the Assistant Division Commander for Support ADC (S) as a friend and confidant. I replaced BG Paul Funk the Assistant Division Commander for Maneuver ADC (M). I was assigned as the ADC (S). J.B. Taylor moved up to the ADC (M) slot. I had oversight for personnel, logistics, and all of the support units within the division. Fort Lewis also was the home fort to the U.S. Army I Corps. I Corps was commanded by LTG William Harrison. Bill Harrison was a tall, lanky leader who it was hard to determine if his cup was half full or half empty. However, he could run for miles and do the show-off stuff that appealed to soldiers. All-in-all he was not a bad guy. His wife Josie was a real character. They treated Olivia and me very well and had us over to their quarters for I Corps events, frequently. We had them over to our quarters also. Once at our house we overheard Josie say to Bill Harrison: "Honey, they've got Lenox." Little did she know that Olivia started planning for that evening when I was a Lieutenant Colonel while we were serving at Fort Lewis the first time? She felt that someday we would have a requirement or an opportunity to display silver accessories, fine china and other elegant furnishings and so she started buying *Autumn* by Lenox literally one place setting at a time when it went on sale at the Army Air Force Exchange Service (AAFES) about once a year. I helped by purchasing a few serving pieces and other little accoutrements. We also had formal napkins, placemats and place tags to match the *Autumn* brand on the china. I was proud of Olivia. She had learned well from people like Ann Berry, Anne Palastra, and Jeannie Werner; however, she had also read a lot on her own. Most of her ideas for entertaining were original. We knew how to do formal entertaining with the best. I must say though, Josie Harrison ranks right up there with the very best military hostesses that we have known. About a week after we arrived at Fort Lewis, MG Shali and his wife Joan, had us over for hamburgers. It was a comfortable evening with their enlisted aid de camp doing the cooking and everyone fixed their own plate. Everything was done outside. We stayed for a comfortable hour or so after dinner, and went home. At our 9th Infantry Division welcome affair held at J.B. Taylor's quarters we were serenaded by the entire command group of the division singing among other songs, *Dixie*. I have often wondered if it was by design to get our reaction or if they were that insensitive. The person who led the *Dixie* choruses was the spouse of a senior officer. They were a fine Christian couple who attended church every Sunday. I wonder if she knew how badly she offended me and Olivia that night. At one point, Olivia came over to me and in a not too subtle way said, "Let's go home!" I felt that the entire group was ignorant of what they were doing and did not really mean any harm so I decided that we would stay. In retrospect, I am glad that we stayed at that party. It was the last time that group of people showed any institutional racism toward us. I think in the final analysis they were embarrassed. For the most part we were treated well in the 9th Infantry Division until Shali and Joan left. The Shalikashvili's were replaced by MG Charles H. Armstrong and his wife, Bunny.

Around 1981 the Chief of Staff of the Army tasked the 9th Infantry Division to develop a high technology light division that could deploy rapidly and still engage heavy threat forces. Moreover, the division was to be fielded more rapidly than the traditional development cycle would support. Accomplishing this demanding task required new methods to determine and test concepts, doctrine, force structure and equipment within a fighting division. Building the new division required a process that had as its core the 9th Infantry Division, working closely with the High Technology Test Bed (HTTB), to find and field quickly the technology needed to "leap ahead" of the normal evolution of combat forces. Thus, was born the motorized division experience. During this process, the 9th Infantry Division evolved from a straight leg Infantry division, like I had commanded in as a lieutenant colonel, to a high technology testing center, to an interim motorized division. Because of affordability problems, the objective motorized division was never achieved. The idea of a motorized division was really foreign to me. I knew how to get troops into combat by parachute, by helicopter air assault, and by air landing and moving to contact. What "motorized" really meant was that troops would be loaded onto trucks and follow tanks into battle. It still does not make a great deal of sense to me, even today. The 9th Infantry Division at the time I joined them, had two fighting brigades; one was an armor brigade equipped with M1 tanks and the other was a motorized brigade equipped with "20-year-old" two and a half ton trucks. The tank brigade was commanded by the flamboyant COL Beau Bergeron. The Infantry brigade was commanded by the staid COL John A. VanAlstyne. We had a

Division Artillery (DIVARTY) commanded by the fair-haired COL Richard Sinnreich and a Division Support Command (DISCOM) commanded by COL Mark Hazen. We also had separate support units, e.g., an Engineer Battalion, an Intelligence Battalion, a Signal Battalion and a Maintenance Battalion. I had supervision for all of the division's support units. Our round-out brigade was assigned from the Washington State National Guard and they had M-60 tanks. Our equipment was old and hard to keep functional. We barely had enough training money to go to Yakima Firing Range once a year to fire the tank tables and conduct a division maneuver exercise. The rest of the time we were doing things to support I Corps and Fort Lewis. On one of the trips to Yakima I shared the VIP Cottage with BG J.B. Taylor. Because he was senior to me I gave up the single bedroom to him and I slept on the couch in the living room. Of course, there was only one television in the cottage and he always stayed up to watch the late news so I was awake and could not turn down the bed until he left the room. After I was in the 9th Division about nine months, J.B. left the Division for Saudi Arabia and for a while I was the lone ADC.

Upon his arrival, MG Charles H. "Chuck" Armstrong informed me right away that he was bringing in a colonel to be the Assistant Division Commander for Maneuver ADC (M). I objected. Everyone knew that the best job and normally the senior job for a Brigadier General was Assistant Division Commander for Operation, ADC (O) or in some Divisions it was referred to as ADC (M). It was my turn to get the best job! During the discussion he got angry and said: "Why don't I just call you guys ADC (A) and (B) and you'll be the (B)." I answered him: "Why don't you call us ADC (1) and (2) and designate me (2)?" He was really mad at this point and it showed. When I offered the 1 and 2 solution he probably harkened back to the time that the Army actually categorized whites and blacks as 1's and 2's. He ended the discussion without making a decision. Sometime later, that week he told me that he was going to give me the ADC (O) position. In retrospect, maybe I should not have fallen on my sword for the sake of a title. However, at the time it was a matter of principle and pride. I felt that I had earned the right to have the senior job and I remembered back very quickly to the days when CPT Sloan, LT Shipley, and CPT Damron had given me the second choice positions in C Company, 327th Battle Group as a Lieutenant. I was not about to take a second tier seat to a colonel at that point in my career. I had nothing against the colonel, in fact, I had never met him. It was not personal. It was just business. I was told by MG Armstrong that he, had been the colonel's roommate at the U.S. Military Academy at West Point. So what! That meant nothing to me. The colonel and his wife turned out to be good folks. In fact, we are still friends today. The 9th Division Chief of Staff position also changed when Shali left. Colonel Tommy Stiner, the Chief of Staff, was replaced by Colonel Richard Sinnreich, the former DIVARTY Commander. Sinnreich and Armstrong were always at each other's throat. With these two guys around in leadership roles, the 9th Division was not a pleasant place to work. Armstrong attempted to run with the troops at morning formations each day. He said to me one day: "I did not see you this morning during the run." The implication was that I was not running. Little did he know that I was a marathon runner and in great shape. I answered that I had been running with one of the separate units, everyday. He said: "I want you to take your flag and have one of the soldiers carry it for you." I told him that I would not do that. He was angry again. I never felt that I needed a soldier to carry my colors during the morning runs. Soldiers don't mind being asked to do normal things but carrying the general's flag on a run probably falls into the category of "bullshit" for soldiers. Finally, one day around the middle of November I informed him that Olivia and I would be going to Oakland, CA, to visit her sister for Thanksgiving. He told me that I needed to have Thanksgiving dinner with the troops. I tried to tell him that Olivia's sister and her husband had come to Fort Lewis the previous year for Thanksgiving and we had eaten, as a family, with the troops. We promised them that we would visit them the next year in Oakland, CA, as a family event. He said, angrily: "The soldiers of this division are your family!" I ignored him and went to Oakland. When we arrived from the airport at Olivia's sister's house the telephone was ringing. She answered and it was Armstrong. She passed me the telephone. He asked me: "Are you sitting down?" I said no and at this point with three children away from home, I was starting to get worried. He said: "You just got orders to Thailand." I was shocked. It was the day before Thanksgiving, November 22, 1989. Who was working at GOMO in the pentagon on that day? My gut feeling is nobody. My conjecture is: Armstrong sold me out with a telephone call to the Pentagon, as soon as I left his office that morning we discussed Thanksgiving dinner in Oakland, CA.

In spite of Armstrong, I continued to have a good time at Fort Lewis. I played golf almost every Saturday morning with COL Tommy Stiner, LTC Larry Fulbright who we affectionately called, "Halfbright," and BG Gary Sausser. We were a regular foursome, no matter how bad the weather got, including playing in snow. We always had the same order at the refreshment stand on the turn at the ninth hole: a hotdog, a coke, and a Snickers bar of candy. Occasionally, we had an additional player in Colonel Douglas Cobb the Commander of the I Corps Law Enforcement Command. We could go out there and literally forget everything that was going wrong at work. I never had so much genuine fun with a bunch of guys as I did with that crew. People who did not play golf regularly probably thought we were insane the way we played in the rain, the hot sunshine and even the snow. We'd just put on gloves, long johns, and galoshes with golf spikes in them and continue to play. I'll never forget the morning that we were teeing off on a short par three over a pond and COL Cobb hit his tee shot into the water. We snickered a little bit. He pulled out another brand new ball and hit it short, into the water. By this time we were laughing openly. He threw out another new ball and, you guessed it…it went into the pond. We were howling! He got so angry that he threw the iron that he was using into the pond. Well, that did it; we were guffawing and screaming out loud. He looked at us with an angry sneer and picked up his bag and threw it into the pond. By now BG Gary Sausser and I were screaming out loud with laughter and holding our stomachs. Doug Cobb walked away for about 25 yards and headed back towards us. We did not know what to think. He was a pretty good sized guy. Maybe he was coming back to fight us. He passed by us and waded into the pond, picked up his golf bag and took his car keys out of the side pocket. I thought I would have a heart attack I was laughing so hard. On another Saturday, Fulbright and Cobb were partners and Fulbright hit a ball under a tree. They went in and found the ball and Cobb laid down and held the tree branches up while Fulbright hit the golf ball about three inches above his head. If he had missed it, he probably would have killed Cobb. On yet another Saturday, at Hole number 18 which had a sharp dogleg to the left. The trick was to draw the ball around a corner about 125 yards away. I got up to hit and somehow I topped the ball and it bounced once and went into a trash barrel about twenty feet behind the tee. Well, these guys were laying out on the ground laughing. Fulbright said finally, "I can't wait to see you hit your second shot out of that barrel." I could spend the next twenty-five paragraphs telling stories about golf at Fort Lewis, but I'll move on.

In the field, we had a good Division. The training reputation from the days of GEN Richard Cavazos remained and we were well thought of throughout FORSCOM. Everyone wanted to visit us and observe the Army's only Motorized Division in the Continental United States. We trained hard at the Yakima Firing Range and at the National Training Center at Fort Erwin, California. When MG Shali was the Division Commander, we had a daily routine in the field that facilitated leaders doing their jobs. I knew how to function in the field and had proven my skills as a Commander of a Separate Brigade in Panama. With MG Shali in command we had a morning briefing at about 0700 every morning and an evening briefing at about 1800 and just before we went to bed we huddled for a briefing at about 2200 hours. This was essentially the model that evolved in Vietnam and was used almost universally for Army divisions. When Armstrong took over he announced that he did not like to have meetings. So we would dispense with having regularly scheduled meetings in the field; but rather, we would meet when he thought it was appropriate or "necessary." However, he wanted the leaders to eat breakfast together, lunch together and dinner together. We also had coffee in the Main Command Post in late evening. Normally, combat divisions operated a main command post (Main CP), a forward command post (Forward CP), and a rear area command post (Rear Area). These command posts were referred to as the "the Main, the Forward, and the Rear." The division commander was expected to be where he could best influence the action. Generally speaking the Forward CP was where the commander was located with minimal staff and support. The Main CP was where the tactical operations center (TOC) was located. The Rear Area was where the logistical planning functions took place. Generally, I was visiting one of these locations in the field and did not have time to meet someone for a meal. I normally ate Meals Ready to Eat (MRE) on the run. I had learned that as a young soldier in the 101st Airborne Division. With the cancellation of three regularly scheduled briefings at a specified time we were now on call and met about five times a day on short notice. That meant that one could never be too far away from the Main CP, i.e., no more than a fifteen minute helicopter ride away. Needless to say I was not too disappointed to get the Thanksgiving telephone call from Armstrong. He had become a pain in my rear-end.

When we returned from visiting Olivia's sister in Oakland, CA, for Thanksgiving we stopped in Seattle, WA, to attend a black tie event of the Northwest Officers Association. I had been a major part of the formation of this group when it was formed in 1980. It was an unofficial spur of the ROCKS, Inc., from the Washington, DC, area. The speaker for the evening was LTG Calvin A.H. Waller, the new commander of I Corps. I was on the program to install the new slate of officers. The newly elected president of the Association was my friend and mentor, Lieutenant Colonel (Retired) Samuel Kelly. Sam had been so instrumental in my life when I was a cadet at West Virginia State College. He introduced me that night and got choked up doing it and I responded and got choked up as well. For a moment we were like a father and son act because of our mutual admiration for each other. During the course of the evening I spoke at length with LTG Waller. LTG Calvin A.H. Waller had arrived at Fort Lewis in March of 1991 and replaced LTG Bill Harrison as the I Corps Commander. He and his wife Marion were a welcome change to the social life of the post. They were down to earth and no nonsense. When I told him about the telephone call that I had received two days previously from Armstrong he was totally surprised. He did not comment about it but I could sense that he was not in the loop. The evening passed and Olivia and I eventually returned to Fort Lewis. When I went in on Monday and asked Armstrong about the news of my assignment, he said: "The boss and I discussed it and we felt it was a good time for you to be reassigned and this is a perfect assignment. You'll love it in Thailand." I felt at the time that I was being screwed. I knew that the assignment would be the kiss of death but I felt if General Waller, was in on the decision I would have a hard time fighting it. So Olivia and I prepared to move. It was not until after I retired and invited Cal Waller to speak in West Virginia. He and Marion stayed in our house in Charleston, WV. I asked Cal point blank, about that decision. He told me that he knew nothing about it. So, MG Armstrong's comment about "the boss and I discussed it" must have referred to another "boss," possibly the VCSA who was a good friend of his.

Armstrong brought up the discussion about him and the "boss" discussing my future in his office that was decorated with memorabilia about General Robert E. Lee and the United States Civil War. I do not remember if he had a confederate flag prominently displayed or not. He kept a copy of Robert E. Lee's biography on the corner of his desk appropriately opened and bookmarked as if he read it during his spare time. He often attempted to engage me in conversations about the greatness of Robert E. Lee and the Confederate Army. Fortunately, I had read a great deal about Robert E. Lee. I had even visited the Lee mansion on Fort Myer. I was not then nor am I now a fan of Robert E. Lee. Did Armstrong really think that I would engage in a favorable conversation about the greatness of General Robert E. Lee the general who led the army hell bent on preserving slavery in the South? Did he think I was an idiot? Certainly he had to know that if Lee and the Confederate Army had won the Civil War, he and I would not be having a conversation at all. I would have been picking cotton somewhere in the south. LTG Waller spoke to me about the civil war motif of Armstrong's office. We laughed about it. Waller had seen it and remarked to me "I wonder how he would feel if I decorated my office around a Martin Luther King theme." It always amazed me how many insensitive white officers praised confederate army leaders and expected people like me to agree with them. I think they did it to get an irrational reaction from me. One of my Aides de Camp once remarked to me that he thought Stonewall Jackson was the greatest general that ever lived. I simply said to him, "If Stonewall Jackson and the Confederacy had won the war you would not have this job." He never mentioned it again. I had gotten beyond the race thing a long time before I met these guys. I never selected an officer as my Aide de Camp simply because he was black. I selected what I felt was the best qualified and the best fit for me. Neither color nor ethnic background was part of the selection criteria.

Christa, our youngest daughter left home in the early fall of 1989 to study at the University of Virginia (UVA) and Stephanie had been accepted into the DOD Fully Funded Law Program for Army officers and she was also at UVA attending law school. Bob was still with the Airline Transport Association and living in the Woodbridge, VA, area. We were given a few Fort Lewis farewell parties and finally a departure ceremony with only sergeants major present on the parade field. It was nice and fitting considering my respect and admiration for the Noncommissioned Officer Corps and my disdain for wasting soldiers' time in parades for departing officers. As for the 9th Division Command Group farewell to us, it was decided, by MG Armstrong, that Colonel Billy Gavin and his spouse Katie would have a farewell event for us at their quarters. There would not be the traditional farewell dinner at the Fort Lewis Officers Open Mess (FLOOM). Every general officer with whom I have served in the past was given a farewell dinner with the entire command group in attendance, in dress uniforms and a mock "roasting" was done by the staff. Armstrong announced my departure party in a staff meeting as if he were doing me a favor. The traditional farewell gift of a replica of the Assistant Division Commander's colors was also omitted and I was given instead, a reproduction of Infantrymen participating in the Spanish American War, part of the series of free posters that were distributed by the Army Public Information Office. It was placed in a cheap frame and someone put a plaque on it. The support unit commanders and command sergeants major gave me the traditional stuff that departing general officers received. As an afterthought, Olivia and I were invited, on about 18 hours notice, to a breakfast in our honor, at Armstrong's quarters on the morning that our movers were arriving to pack our household goods. Anyone who has served a year on active duty knows how crucial one's presence is on moving day. It was perhaps, the most inconsiderate thing that happened to me and Olivia since our first assignment with Captain John Sloan in 1962. We kept our cool and attended but I had some choice thoughts in my head for that distinguished gentleman and his spouse. The division staff and their spouses had a separate farewell happy hour for us later and did present me with the traditional replica of the general officer's colors. They also asked that I not inform the CG that they had done so. I left Fort Lewis with a sharp revival of my disdain and distrust of Army senior leaders. However, I also knew what goes around comes around.

During that assignment at Fort Lewis Olivia and had I some great associations with the other general officers and their spouses. LTG Bill Harrison and his wife Josie were always entertaining the group at their home and when LTG Calvin Waller and his wife Marion arrived they continued to have quite a few get-togethers for all of us. One of the couples that we met was BG John Hutton and his wife. What a classy couple they were. John had been the white house physician for President Ronald Reagan. We remember some of our best times in the Army from those general officer social gatherings at the home of the I Corps Commander at Fort Lewis.

THE KINGDOM OF THAILAND

When Olivia and I left Fort Lewis in January 1990, we went into training at the Anti-Terrorism School at Fort Bragg, NC, in preparation for our overseas assignment in The Kingdom of Thailand. Both Olivia and I attended classes on how to inspect our quarters and our cars for explosive devices, how to crash through a highway traffic roadblock, and how to fire effectively a 9mm pistol. Olivia was great at all of this stuff. She, unlike me had no bad habits to break and did exactly what she was taught. She even fired a better score than I did on the pistol range. She also learned to do satisfactory "J" turns in a car before I did. She was having a ball. We made it fun and the two weeks passed very fast. Over the weekend we rented a car and went to see her parents in Bishop, VA, since we would be out-of-the-country for a couple of years. We also had classroom work none of which I remember at this time.

We left Fort Brag and went to Washington, DC, for a series of orientations from the Defense Security Agency, the U.S. State Department and the Central Intelligence Agency (CIA). I remember that the CIA folks wanted me to sign a form that said that I would cooperate with the local DOD Attache in Thailand. I told them that I was not going to sign a document that mandated that I cooperate with another American. They appeared to be upset but did not argue. Somehow signing a form to cooperate with another American made no sense to me. The Attache was an Air Force Colonel that I felt was trying to manipulate me, for some reason. Olivia and I had to get passports and international drivers licenses. I also had a series of cultural briefings and an orientation from the United States Army Security Assistance Agency where I bumped into Colonel Richard Jarrett, my former brigade commander from my first tour at Fort Lewis. Jarrett and I talked briefly and he appeared to be a little uncomfortable talking about old times. He had given me a lukewarm evaluation when he left the 9th Division and there I was bigger than life wearing the insignia of a brigadier general. Olivia had a chance to go and visit our daughters at UVA and say hello to some other friends in the NCR. I also had lunch in the pentagon executive dining room with Rear Admiral Robert Toney, who was going to be my new rater in Hawaii. I don't know if he was upper half or lower half. The way the Navy frocked their guys he could have been an 06 wearing two stars. When it came time to depart Washington, DC, for the Kingdom of Thailand the State Department was unable to get our passports to us on time. I asked if there was a problem and was assured there was not a problem except they were backlogged and could not get our passports out in a timely manner. So, I decided we would leave Washington, DC, and fly to Hawaii to wait for our passports to catch up to us. It only took about a week for them to get them to us. It was a great ten days or so for us in Honolulu, HI, however, someone had to do it.

Waiting in Hawaii was great! It was the home of the Commander in Chief, Pacific (CINCPAC), the parent unit to which I was assigned. The CINCPAC Commander was Admiral Huntington Hardesty. I met almost daily with my CINCPAC desk officer, LTC Lyn Stull. What a great friend he and his wife Carol turned out to be for us. Even today Olivia and I count Colonel (Ret) Lyn Stull and his wife Carol among our closest friends He scheduled me for the normal round of briefings from all of the CINCPAC staff and he took me out on the golf course at Fort Shafter in the afternoons. It was so relaxing that Olivia even played golf about three days. While we were there we ran into MG Joe Turner and his wife, Norma. They were visiting Honolulu on vacation. We had dinner with them at Fort DeRussey. Joe is a West Virginia State College graduate that I knew as a cadet. After our passports arrived, we departed for Bangkok, Thailand. The multiple hour airplane ride was softened a bit by being upgraded to first class seating. During the plane ride we continued to study the folkways and mores of the Thai people. We also studied Thai history and found out that they had never been conquered. We also learned that when visiting with them you always keep both feet on the floor. One of the final things we learned was that patting children on the head was offensive to them. We were trying to get as much cultural indoctrination under our belts as we possibly could before we arrived. We knew that we were entering a foreign country and the last thing we wanted, was to be perceived as ugly Americans. The airplane ride was absolutely grueling. The worst part was the stop at Narita Airport, in the greater Tokyo area of Japan. We eventually named that stop the "black hole." When you arrived there you would have at least a three hour wait and the accommodations were terrible. We arrived in Bangkok, Thailand late at night on the night of February 09, 1990, one day before Nelson Mandella was released from prison in South Africa.

We were met in Thailand by a large delegation of American and Thai officers and their spouses. The Americans were the people who were assigned to the Joint United States Military Advisory Group, Thailand (JUSMAGTHAI). The Thais were from the Office of the Foreign Ministry and the Ministry of Defense. Our entry into the country went very smoothly. As we exited the airplane someone took our passports and we were ushered into a small waiting room that had warm hand towels, a restroom, and refreshments. I met the senior staff and their spouses and the outgoing Chief JUSMAGTHAI, BG Peter Lash and his spouse, Ginger. Since it was late evening and dark we did not see much of the city on the way to our hotel. We were taken to a penthouse suite in a new hotel owned by a Japanese company. The accommodations were comfortable and rated at about the four stars level. Because of the jet lag from our trip we were wide awake and did not sleep very much that first night.

Colonel Paul Courtney, the JUSMAGTHAI Chief of Staff, and his spouse Diane picked us up for lunch and house hunting the next morning. The plan was for me to choose a new location to be the home of the Chief, JUSMAGTHAI. COL Courtney was a Marine Corps fighter pilot. He was loyal and very supportive of everything I did at the Joint United States Military Advisory Group (JUSMAG) headquarters. I had a lot of overseas experience in command and decided that I did not want to change the location of the Chief, JUSMAGTHAI quarters. Over time, one of the changes that I made at JUSMAG was to establish an Exercise Division. I put Colonel Courtney in charge of that division and eliminated the Chief of Staff position. In place of the Chief's job I created an Executive Assistant position and put an Army lieutenant colonel in the position. The Joint Advisory Group traditionally had an Army Division, an Air Force Division, and a Navy Division. All of the Divisions were led by an O6. For the most part the Colonels and the Navy Captain were all very capable leaders and knew their social responsibilities very well. Thailand was very taxing from a social and entertaining standpoint. I took the liberty to let the Division Directors use their drivers and sedans from JUSMAG to attend social functions in the evening. This was one of the common sense decisions that may have violated some obscure military rule but it met the "makes sense test." Prior to my arrival one of the O6's had an automobile accident one evening while returning from a social event and his spouse was killed. This was another situation where I was in charge and made a decision. In order to attempt to get a modicum of control on our participation in social events I put out a directive to my secretaries stating Olivia and I would not accept more than four invitations in one week unless it was from His Royal Highness (HRH) The King, the American Ambassador, or the Thai military equivalent to the United States Chairman of the Joint Chiefs of Staff.

Our accommodations in Bangkok were great. The house was not a mansion but it had the history of being the quarters of the Chief, JUSMAGTHAI since its inception during the Vietnam

War. The landlord was Kuhn Sonya. He had a government contract from the United States to rent the place. The maintenance crew at JUSMAG kept up the maintenance. When we arrived it appeared that nothing had been done to improve the place for ten or more years. I had learned about renovating commander's quarters during my stint as an IG in MDW. One of my duties as an IG was to review the repair and renovation of the quarters of the Chief of Staff of the Army. Believe me I learned a lot in that process. Anyway, Olivia and I set out to cleanup and renovate Quarters Number 33 Sukumvit. First we painted the place inside and outside. This, of course excited all of the Thais that worked at the JUSMAG and gave them hope that the Americans were not going to completely pull out of Bangkok. We had closed all of the other JUSMAGTHAI locations throughout Thailand and the Thai employees appeared to be waiting for the final shoe to drop. Prior to commencing any of the work we did a complete inventory of the quarters furnishings. During the inventory we discovered that the former Chief, JUSMAG shipped a couple of teakwood monk's chairs to the United States with his household goods. The maid, who had been in the house since it opened, was beside herself about the chairs being missing. So, I went to the JUSMAG property officer and inquired how that could have occurred. It appeared that there had been a short period when members of the JUSMAG could purchase excess furniture from the Advisory Group in an effort to reduce the property inventory. My predecessor had actually purchased the chairs for a pittance. It appeared that the purchase was legal, but in my opinion, not necessarily ethical. I chalked that little experience up to the infamous West Point cadet slogan, "don't lie, cheat or steal, nor tolerate those who do—unless it is to your advantage." Next, we replaced all of the drapes and the worn out carpet. We planted orchids in the yard and revived the artificial waterfalls and the fountains. We settled in for what turned out to be one of the best assignments we ever had. The Thai people were wonderful to us. They treated us like we were family and I will be appreciative to them forever for their kindness. Our maid at our quarters was named Pernohm.

My Thai secretary at the office was named Phoonsap, and my driver was named Wan. They were like family to me and Olivia.

Part of my job in Thailand was to sell excess American military equipment. As part of the duty I helped sell among other things, two squadrons of F-16 fighter planes, some excess battle ships, and more than a hundred M60 tanks. I also tell people that part of the job was playing golf. You didn't have to be good at it but you had to play, regularly. Sometimes I would play as much as four times a week. I know! It was tough duty, but somebody had to do it. All of our visitors from the United States also wanted to play golf. The Thai officers always invited the visiting general and flag officers from the United States to play golf. There was one time that a U.S. Navy Admiral was trying so hard to win the match that I pulled him aside and said "Sir, we are not here to embarrass these guys." We were trying to sell excess military equipment. I think that the Thai officers appreciated the fact that the U.S. Ambassador and I were mediocre to average golfers and seldom won the matches. In fact, the Ambassador, Daniel O'Donohue, might well have been one of the worst golfers with whom I have ever played. He was good natured about it though. We always had fun.

During our first week in Thailand we had a visit from the CINCPAC and his spouse. He had about twenty other people in his party. Admiral Hardesty was a Navy pilot and therefore always taxied his aircraft into the chock area on the military side of the airport, himself. Of course the Thais acted as if they thought he had actually flown the aircraft from Hawaii to Bangkok. It turned out that this was sort of an "elephant on the tarmac" that everyone signed up for. It also happened with most of the other dignitaries that had a pilot's license and flew into Bangkok. After the CINCPAC and his party landed, Olivia and I got a real lesson in why so many people visited Bangkok, Thailand. Almost immediately, the straphangers and aides traveling with him wanted transportation to either Johnny's Gems or Venus Jewelers. These were the two most popular Thai jewelry shops that were remnants from the Vietnam War. The quality of the jewelry was very good, the prices were rather reasonable, and the customer service was absolutely outstanding. All of the straphangers had shopping lists from the military communities in Hawaii. Sometimes, I surmised that the reason some of the dignitaries, including members of the United States Congress put Bangkok on their schedule was for the Thai jewelry shopping.

As it turned out Admiral Hardesty and his wife visited us about three times. They were wonderful. I never saw anything out of the ordinary happen when they were visiting. He was always a gentleman and she was the quintessential flag officer's spouse. Admiral Bob Toney, my rater, also visited us a couple of times. He was very demanding of my staff, including our house staff. Of course during the big CINCPAC Exercise, COBRA GOLD, we would swell to approximately ten thousand soldiers, airmen, sailors and marines on station for about two to three weeks. Our quarters were always open to the brass including the Commanding General of the 25th Infantry Division from Schofield Barracks, Hawaii. Major General Fred A. Gordon was the commander during my years in Thailand. We would also occasionally get a visit from the CINCPAC Component Commanders. They were always very demanding and required us to jump through hoops to accommodate them. The U.S. Army Security Assistance Agency Directors also made annual visits. Theirs was strictly a routine visit normally no more than two days. We were visited by LTG Teddy Allen who was an aviation battalion commander back in the 101st Airborne Division when I was a Major. The Commanding General of the U.S. Army Special Operations Command, LTG Wayne Downing, also came into country to visit some of his troops. Aside from being an official protocol officer for the United States military visitors I spent a fair amount of time with the Thai military hierarchy. The Chief of Staff of the Thai Army and the Supreme Command Headquarters Commander when I arrived was dual hated under General Chavalit Yongchaiyudh. He was absolutely great to us. He treated us like we were Thai natives. He was replaced by General Suchinda Kraprayoon who along with his wife was equally accommodating. Another major player in the Thai Military was General Sunthorn Kongsompong who succeeded General Chavalit as Commander of the Supreme Command Headquarters and later took charge as the Chairman of the National Peacekeeping Council after the 1992 Coup d'e-tat. I consider all of these men and their spouses as friends.

At some point during the Thailand tour MG Armstrong contacted me and asked if I would have the Thai Jeweler, Nipon, redefine his West Point class ring. My immediate inclination was to say no. However, I talked to Olivia about it and she said "why not?" I relented and told him I would do it. He sent his ring to me. Well, the Thai Jeweler lost it and I spent a lot of time corresponding with a guy that I literally despised over the loss of his West Point class ring. I forgot about it. Finally, Nipon told me that they would do him an exact replica at no charge. Armstrong's answer to me was no, make them find it. Finally about two weeks before we were to depart, at the end of our tour, the Thais found the ring. I sent it to Armstrong. The lesson learned with that little episode was never get sucked into doing something for someone you don't like. It never works out the way you planned and you will likely spend an inordinate amount of time on it.

A great part of living overseas is the relationships that one establishes with expatriate U.S. citizens. There were more than six hundred expatriates in Thailand and the JUSMAGTHAI Headquarters was their life line to the "real world." The JUSMAG compound consisted of several buildings which included a post office, a barber shop, a medical clinic with a dentistry component, a tailor shop, a motor pool, a restaurant and a bar. All of these entities were located on the first level of the compound. For athletics, in addition to a racquet ball court, tennis courts and a basketball hoop area we had a complete weight room. We installed a sauna while I was there. Upstairs, we had all of the offices of the military component divisions, my command suite and conference rooms. A good portion of my suite was done in teakwood and was absolutely gorgeous. We had movies on two or three nights a week in the restaurant/bar which was open seven days a week. When I arrived the bar was opening at nine o'clock in the morning. Many of the expatriates were there to start drinking when the door opened and by noon many of them were becoming incoherent. The drinks were priced extremely well at about .35–.50 cents a shot. During Happy Hour which started at three o'clock in the afternoon every day and ran until about seven o'clock in the evening the price was even lower. The bar's hours of operation were from 0900 hours until 0200 hours the next day. The first thing I did was adjust the hours of operation to start at 1200 noon until 2400 hours midnight. That did not go over well with the patrons at first. When the "expats" put together a group to come in and complain, I threatened to shorten the bar's hours even further and restrict the hours that they could visit the JUSMAGTHAI compound. I got their attention rather quickly and we started to reform the way we would allow business to be conducted on the JUSMAG compound. I put instructions at the main gate that said if a person was not registered on an access roster they could not bring a car on the compound. That decision did not go over very well either. What was happening was the "expats" would drive into the JUSMAG compound and park and go shopping for three or four hours in Bangkok. Late one Saturday night I went into the compound after midnight to check and see if my policies were being carried out. They were not! I closed the bar immediately. One of the visitors that evening was a young American woman from the Peace Corps, who came over and got in my face and started yelling and cursing at me about closing the bar. Her ending words were something like: "Who in the hell are you anyway?" I answered very calmly, "I am the new Mayor in this compound, and you're under arrest." That action got everyone's attention, and from that night on, the new rules were in effect. During the course of my tenure I remodeled the restaurant to look as much as possible like a stateside McDonald's. I had it dedicated and blessed by the Buddhist monks and we also began serving Thai food on a regular basis. Not only could you get a hamburger and French fries you could get noodles, sushi, and fried rice. The business results were overwhelming. Families from the U.S. Embassy staff started bringing their children over on Saturdays for an American style hamburger and fries. The Thais on my staff also felt like they had a place to go and socialize and bring their families for lunch, and on the weekends. I also invited the Thai employees to attend the annual JUSMAGTHAI Christmas party for the first time. On my birthday they gave me a Thai shirt and a sarong as a symbol of their acceptance and affection for me and Olivia. There was a kindred established there that far exceeds normal superlatives.

There were good times and a few unpleasant times in Thailand. Being in charge of a large American contingent overseas was not easy work for me or Olivia. In order to assist her with spousal activities for the ladies I allowed the JUSMAG fourteen passenger van to be used once a week to take them to the Thai Navy Golf Course in Bangkok to play golf. That was another case of an action that was probably not authorized by CINCPAC Regulations. However, for me it met the "makes sense" test. The ladies had a great time for about six months and then the bickering started and I discontinued it.

Our day normally started with a wake up at about 0530. Olivia and I would leave the house at about 0600 and ride with her driver, Somsak, to Lumpini Park to start our exercise regime. Lumpini Park is located in the heart of Bangkok. Usually, I ran about six miles and Olivia walked two or three miles. We did this routine five to six days a week. I would then go to the office and shower and get dressed for the day. I had a sedan and driver available for conducting business and therefore, Olivia and her driver went back to our quarters so she could clean up and begin her day. The Thai Supreme Command headquarters supplied Olivia with a driver/bodyguard from the Royal Thai Navy whom we paid out of my pocket. I was told that since he was a Thai sailor that I did not need to pay him. However, to avoid even the slightest perception that I was taking anything from the Thai government, I paid him his regular Thai salary. I also refused to accept a Thai Aide de Camp from the Supreme Command Headquarters. Somehow I knew that I didn't need that kind of personal scrutiny. I felt that the routine Thai help, i.e., maids and drivers, was enough intelligence gathering sources for that tour. Many of our Saturday morning activities started as early as 0500. We would get dressed and get in the car for a one hour drive to the Rose Garden Country Club or some other plush venue and have breakfast with other members of the international community and tee off at 0700 in groups of four. At the Ninth Hole turn, at about 11:00 o'clock, we would have refreshments and a light lunch. We would start back out on the golf course at about 1:00 PM and finish around four o'clock in the afternoon. We were then assigned to a room in the clubhouse with two young people to help us shower and get dressed. We would get back into our car and head back to Bangkok. By this time the traffic would be horrendous. If possible we would catch a few winks of sleep. Upon arriving home, we would often shower and get dressed again for an evening event that would end around midnight.

A highlight of the tour that cannot be ignored was our participation in the celebration of the King's birthday. My day's activities began at about seven o'clock in the morning going to a breakfast event in full official dress uniform. I would be joined at about 10:00 o'clock by Olivia at a parade field near the Royal Thai Palace. It appeared that we were assembled and waited for hours but it was really only about one hour before the festivities started. First, all of the available soldiers from the Ministry of Defense were marched onto the parade field and prepared for the arrival of the King and the Queen. The King and Queen arrived in a yellow convertible Rolls Royce Corniche from which they reviewed the troops on the parade field. The King always stood tall in the front compartment of the car and the Queen was regally seated in the back seat. Upon completion of the review of the troops, the King gave remarks and then the troops passed in review, I think two times. As the senior member of the Thai

Foreign Military Diplomatic Corp, Olivia and I always occupied the place of honor among the foreign military attendees at these events. At the end of the day's festivities the members of the diplomatic community scrambled back to their quarters and changed clothes into formal clothes for the evening's events. I normally changed into a mess white uniform for the evening festivities. The Official Diplomatic Corps, i.e., the Ambassadors were in white tie and tails. The evening events for the King's birthday were normally hosted by either the Crown Prince or the Princess.

The two years in Thailand passed very fast and it was time to move on far sooner than we wanted to go. One evening, I received a telephone call from CINCPAC Headquarters in Hawaii and I was told that I should expect to hear from the Commander of the Military District of Washington concerning my next assignment. I knew what to expect because we were coming up on an election year and the timing for my reassignment was perfect. Sure enough I received a call from MG William Streeter. He offered me the job of Director of the Joint Military Armed Forces Inaugural Committee. MG Streeter was the designated Chairman of the joint committee. During the course of our telephone call, I negotiated getting quarters at Fort Myer, Virginia. We were elated to be coming back to the United States and especially to such a historic location. A brief historic sketch on the Fort Myer Military Community website states:

"Fort Myer, Virginia, traces its origin as a military post to the Civil War. Since then it has been an important Signal Corps post, a showcase for Army cavalry and site of the first flight of an aircraft at a military installation and the first military air fatality.

The acres encompassing Fort Myer and Arlington National Cemetery were called Arlington Heights when they were owned in the 1800s by Mary Anna Randolph, granddaughter of George Washington Parke Custis. Custis was Martha Washington's grandson. Mary Anna Randolph married Robert E. Lee when he was a young Army lieutenant. Lee helped rescue the estate from financial disaster in 1858, left the area in April 1861 to lead the Confederate Army, never to return.

The land was confiscated by the government for military purposes when the Lees were unable to pay their property taxes in person. Part of the estate became Arlington National Cemetery and the remainder Fort Whipple, named in honor of Maj. Gen. Amiel Weeks Whipple, a division commander at Fort Cass which was established where the stables are today in August 1861. Gen. Whipple fought in the Civil War battles of Fredericksburg and Chancellorsville in Virginia. He died of his wounds from Chancellorsville in 1863.

Fort Whipple, on 256 acres, was one of the stronger fortifications built to defend the Union capital across the Potomac River. Units stationed there lived in tents and temporary frame structures. The fledgling post's high elevation made it ideal for visual communication, and the Signal Corps took it over in the late 1860s. Brig. Gen. Albert J. Myer commanded Fort Whipple and, in 1866, was appointed the Army's first chief signal officer, a post he held until his death in 1880. The post was renamed Fort Myer the next year, primarily to honor the late chief signal officer, but also to eliminate confusion created by the existence of another Fort Whipple in Arizona.

In 1887, Gen. Philip H. Sheridan, the Army's commanding general, decided Fort Myer should become the nation's cavalry showplace. Communications people moved out and cavalrymen moved in, including the 3rd Cavalry Regiment, supported by the 16th Field Artillery Regiment. As many as 1,500 horses were stabled at the fort during any given time from 1887 to 1949, and Army horsemanship became an important part of Washington's official and social life.

Most of the buildings at the north end of Fort Myer were built between 1895 and 1908. Many of those still standing have been designated historic landmarks by the U.S. Department of the Interior and the state of Virginia. "Quarters One" was completed in 1899 as the post commander's house, but since 1908, it has been the home of Army chiefs of staff, including Generals George C. Marshall, Omar N. Bradley, Douglas MacArthur and Dwight D. Eisenhower.

The first military test flight of an aircraft was made from the Fort Myer parade ground on Sept. 9, 1908, when Orville Wright kept one of his planes in the air for a minute and 11 seconds. The second test flight ended in tragedy when, after four minutes aloft, the aircraft crashed. Wright was severely cut and bruised, and a passenger, Lt. Thomas Selfridge, became the first powered aviation fatality.

Defensive troops were stationed at Fort Myer during World War II, when it also served as a processing station for soldiers entering and leaving the Army. The U.S. Army Band (Pershing's Own) and the U.S. Army School of Music moved to the post in 1942, joined later by the U.S. Army Chorus. The Army's oldest infantry unit, the 3rd U.S. Infantry (The Old Guard) was reactivated in 1948 and assigned to Forts Myer and Lesley J. McNair in Washington to become the Army's official ceremonial unit and security force in the Washington metropolitan area."

Later, I received another telephone call from BG Clara Adams Ender. She was the Deputy Commanding General of MDW and also serving as the Commander of Fort Belvoir, Virginia. She indicated in her call I was in for a real surprise working at MDW. I informed the new U.S. Ambassador to Thailand of my new assignment and he immediately started telling everyone that I had been picked to assist with the planning and conduct of the inauguration of George Herbert Walker Bush. He was obviously a Republican.

THE ARMED FORCES INAUGURAL COMMITTEE

Our send off from Thailand was unforgettable. Of the last thirty evenings that we were in country, more than twenty were spent at farewell parties of every variety imaginable. The Thai military officers and their spouses were unbelievably nice to us. Our Thai civilian friends were equally as gracious. Although it was trying, we attended every single event that our hosts planned. The American diplomatic and expatriate community was also very kind to us. We arrived back in the United States in March 1992. The Armed Forces Inaugural Committee was already starting to assemble. Since the inauguration of President George Washington, the United States military has participated in presidential inaugural celebrations. It became more involved in the 1950s, when legislation was passed that specifically authorized the Secretary of Defense to provide military ceremonial support to the presidential inaugural events. For the last half century, this support has been coordinated through the Armed Forces Inaugural Committee, now called the Joint Task Force-Armed Forces Inaugural Committee (JTF-AFIC) with the Army in the lead.

The AFIC, as we shortened the name, coordinated all military ceremonial support of the inaugural events, which traditionally included musical units, marching bands, color guards, ushers, firing details and salute batteries. The AFIC also provided a very limited amount of approved logistical support to the official inaugural ball celebrations.

JTF-AFIC is a temporary joint military command established every four years at the direction of the Secretary of

Defense. It is comprised of military and civilian members of the Army, Navy, Air Force, Marine Corps, and Coast Guard. The organization is formed several months before the presidential election for the sole purpose of coordinating military support of the inauguration and the related activities during the Inaugural Period defined as "the day on which the ceremony inaugurating the President is held, five days immediately preceding that day and the four calendar days immediately subsequent to that day." The Inaugural Period for the first inauguration for President Bill Clinton was January 15–24, 1993. My job began on or about March 9, 1992. Until that time the unit was being led by an Air Force Colonel named Victor Tambone. Vic was a great guy and a superb organizer. He was a U.S. Airforce Academy graduate. He drove a classic, anniversary model Corvette. He was a former B-52 airplane pilot in Vietnam and, a workaholic. We hit it off perfectly. After a short period, I learned to love him like a brother. When I arrived, he was being assisted by an Army Sergeant Major, Joe E. Neely, who was a logistics expert. I had my initial meetings with everyone and we started to build the AFIC team. It did not take me long to realize why BG Clara Adams Ender had called me early in Thailand. I reported to Major General William F. Streeter. Streeter was a graduate of Norwich University and a classmate of the Army Chief of Staff, General Gordon R. Sullivan, a fact that he would tell you within five minutes of meeting him, and remind you every time he saw you, thereafter. Thank God, his duties of commanding the Military District kept him out of our hair most of the time. I was never able to figure him out but it was not difficult to surmise that this man just didn't like me, and he didn't try to hide it.

The AFIC was located at the Washington Navy Yard. Because Sergeant Major Neely knew logistics so well, and had the proper connections, we were able to secure our office furnishings through the U.S. Army Surplus System and consequently saved a large amount of money. We were allocated approximately $1.5 million to accomplish our inaugural mission. When the dust settled in 1993, we turned back approximately $500 thousand dollars to the MDW headquarters. We required everyone to be checked out on a computer before we hired them. Eventually I was assigned a joint coordinating staff of six colonels, a Navy captain, and a Coast Guard captain. My first personnel challenge came when the Marine Corps sent me a lawyer to be the AFIC operations officer. At first, I refused him. That resulted in a call from MG Krulak, the Marine Corps Assistant Deputy Chief of Staff for Manpower and Reserve Affairs (Personnel Management/Personnel Procurement) at that time. He tried to convince me that he was sending me an outstanding officer who would do great things for the JTF-AFIC. MG Streeter also got on the band wagon and asked me to accept this guy. I took him. On his first day at work I invited him into my office, interviewed him and said, "You'd better be good at this or you will regret the day that they forced you upon me." About a week later he was reassigned. Then they sent me a promotable lieutenant colonel, Jim Eicher, who knew what he was doing. Within that staff group, I had a Coast Guard Captain that was a personal friend of Walter Cronkite. I also had an Army O6 for a Public Affairs Officer who was a marathon runner. Many of the folks were hand picked by their Service personnel departments and for the most part, they sent me their absolute best. The AFIC joint military staff grew in leaps and bounds to about 400 permanent staff in the summer of 1992 and later, to approximately 5,000 on the day of the inauguration.

There were three inaugural committees working to ensure that everything went well for the presidential inauguration. They were the Presidential Inaugural Committee (PIC) that was led by Ronald Brown then the president of the Democratic National Committee (DNC). That particular inaugural committee was charged with the overall planning of the presidential inauguration and the events surrounding it. The Joint Congressional Committee on Inaugural Ceremonies (JCCIC) was under the tutelage of Senator Wendell H. Ford (D-KY). They were responsible for the planning and execution of the swearing-in ceremonies and the Congressional Luncheon for the Inauguration of the President at the nation's Capitol. My committee, the JTF-AFIC was charged with coordinating all of these activities. There were several key events that had to be done to perfection. There was no margin for error! Since the president elect was not the sitting President of the United States the first "no error" event was the arrival ceremony on Sunday the 15th of January 1993. The most critical event of that day was the fly over by aircraft representing all of the Services. The next critical event was the swearing-in ceremony which, by law, is required to take place at 12 o'clock noon on the 20th of January in the year following a general election. Those 105 mm howitzer artillery pieces did not malfunction that day and the swearing-in went off perfectly. The next event was the departure ceremony for the outgoing President of the United States both, by helicopter from the Capitol, and onto the presidential airplane from Andrews Air Force Base. Notice I did not say on Air Force One because it is only Air Force One when the sitting President of the United States is aboard. Past presidents do not ride Air Force One, except as passengers. Fortunately, with the help of dedicated police escorts, I was able to navigate the Washington, DC, traffic and get to Andrews, AFB in time for the departure of President George H.W. Bush. Then I rushed back for the critical coordination and start of the parade and escort for President Bill Clinton to the White House. MG Streeter, as the Commander of MDW and Chairman of the JTF-AFIC, walked up the Capitol steps to meet and welcome President Clinton to the Military District of Washington. After they shook hands and started down the steps of the Capitol, I started the inaugural parade as the Commander of Troops. I led the parade for about a half mile before MG Streeter melded in from the side and I merged back into the joint staff. About a month before the parade MG Streeter approached me and asked if I would let his Deputy Commander, BG Clara Adams-Ender march in my place in the parade. I answered him with an unqualified, no. He said, as he did often, "Gordy and I thought it might be good for the Army's image to have a woman in the staff at the inaugural parade." I gave him a short simple answer: "Let her march in your place, after all she's your deputy." He never answered me. He dropped the Chief of Staff's name all the time to give the impression that they were bosom buddies. Maybe they were.

One of my first requirements as the AFIC Director was to pick an Aide de Camp. An officer was sent over from the 3rd Infantry (The Old Guard) and I interviewed him. I had just spent two years operating very well without an Aide de Camp and quite frankly did not want one. First Lieutenant Matthew Canfield was sent over to my office at the Navy Yard and we hit it off right away. He was energetic, thin, and extremely neat. My philosophy with aides was always to select a sharp, good looking officer and I would teach them what I wanted them to know. Matt asked if he could be called "Koolaide." I was amused but I always called him Matt. Others called him "The Koolaide." Early on I received a telephone call from then Master Sergeant Paula Brock, from Task Force Bravo in Tegucigalpa, Honduras saying "Sir, can you get me out of here?" I brought her on board and put her in my front office as an administrator. She had tremendous computer skills, a college degree, and a lively presence. She was there to protect me from everyone else and she knew it! Thanks to her I never had to look over my shoulder. I felt that she always had my back. Paula Brock's husband had worked for me in Panama years before. She became almost like family with me and Olivia. I still correspond with her today, sporadically by email.

While making my rounds through the pentagon I stopped by to see the Under Secretary of the Army, John Shannon. Shannon had been the first guy to welcome me to the pentagon on the 7th of July, 1976. In my conversation with him that day he asked me to hire Colonel George Hudgens as the Deputy Director of the Inaugural Committee. I told him that I did not need a deputy. He was very insistent and made it clear that he wanted George to have the job. I finally agreed not so much because I knew George, but I always felt kind of beholding to John Shannon for his acts of kindness to me twelve years earlier. I immediately went to COL George Hudgens' office and informed him that he would be working for me. I said to him: "You'd better be damn good or your life with me will be miserable." He answered with a phrase that I will never forget and in fact use it myself quite a bit, he said, "There is no telling how far you can go in life as long as you don't care who gets the credit." From that meeting forward George and I forged a friendship that is still alive today. I consider him to be among my closest friends and confidants. He moved into one of the large connecting offices that we had at the Navy Yard.

The Directors suite of the AFIC was really nice. I had a corner office that overlooked the Washington Navy Yard Cantonment Area and the loading docks along the Potomac River. I also had a clear view of the other side of the river and a fair portion of downtown Washington, DC. Adjacent to my office with interlocking doors was COL Vic Tambone's office. On the other side of Vic's office were interlocking doors to COL Hudgen's office. The three of us could meet and never open the front doors to our offices. It was very efficient. We kept a smaller office for MG Streeter in the suite that was across the room. Matt Canfield told me that Streeter's Aide de Camp told him that Streeter wanted my office and that I should take the small space that we had set aside for him. I ignored the request until it went away. He was only on the premises about two to three hours a week and I was there full time. I felt the old cliché "possession is nine tenths of the law" was in affect. I kept the large office. After all, I was in charge. Another major run-in with MG Streeter was when Vic Tambone and I went over to the pentagon to brief Pete Williams who was the Deputy Secretary of Defense for Public Affairs at the time. We did not tell Streeter that we were going and he came in as we were wrapping it up. He was livid. However, he did not say anything until we went into the pentagon corridor. He was pointing his fingers at me and making it clear to everyone within earshot or eyesight that he was in charge of the inaugural committee and he wanted to be invited to all of the meetings that we held in the pentagon. I got ticked off also and we had words. I knew that I could not win in that hallway so I walked away while he was still talking. By the way, I continued to have meetings all over the NCR and sometimes I invited him and sometimes I did not.

After the general election on November 3, 1992, we prepared for our first meeting with the PIC headed up by Ronald Brown. Ron Brown was a charismatic, high energy person who displayed the self confidence of a chief executive officer. He was clearly in charge of the inauguration from the beginning. His immediate circle of associates included Rahm Emmanuel, Harry Thomason and Linda Bloodworth-Thomason. The presidential inaugural committee held a meeting every morning that was chaired by Rahm Emmanuel who was Ron Brown's executive assistant and operations officer. Colonel Tambone and the AFIC operations officer attended those meetings. I did not attend every day. The purpose of the meetings was to plan and coordinate all of the inauguration events. About once a week we would meet in a joint session in our area and Ron Brown and I would attend. If MG Streeter had known we were meeting he surely would have wanted to add his two cents. On one of those occasions Ron Brown allowed as how he thought I had been sent by the Bush Forty-One Administration to sabotage Bill Clinton's inauguration. I was furious but I kept my cool until the meeting was over. I followed him into his office and closed the door. He was visibly nervous. The first thing that I told him was that I was a registered democrat and that my political affiliation did not have anything to do with my selection for the job, nor would it have anything to do with how well I performed. I let him know in no uncertain terms that I did not appreciate his public insinuation at the meeting and I would not stand for him implying such in the future. After that little session he and I became very good friends and he included me in every planning session he attended. The AFIC worked well with the presidential inaugural committee folks. They had some weird folks working for them but I am sure that they felt that some of our folks were weird also.

The backward planning process was our key to success. We started with the "show" that would be held at noon on the January 20, 1993. Everything revolved around that event. We made a large wall poster (20 feet tall) with data and timelines with everything converging on Inauguration Day. This board was placed in the AFIC Operations Center which resembled a microcosm of the U.S. Army and Joint Chiefs of Staff Operations Centers in the pentagon. We also had an observation deck that was equipped with one-way glass so that visitors could see but not disturb the people on duty on the floor. We coordinated the activities of all of the Uniform Services including the U.S. Coast Guard, the Law Enforcement Agencies of the District of Columbia, Maryland and Virginia, and all of the Federal Agencies including the Treasury Department, the Secret Service, the Capitol Hill Police, the Park Service, the Federal Protective Service, and etc. We counted twenty-six different agencies with whom we had to do business regularly. We were busy with the District of Columbia government coordinating route reconnaissance, emergency aid stations and egress routes to the nearest medical facilities, if needed.

Sharon Pratt-Kelly was the Mayor of Washington, DC, and her contact person was Mr. Sam Jordan, a person who had attended West Virginia State College. My entree with him was not difficult. I spent a lot of time going around and meeting with folks who had a piece of the inauguration. For example, I made a trip one day to the U.S. Navy Medical Facility that was located in the U.S. Capitol for Congressional members' use. We figured that on Inauguration Day we would plan for a minimum of 8–10 heart attacks during the activities. Other trips included visiting the Office of the Police Chief and Fire Chief of the Washington, DC, Government. I also visited all of the venues where the ten official presidential balls were to be held. One of the best coordination visits that I made was with Quincy Jones as he was preparing the music for the Opening Ceremony to be held on Sunday, the 17th of January 1993. When I reached his modular office (trailer) in the vicinity of the Lincoln

Memorial it was Friday afternoon on the 15th of January and freezing cold on the National Mall. I do not know what I expected but I did not expect to see the great Quincy Jones dressed in common clothes wearing a baseball cap, with a runny nose pouring over musical scores. I was impressed and I told him so. He appeared to be amused. It was another reinforcing lesson that proved to me that the great ones did their own fundamental work. The great ones leave nothing to chance! The pay off came two days later when the President Elect and Vice President Elect and their spouses arrived from Charlottesville, Virginia, at the back of the Lincoln Memorial and were raised by a portable elevator to a back entrance. They emerged to the voice of James Earl Jones announcing: "Ladies and Gentlemen the President Elect William Jefferson Clinton and Mrs. Clinton and the Vice President Elect Albert Arnold Gore, Jr and Mrs. Gore." At the precise moment of the conclusion of those words Quincy Jones signaled the assembled national orchestra to begin the opening fanfare from *2001: A Space Odyssey*. What an emotional moment that was for a little skinny black kid born in a one bedroom house on Court Street in Welch, WV. I was on hand to witness and to a large extent, direct the official opening ceremony of the inauguration of the Forty-Second president of the United States of America. The significance of that event may be lost to the reader but it will always be special to me.

That was the kickoff to one of the most memorable weeks of my life. LT Matt Canfield and I went to almost every event if only for a few minutes. After the Opening Ceremony at the Lincoln Memorial we raced ahead of the main traffic to Arlington Cemetery where the president elect and the vice president elect visited the President John F. Kennedy Memorial. I was off then to Quarters 14-Fort Myer, just above the cemetery grounds to change clothes and attend the Presidential Youth Inaugural Dinner at the Marriott Hotel on Connecticut Avenue along with The Reverend Jesse Jackson. What an experience that was! Jesse was...Jesse. Early the next morning I spoke at the Presidential Youth Inaugural Conference. Earlier that day I was interviewed by a local TV station on a show called *Coffee with Jess*. The next night Ron Brown threw a bash at his northwest DC townhouse. Notables in attendance at that event were Vernon Jordan, Senator Ted Kennedy with his new wife, Tim Russert and Joe Johns, Attorney Togo West and a host of others. Olivia and I had a great time. In fact, we started to leave about three times and we would see someone that we recognized from television and stayed just to say hello to them. Olivia's enthusiasm for those kinds of events always amazed me. She is really an introvert except in social situations, she simply blossoms. On another evening we also went to the rehearsal for the Presidential Inaugural Gala Celebration. The featured performers were Barbra Streisand and Michael Jackson. The tickets for the real thing event were hard to come by, however, as the Director of the AFIC I was able to go into the rehearsal without being challenged. At one point someone in the Presidential Inaugural Committee asked if I wanted tickets to an official ball. I requested four tickets to the MTV Ball. I gave them to Bob and Christa. Both of them invited friends and they went to what many people considered the biggest show in town that night. On the street those tickets were going for about $2,000 each. Olivia and I went to the Presidential Ball that was sponsored by the combined military organizations, e.g. the American Legion, the Veterans of Foreign Wars, The Order of the Purple, and etc. General Colin Powell was there with all of the Service Chiefs and several other military dignitaries. I took my daughter, Stephanie who was an Army Captain at the time and we were joined by LTC (Ret) John Malloy from the Fort Lewis Washington area and his son Major Brian Malloy. I introduced Stephanie to LTG Ron Griffith who at that time was The Inspector General of the Army. I also took her to the head table and introduced her to General Powell and the Service Chiefs. The President and Ms. Clinton arrived at around nine o'clock. We had a good evening but I turned in early because I had been up since about 0300 that morning. The one thing I learned was that if you do the proper planning everything will go smoothly. The fact of the matter was that we were just trying to get through the day after about eight o'clock in the morning.

There was not much going on in Washington on the morning after the inauguration except I knew the morning briefing at the Army Operations Center at the pentagon would feature the Army's role in the inauguration activities. The briefing was held at 0600 and I did not want to miss it. The Acting Secretary of the Army, now John Shannon was there and he made special note of my presence and the Army's participation in the Inauguration. He also said in passing that he had visited the AFIC Headquarters and was handled by the Chief of Staff instead of me. I thought nothing of it that day. At that moment the Chief of Chaplains, MG Matthew Zimmerman leaned over and said something that I've thought about a lot since then. Matt said: "Enjoy the moment, fame can be fast and fleeting." I did not know what he meant that day. However, it did not take long for me to find out.

The Clintons opened up the White House to visitors on the day after the inauguration. Because I had some time on my hands, Olivia and I took my brother-in-law Rod Bennett and his wife, Edie and my brother, Booker and his wife Gloria to the Officers' Club at Bolling, Air Force Base for lunch. It was the first real relaxation for me in a long time. Our relatives left the city shortly after lunch and Olivia and I went home to relax. Now it became a matter of tying up loose ends and moving on to another job, or so I thought. Not long after the ceremonies were over, maybe a week or two, MG Streeter came to visit me. He said that Gordy wanted to know if I wanted to go to JCS "until they could figure out what to do with me." I asked where in the JCS and he said as a "watch officer in operations." He also said that he had told "them" that I was probably going to retire. I said, that I thought that I would be selected for promotion on the major general selection list. I also said that if I did not make the "two stars" promotion list I would probably retire. He left my office and called me about an hour or so later and said "I told them what you said." I knew instantly that I had been set up. Quite frankly I think that my Aide de Camp and Streeter's Aide de Camp had been talking and my Aide told Streeter's Aide that I was looking at civilian jobs. I was looking but I was also prepared to stay in the Army under the right circumstances. The day that the two stars promotion list was released, I was not on it.

I had an inkling that I would not be on the list from another flag officer who came by our house when he was in town. MG Ernie Harrell was a friend that I had known since my early days in the pentagon, back in 1976. He called me one day and told me to call the two black lieutenant generals—the Army only had two at the time—and solicit their support for the upcoming two stars promotion review board. He said, "Hell, call 'em both. There are only two and surely one of them will sit on the selection board." I talked face to face with LTG Alonzo Short who I had saved the 501st Signal Battalion command job for in the 101st Airborne Division back in 1976. He told me that he had served on the last two stars promotion board and he would probably not be on this one. Beyond that he was completely noncommittal. I had an immediate flashback to the manipulation that I had done to preserve his battalion command position in the 101st Airborne Division. However, I thanked him. He had come to see me to ask for a favor. He asked me to release a young captain to go to work for him. I gave up the captain. In the scheme of things I could not imagine that a captain could be that valuable. I barely knew the captain and when I inquired, I was told that he did a good job but was not exceptional. However, I figured if a lieutenant general took the time to come and ask for him, he must be something special. Then I called LTG Samuel Ebbeson, the other black three star general at the time, and asked for his help. Sam had been a classmate of mine in AOC and CGSC. We knew each well but we were not close friends. In fact we had been Assistant Division Commanders at the same time in I Corps. Sam was very coy with me but finally agreed to support me. I took him at his word.

Two other three star generals that I knew on the board were LTG John Shalikashvili my former division commander and LTG Wayne Downing. I did not ask either of them for their support. In many ways I felt that asking for help from board members was unethical. I was naïve enough to think that everything hinged on merit. I still believe that. The selection board met. I was not selected. I harbor no hard feelings. The competition is very tough at that level and apparently I did not compete well. That was my second pass-over for promotion to major general. The first had come while I was in Thailand and the Commanding General of U.S. Army Pacific did not accept the invitation to go to Washington and sit on the board. Therefore, neither I nor the other two Security Assistance general officers in the Pacific Theater, BG Gary Sausser and BG Robert Jellison, were selected. My guess is that without someone to personally speak in your behalf to the board members you do not have a fair chance at being selected.

During the planning for the Inauguration I met and became friends with a lot of good people. One of them was the Governor of West Virginia, Gaston Caperton. He called me personally and asked if I could arrange for special transportation for his wife's parents during the inauguration festivities. He simply wanted an Americans with Disabilities Act (ADA) equipped van. That was a piece of cake for us and so he sent me a personal thank you note. I asked my brother, Judge Booker T. Stephens, Chief Judge of the 8th Judicial Circuit of West Virginia, if he could arrange an interview for me with the Governor. He did.

Olivia and I went to Charleston, West Virginia, to meet with Governor Caperton. I arrived thirty minutes early for the meeting, parked on one of the side streets at the West Virginia Capitol main campus and asked an elderly black gentleman in a uniform, on duty at the entrance to the capitol, where the Governor's office was located. He gave me a classic answer. He got up and walked out of the guard shack and said pointing, "You see that sidewalk right there?" I answered yes sir, almost bursting with laughter. "Just follow it to that door over yonder and go inside and you'll find the Governor." I was amazed at how simple he made the instructions. I went inside and reported to the receptionist. She said that the Governor would be in shortly. He arrived fifteen minutes late. I was getting irritated and started to wander around the room looking at elementary school art, when he tapped me on the shoulder. He introduced himself to me and said; "You must be the General?" I answered him and he led me into his office. He offered me coffee. I asked if he was going to have a cup and he said that he would be drinking a coke. I took the coffee. After he put my cup down on the coffee table he sat across from me on a facing couch and abruptly said, "Let's cut thru all of the crap and you tell me why I should hire you as opposed to anyone else who would be sitting there." I answered saying that I was well qualified. He interrupted me and said I don't want the standard stuff like "I am well educated, I get along well with people or I have a strong work ethic. Tell me something I don't know." I leaned forward on the couch and, partly because I was a little irritated at him being late, said to him, "I make shit happen!" There was a pause and we both laughed and I knew and he knew that I had a job. We talked a few more minutes and he said that he had two jobs open, Director of Communications and Director of Personnel. He said it as if I had my pick of the two. I left the office feeling rather proud of myself and Olivia and I went to visit her parents and spend the night in Bishop, WV. The next day we retuned to the NCR grinning like the cat that swallowed the canary. At that point, I really did not give a damn if the Army picked me for promotion to two stars or not.

I went about my business as usual until about mid-February and I was in the pentagon one day so I stopped by GOMO and asked the assignment officer what he had planned for me. He said, "The Chief is not going to offer you another assignment. You refused his last offer." I was shocked! I said, what offer? He then told me that MG Streeter was acting on behalf of the Chief of Staff when he came by and made the offer about JCS. I told him that Streeter was not authorized to speak for me and that he should have called me himself. I really tore into him that day. That little episode had all of the signs of a modern day lynching. Those guys had taken me out of the game without letting me touch the ball. I went home and told Olivia and she was as shocked as I was. I was hurt, really hurt! I laid down on a daybed in our den and felt light headed. I had never been closer to fainting in my life. I called Acting Secretary of the Army, John Shannon. I told him what happened and he was completely noncommittal. I asked if he knew about it prior to my call. He said that "they" did not brief him about assignments. While in the pentagon, I asked the jerk that was the assignment officer if I could talk to the Chief of Staff. He told me that the Vice Chief of Staff would contact me later. Sure enough, on April Fools Day, April 1, 1993, I received a call from General Dennis Reimer, the VCSA. He said, "Bob, we'd like to ask you if you can be gone from the Army by the end of August." I dragged it out for a little while. I said, "Gone? My mandatory retirement date is not until July 1994. What's the problem?" He answered "Well we can't find anyone who will take you for a short period of time." I did not answer him immediately. I let it stew for a few seconds. He was completely silent on the other end of the line. Finally I said, "First, my name is not Bob. Everyone who knows me well calls me Steve. Second, I will go home today and I will not return to work, and I will leave the Army sixty days from now." It appeared that I caught him off guard and he said, "Oh we'd like you to stay until August." I am sure that in his mind he thought he was giving me six months or so to get my things in order. I asked if he had anything else to say and he said no. I hung up on him. What he did not know was that I already had a tentative start date of June 1st, for my new job as Director of Personnel, for the great State of West Virginia. I left the AFIC headquarters and went home.

The next morning I went to the weekly staff meeting at MDW Headquarters and my intentions were to announce my retirement to the MDW staff. As usual Streeter was in a mood where he started the meeting with something like "When are you going to get that unit closed?" Usually, general officers are very collegial and do not say demeaning things to each other in public. I never felt that Streeter respected me as a general officer. He always spoke to me in arrogant and demeaning tones. I found that to be true of a number of officers who for one reason or another were not very confident of themselves. I saw him the first time when he was the Director of the Combined Arms Training Integration Directorate at Fort Leavenworth, KS, and I was in the pre-command course for Commanders. I had my doubts about his ability to communicate effectively then and after working with him at the AFIC, I have not changed my mind. It is my opinion a lot of military leaders use their rank as a means to push their agenda. I think they believe that their rank gives them privileges and prerogatives that they could not otherwise acquire. Anyway, I was not in a frame of mind to listen to his drivel that day and I exploded. I said, "Why do you feel that you must display your authority in these meetings? Everyone here knows who you are. Why do you feel that you have to belittle the AFIC in every meeting?" He was embarrassed and said, "Let's go to my office." I am sure all twenty or so of the people, in that room, were shocked and they thought that we were going to fight. When we entered his office I did not give him a chance to speak. I told him that from the beginning, I had tried to make him and the MDW staff, look good in every circumstance. I also told him that I was tired of the insults and barbs about the AFIC. I continued my rant by saying to him that I did not appreciate being set up by him and the GOMO assignment officer. I ended by telling him that Reimer had called me the day before and that I would not be coming back to work after that morning. As I glared at him he seemed to wither and started to deny any complicity in the GOMO assignment officer's snafu. I will always believe that "they" including the assignment officer in GOMO set me up and I'll never forgive them for it. If they wanted me out all they had to do was say it. The under handed stuff was sophomoric and very unprofessional, to say the least. I was not in the mood, that day, to listen to him and I left the room while he was still talking. However, I did not stay at home everyday as I had said I would but instead came in and finished my job. The assignment officer in GOMO sent me a resignation packet. I signed it. Olivia and I went to the pre-retirement briefings and we contacted the transportation folks for the move to West Virginia.

As I was signing out of the Army at Fort Myer I bumped into Colonel Leslie G. Gibbins, a former company commander at Fort Campbell when I was a lieutenant, who was also retiring from the Army that month. For the most part Gibbins had been a good guy. I remember that during Swift Strike III in North Carolina he invited all of the company leaders (officers and senior sergeants) to eat supper at a local roadside restaurant. We went in, sat down and nobody came over to take our order. CPT Gibbins went over to the counter and the person behind the counter told him that they would not serve me. I was the only black person in the group. Gibbins came back to the table and informed us of what the redneck had said and instructed us to leave. I always admired him for his forthrightness that evening. That sort of brought my career full circle and I was ready to leave the Army. In the meantime, my daughters were graduating from the University of Virginia. Stephanie was graduating from the School of Law and Christa from undergraduate school with a degree in Spanish. We went to their commencement ceremonies in Charlottesville, VA, and moved to West (By-God) Virginia to start life anew as civilians.

Both Streeter and I were called to the Office of the Acting Secretary of the Army, John Shannon for an awards ceremony. I really did not want go. I was awarded the second award of the Defense Superior Service Medal. Shannon suggested that I should go back to WV and join the choir in my church. He was trying, without much success, to make small talk with us. I refused to associate with Streeter that day. I deliberately did not take Olivia to the ceremony. I had enough of the Army by that time. I had been deceived one time too many and I did not want to play the accommodating game any longer.

My retirement ceremony was conducted on the 28th of May, 1993 with a full parade at Fort Myer, Virginia. The folks at AFIC arranged a farewell dinner for us at Fort Belvoir and I will never be able to thank them enough for doing that. Initially, I was going to pass up all of the brouhaha that accompanies retirement. I was upset and just wanted to go away quietly. The first person to call me was COL Melvin Smith an African American friend and neighbor from our days in Lake Ridge, and say "It's not about you Steve. You owe it to us to have a retirement parade and reception." Olivia said she wanted to give me a reception. One of the parade ceremonies officers at MDW called and asked if he could arrange something special for me. Finally, I said yes. Besides MSG Paula Brock had written up and gotten approved a U.S. Army Distinguished Service Medal for me. Paula had covered my back again. So Olivia and I participated in a parade hosted by our friend MG Fred A. Gordon who by now had replaced the retired Billy Streeter, and was the Commander of MDW. The 3rd U.S. Infantry Regiment (The Old Guard) the oldest active unit of infantry in the army having been first organized as the First American Regiment in 1784 was the host unit. Of course that meant that the Fife and Drum Corps and all of the other accoutrements such as the gun salute platoon were present. What a way for a little skinny kid from War, West Virginia, to go out of the Army. I will admit that Olivia and I had come a long way. She joined me on the reviewing stand after I presented her with a large bouquet of red roses. I was retired along with a major general from the Corps of Engineers so I was not the ranking retiree on the reviewing stand that day. I was a little disappointed but it made for a good transition into the impersonal world of civilian life. It was, however, fitting and proper and I left the parade field, went into the Fort Myer Officers' Club hosted my reception, had a couple of drinks and went home.

That was a tough day for me. I had spent my entire adult life to that point in uniform, on active duty—thirty years, nine months and twenty-one days. Since commissioning day from WVSC I had never had another job. The Army was my life and it was difficult for me to imagine life without it. However, Olivia put it all into perspective as only she can for me. She simply said, "It had to end sometime and now is as good a time as any." She was right! We began packing to leave the next day.

EPILOGUE

Life in the military was not easy even for those of us who loved it. I dearly loved being in the Army. I was devastated at the way they pushed me out. Not only did I love it but my family loved it as well. Olivia and I used to joke that they, the government, got two of us for the price of one. After I became a field grade officer, Olivia's days for the military were just as long and arduous as mine. Unfortunately, the military system of duty and protocol demands a great deal from Army families that is never repaid. My children took heat at Fort Lewis because their father was a battalion commander. Bob took undue harassment from noncommissioned officers at the West Point Preparatory School because his father was an officer. Christa took heat in a local beauty contest in Tacoma, Washington, because her father was an officer. However, through it all, we survived as a family.

As I look back over my military career, I am struck by how well we did as a family. Olivia taught school full-time in Ohio, Kentucky, the Panama Canal Zone, West Virginia, Virginia, Washington, Georgia, and even Bangkok, Thailand. I believe she could teach anyone to read. She is that good as a reading instructor. She is the strongest woman that I have ever known. She deserves all of the credit for the success of our children. Bob, although it took a while, is a college graduate. He is probably the most talented of our children but failed to apply himself early in life. He certainly has the most extensive vocabulary and he can do the most in mathematics very quickly. When he was in grade school, he scored 127 plus on the Stanford-Binet Intelligence Quotient Test. He is really smart and finally in his mid-forties is starting to come into his own. Currently he is managing a multimillion dollar contract for a transportation company in

Kuwait. He is married to a young woman, Marlyn, from Manila, Republic of the Philippines, who also works in Kuwait.

Stephanie is the one who followed my career path. She set records in high school track, served as the player coach for her high school gymnastics team as a junior, entered The U.S. Military Academy and graduated with a major in Psychology and the normal number of math courses and took a commission in the Military Police Corps. After a couple of years in the Army, she competed for and was selected for the military's Fully Funded Law Program (FLEP). She entered Virginia Law at UVA became a military law expert. As an Army lawyer, she excelled and after going to the JAG Advance Course was selected to serve on the staff of the Judge Advocate General Law School at Charlottesville, Virginia. Oh, did I mention that she also has a Master's degree in Administrative Law? She is currently serving as a Colonel, on active duty for the 3rd U.S. Army, a major military command, at Fort Mcpherson, GA. She has more than twenty-five continuous years of active service. Above all, she is the mother of our only granddaughter, Olivia Pearl. Stephanie's husband LTC (Ret) Kevin Henderson recently retired from the Army after serving more than twenty-five years.

Christa, our third child, was born with a silver spoon in her mouth. I was a Major on active duty when she was born. There are seven years difference between her age and Stephanie's. With a UVA undergraduate degree in Spanish and a Master's degree in International Relations and Public Affairs from Columbia University, she is always in high demand for her talent. She is fluent in several languages. Her disposition is so steady that she deceives most people into thinking that she is timid. She is quite the opposite. She is the fourth strongest woman that I have ever known, including my mother. She is also the mother of my grandson, Kayo. Her Husband, Erwan Pouchous, is from Brussels, Belgium, and works at the United Nations in New York City. So, we have three well educated, well adjusted and self-sufficient offspring. All of their success is due to the amount of attention and care afforded them by their mother. I was always working for the next promotion and did not always have time for them. I have tried to make it up to them but I am sure that I have failed miserably in my attempts.

It is apparent, at least to me, that I have achieved a modicum of success in my lifetime. In my own head, my accomplishments boil down to three. The first big accomplishment was to marry an intelligent, supportive woman who has kept me as a priority in her life. I can never thank her enough for allowing me to grow old, without having to grow up. Second, I stopped smoking cigarettes on the 4th of December, 1984 which will probably extend my life for about five years. Third, I ran a marathon in November of the following year, 1985. Those are what I consider to be my greatest accomplishments. I don't have to tell you which of these is number one. Olivia continues to be as pretty to me today as she was when I saw her the first time in the seventh grade. I know this is an over used cliché, but she is truly the wind beneath my wings!

If I had to define the word life it would be easy for me. Life is simply a series of choices. I believe that 98% of the choices we make range somewhere between average and mediocre. About one percent of our choices are brilliant. The brilliant choices are so rare that we hardly recognize them when they occur. We normally look back and say words to the effect, "That was a great choice!" Another one percent or so is disastrous. Sometimes we never completely recover from some of them. We look back and say, "That was a poor choice!" The remaining mediocre to average 98 percent of our choices are what we make work. All of the choices we attempt can be satisfactorily accomplished. It depends on how much time, and resources, i.e., money, people, and or other materials we want to expend to make them work. We make them work right from their mediocre to average beginning. In the final analysis, we are simply the sum total of all of our experiences and choices. It was my choice to go in and threaten the housing officer at Fort Campbell when I was a second lieutenant. It was my choice to go into Special Forces as a young officer and become a very highly skilled soldier wearing officer's brass. It was my choice to volunteer for duty in Vietnam because I wanted to obtain a chest full of medals. It was my choice to enter graduate school against COL Shumacher's orders. It was my choice to fight the bad efficiency report that LTC Tausch gave me in Vietnam. It was my choice to leave the solitude of Fort Campbell Kentucky and go to work at the pentagon as a Major. It was my choice as an evaluator of an Annual Training Test to score two events unsatisfactory. It was my choice to go to the National War College instead of the Army War College. It was my choice to get drunk at LTC Sam Howell's house and try to drive home and wreck my car. It was my choice to stand up to the commanding general of USARSO and design, have made, and openly display a set of colors for The Task Force of the 193rd Infantry Brigade (Separate).

It was my choice to take my wife to visit her sister on Thanksgiving Day against the desires of the distinguished gentleman that was commanding the 9th Infantry Division at that time. It was my choice to leave USJUSMAGTHAI better than I found it and restore dignity and pride to its staff. Finally, it was my choice to attempt to make Bill Clinton's first inauguration the best one on record. Every choice, right or wrong, made me more knowledgeable about myself and my surroundings. That's what the military did for me. I am far richer for having served in the Army. I met tens of thousands of wonderful people and a few jackasses. Our family traveled a bit and we saw a few of the world's wonders. Olivia and I, mostly Olivia, raised a wonderful, productive family. Through it all, we held our marriage together under some trying circumstances.

There are a lot of people that I need to thank for my success in the Army, but at the risk of overlooking someone I will decline mentioning names except Olivia. I'll just say that all of you know who you are and you also know that I will be eternally grateful to you. The Army was a helluva ride for me and Olivia and we enjoyed most of it. We retired and moved on!

Our first stop was Charleston, WV, where I worked for Governor Gaston Caperton for almost four years and became a Toll Fellow in The Council of State Governments. Governor Caperton did not tell me the complete truth about my salary for that job in West Virginia, something I used as a learning experience for future civilian employment. When the Republicans came into power in West Virginia in 1997 I stayed with Governor Underwood until I figured out how unethical that administration could become and I resigned. I moved on to the State of Georgia and became the Assistant Commissioner to Dan Ebersole in the Georgia Merit System of Personnel Management. Ebersole gave me a thirty thousand dollar a year increase in pay over what they paid me in West Virginia. When Dan left to become the Treasurer of the State of Georgia a young, connected policywonk named Dana Russell became the Commissioner of the Merit System and I was promoted to Deputy Commissioner.

Zell Miller was in his last term as the Governor of Georgia at the time. Roy Barnes was elected and became the next Governor of Georgia. He appointed a well positioned, politically savvy, black female as the Commissioner of the Merit System. Without warning, notice, or a reason she called me in and fired me six months later. At the time I was fired I was the sitting president of the National Association of State Personnel Executives (NASPE). The person who fired me had no state level personnel management experience and therefore, she had no inkling of what having the President of NASPE in Georgia meant at the Council of State Governments (CSG). I had an active seat on that council. I tried working for another woman in the Georgia Building Authority. That lasted about forty-five days and I left on my own. It was probably the worst job fit that I ever had. It is a pleasure to work for someone who knows their job and does it well. On the contrary, it was absolutely hell to work for an incompetent, blustering, braggart who did not have a clue about what she was doing. She bragged to me once that the only reason that she got the job was because she was the

Governor's wife's best friend. That kind of honesty on her part was too dishonest for me to accept or respect. She also lied to me about my salary, and I was determined that I was not going to let a second person lie to me about the amount of money I was going to be paid (even though it was an insignificant amount).

I went home and did household chores for about two months while Olivia taught school. I cleaned house, prepared meals and cut the grass. I put in several resumes a week and finally landed a job teaching defensive driving to corporate executives and regular fleet truck drivers for a company out of Arlington, Texas. That was probably the best job that I ever had after the Army but the pay was not that good. After a month or two of that I started looking again and landed a job with a former college friend, BG (Ret) Walter F. Johnson. I will always be grateful to Wally and Doris Johnson for rescuing me and assisting me in regaining my dignity, self respect, and pride. Wally made me a Project Manager for a Command Post Exercise Program for the U.S. Army Reserves. I had fun in that job. I worked with a group of whining and moaning colonels and traveled on weekends all over the United States and to Puerto Rico.

Upon moving to Georgia in 1997, I became part of a Saturday morning golf group at Fort McPherson called the "Command Group." We played every weekend come hell or high water, rain or shine. On one of those Saturday's I overheard a retired lieutenant colonel say that he was going to retire for the second time. I asked what he did for a living and he said, "I advise students at a small university, south of the Atlanta Airport." I told him that I had a Master's degree in that stuff but had never used it. He asked if I would send him my resume. When I returned to the office on Monday I emailed him my resume and forgot about it. In about a week to ten days he called me and asked if I had time for lunch. I went to lunch with him, the Dean and the Associate Dean of the School of Business at Clayton State University. A week later I met the university president and they hired me as a student advisor and visiting assistant professor of management in the School of

Business. I took a substantial cut in pay when I accepted that job. Three years later I applied for the position of Executive Assistant to the President at Clayton State and that's one of the jobs that I am doing now. What does an Executive Assistant to the President do? Anything the president wants me to do. Later, I was also appointed to the university position of Vice President for External Relations. I was always a dreamer and so my dream goes on. How much longer will I continue to dream? I do not know. I still have lots of choices.

INDEX